TEACHER GUIDE

Includes: Answer Keys
...n Guide
...ept Builders
...ments

James P. Stobaugh

1 Credit -

Skills for
LITERARY
analysis

Lessons in
Assessing
Writing
Structures

First printing: August 2013
Third printing: January 2017

Master Books®, P.O. Box 726, Green Forest, AR 72638
Master Books® is a division of the New Leaf Publishing Group, Inc.

ISBN: 978-0-89051-713-0
ISBN: 978-1-61458-321-9 (digital)

Cover design by Diana Bogardus.
Interior design by Terry White.

Scripture quotations taken from The Holy Bible, New International Version®, Copyright © 1973, 1978, 1984, 2011 by Biblica, Inc.™ Used by permission of Zondervan, All rights reserved worldwide.

Please consider requesting that a copy of this volume be purchased by your local library system.

Printed in the United States of America

Please visit our website for other great titles:
www.masterbooks.com

For information regarding author interviews, please contact the publicity department at (870) 438-5288

Acknowledgments

I thank my four children and my distance-learning students who so graciously allowed me to use their essays. Over the last 15 years it has been my great honor to teach some of the best writers in America. Finally, and most of all, I want to thank my best friend and lifelong editor, my wife, Karen. I also want to thank the students who have contributed to this book as well: J.B. Rutlemann, Joseph Stahl, Emily Miller, Benjamin Cobb, Rebecca Holscher, Sheridan Swathmore, Catelyn Mast, Ian Elliott Smith, Hannah Huynh, Daphnide McDermet, John Micah Braswell, Faith Baumann, Bethany Rishell, Anna Grace Knudsten, Stacia Hiramine, Megan Norman, Austin Allen, James Grinalds, Daniel Greenidge, Claire Atwood, Jaime Schimmer, Chris Loyd, Alouette Greenidge, and Josiah Keiter.

Everything is from God, who . . . gave us the ministry of reconciliation (2 Corinthians 5:18).

Master Books®
A Division of New Leaf Publishing Group
www.masterbooks.com

Contents

Using Your Teacher Guide

How this course has been developed:

1. **Chapters:** This course has 34 chapters (representing 34 weeks of study).

2. **Lessons:** Each chapter has four instructive lessons, taking approximately 45 to 60 minutes each, with an exam and/or writing assignment due on Friday.

3. **Grading:** Depending on the grading option chosen, the parent/educator will grade the daily concept builders, and the weekly tests and/or essays.

4. **Course credit:** If a student has satisfactorily completed all assignments for this course, it is equivalent to one credit of writing and one credit of literature.

Throughout this course, you will find the following:

1. **Chapter learning objectives:** Always read the "First Thoughts" and "Chapter Learning Objectives" to comprehend the scope of the material to be covered in a particular week.

2. **Concept builders:** Students should complete a daily concept builder Monday through Thursday. These activities take 15 minutes or less and emphasize a particular concept that is vital to that particular chapter topic. These will relate to a subject covered in the chapter, though not necessarily in that day's lesson. Answers are available in this teacher guide with each lesson.

3. **Weekly essay/tests:** Students have weekly evaluations. These are available in this teacher guide (starting on page 223). With each chapter introduction, the "Look Ahead for Friday" is a reminder that every Friday the essay can be turned in for the week and a test taken as well (if separate from the essay). A parent/educator can also assign a separate essay based on the daily warm-ups (Monday through Thursday) if they desire.

4. **Daily prayer journal:** Students are encouraged to write in a prayer journal every day. A parent/ educator may include this in the overall grade. If so, it is encouraged that the grade be based on participation rather than on the content, since this is a deeply personal expression of a student's walk with God.

5. **Final project/portfolio:** Students will correct and rewrite their weekly essays for their final portfolio (100 points total).

6. **Warm-ups:** Daily warm up exercises will start each lesson, setting the tone of thought for the day.

Grading Record Options (See chart on following page.)

This course has been developed to allow two grading options for a parent/educator. This allows one the flexibility to adjust the usage of the course content to individual situations and varying requirements. For ease of grading, **Option A** includes the grading of the weekly essay/test and final portfolio. **Option B** includes the grading of the weekly essay/ test final portfolio, and concept builders. Both provide a total weekly score of 100 points for a course total of 3,500 possible points. Dividing the total score at the end of the course by 35 will provide a percentage grade for the student. You may use the standard system (90-100 = A, 80-89 = B, 70-79 = C, 60-69 = D, below 60 = F), or you may use your own personal grading system. An additional option includes additional credit for the student's prayer journal, which can be done at the educator's discretion and be added into the overall score of Option A or Option B. An additional 10 percent bonus can be awarded for the prayer journal, in the extra credit column.

week	Option A	Option B	
	Essay /Test = 100	Essay/Test (80 points)	CB (20 points)
1			
2			
3			
4			
5			
6			
7			
8			
9			
10			
11			
12			
13			
14			
15			
16			
17			
18			
19			
20			
21			
22			
23			
24			
25			
26			
27			
28			
29			
30			
31			
32			
33			
34			
Subtotal			
Final Portfolio			
Total			
	Divide by 36 for grade	Divide by 36 for grade	
Credit (optional)			
Final Grade			

Preface

Skills for Literary Analysis is a dialectic (examining opinion or ideas logically, often by the method of question and answer) or early rhetoric (using words effectively in writing or speaking) level, middle school or early high school, basic course. It is for the reluctant writer who nonetheless must be equipped with writing skills requisite for college and for the eager student who needs the same. Most college English professors do not assign essays with such titles as "What Did You Do for Summer Vacation?" Instead, they will ask you to write essay papers about literature. *Skills for Literary Analysis* teaches you how to write sophisticated literary analyses or criticisms.

Literary analysis or criticism is a way to talk about literature. It is a way to understand literature better so that we can tell others about it.

Charles Osgood in his preface to Boswell's *Life of Johnson* states:

> Phillips Brooks once told the boys at Exeter that in reading a biography three men meet one another in close intimacy — the subject of the biography, the author, and the reader. Of the three, the most interesting is, of course, the man about whom the book is written. The most privileged is the reader, who is thus allowed to live familiarly with an eminent man. Least regarded of the three is the author. It is his part to introduce the others, and to develop between them an acquaintance, perhaps a friendship, while he, though ever busy and solicitous, withdraws into the background.[1]

Our task, likewise, is to bring the subject, the author, and the reader together. We presume to offer insights about different literature that will edify all three.

Every literary piece and every analysis of a literary piece concerns three elements: *ethos, logos,* and *pathos.*

Ethos means "character," and it implies "credibility." Great literature exhibits ethos, and great literary criticism exudes *ethos,* too! Ethos evidences beliefs or ideals that characterize a community, nation, or worldview. Literary criticism rises or falls on its ability to exhibit believable, credible analysis. For instance, the reader must ask, "Is Huw in *How Green Was my Valley* a credible, believable narrator?"

Logos concerns the argument. Every literary critical essay that you write will have an argument. What is the theme? What narrative approach does the author take? Does it work? These are only a few examples that a literary critic might argue. *Logos,* like all argumentation, must be mindful of logic and rhetoric. For instance, Jack London's *Call of the Wild* is not merely an adventure story about a sled dog — it is a book that presents an argument: a naturalistic argument. Readers and literary critics must be able to discern and to write about these arguments. No serious literary discussion of *Call of the Wild* can ignore the fact that London is advancing an evolutionary, naturalistic agenda.

Finally, every trustworthy literary piece has pathos, or "heart." Literary critics, and the literary pieces they are analyzing, should offer much more than sterile, persuasive rhetoric. Great literature, and effective literary analysis, exhibits empathy with the reader and insights about the human condition. For example, George Eliot's *Silas Marner* skillfully invites readers to enter the lonely world of old Silas Marner. Eliot causes the reader to feel, not simply to understand, the tragedy that drives Marner from his loving God and human community.

---

1   James Boswell, edited by Charles Osgood, *The Life of Samuel Johnson* (1917), preface.

Schedule and Study Guidelines

The following guidelines were developed to help make this course manageable for students.

Weekly study pattern: Each chapter equals one week, and every lesson is a day, which includes warm-up exercises and concept builders Monday through Thursday, and an essay due every Friday.

Readings: If a student is given a set time in their day to read, they should be able to sample a good majority of the texts mentioned. The following is a synopsis of the readings required throughout the course. Most will be available either in the student book, at local libraries, or as free downloads at Bartleby (www.bartleby.com/), The Online Books Page (onlinebooks.library.upenn.edu/lists.html), or Project Gutenberg (www.gutenberg.org/wiki/ Main_Page). When the assignment states to read or "review the assigned text" it is referring to the following assigned reading portions.

It should be noted that students most likely will not be able to complete all the readings within the year, since several fairly large novels are included, so a teacher can help students select the books that they want to put the most effort into finishing. (These large readings are marked below with an "*".) If a student cannot finish a book in the given time, they might check for book summaries on online sites (such as SparkNotes.com) that offer vital summaries of the characters, context, and stories. There is no comprehensive test evaluating a student's knowledge of the books discussed in this course.

Chapter 1. Reading *The Call of the Wild*. Student could begin reading *The Call of the Wild*. This would allow up to four weeks to complete the book.
Chapter 2. Reading Worldviews (contained in the text).
Chapter 3. Reading *The Call of the Wild*. Continue reading the book.
Chapter 4. Reading *The Call of the Wild*. Finish reading the book.
Chapter 5. Reading *Joseph Narrative*, Genesis 37, 39:1-8, 19-45:9. Student could begin reading *The Adventures of Tom Sawyer*. This would allow up to three weeks to complete the book.
Chapter 6. Reading *Joseph Narrative*, finish Genesis 37, 39:1-8, 19-45:9. Continue reading *The Adventures of Tom Sawyer*.
Chapter 7. *Reading *The Adventures of Tom Sawyer*. Finish reading the book. Student could begin reading *Idylls of the King*. This would allow up to three weeks to complete the book.
Chapter 8. *Reading *Idylls of the King*. Continue reading the book.
Chapter 9. Reading *Idylls of the King*. Finish the book. Student could begin reading *Treasure Island*. This would allow up to three weeks to complete the book.
Chapter 10. Reading *Treasure Island*. Continue reading the book.
Chapter 11. Reading *Treasure Island*. Finish the book. Student could begin reading *How Green Was My Valley*. This would allow up to two weeks to complete the book.
Chapter 12. *Reading *How Green Was My Valley*. Finish the book. Student could begin reading *Alice in Wonderland*. This would allow up to three weeks to complete the book.
Chapter 13. Reading *Alice in Wonderland*. Continue reading the book.
Chapter 14. Reading *Alice in Wonderland*. Finish the book.
Chapter 15. Reading "Oracle of the Dog" (contained in the text). Student could begin reading *The Screwtape Letters*. This would allow up to two weeks to complete the book.

Chapter 16. Reading *The Screwtape Letters*. Finish the book. Student could begin reading *Uncle Tom's Cabin*. This would allow up to three weeks to complete the book.
Chapter 17. *Reading *Uncle Tom's Cabin*. Continue reading the book.
Chapter 18. Reading *Uncle Tom's Cabin*. Finish the book. Student could begin reading *Anne Frank: The Diary of a Young Girl*. This would allow up to three weeks to complete the book.
Chapter 19. *Reading *Anne Frank: The Diary of a Young Girl*. Continue reading the book.
Chapter 20. Reading *Anne Frank: The Diary of a Young Girl*. Finish the book. Student could begin reading *Silas Marner*. This would allow up to four weeks to complete the book.
Chapter 21. Reading *Silas Marner*. Continue reading the book.
Chapter 22. Reading *Silas Marner*. Continue reading the book.
Chapter 23. Reading *Silas Marner*. Finish the book. Student could begin reading "The Religious Life of the Negro." This would allow up to two weeks to complete the text.
Chapter 24. Reading "The Religious Life of the Negro." Finish the text. Student could begin reading *Anne of Green Gables*. This would allow up to three weeks to complete the book.
Chapter 25. Reading *Anne of Green Gables*. Continue reading the book.
Chapter 26. Reading *Anne of Green Gables*. Finish the book. Student could begin reading *Ivanhoe*. This would allow up to three weeks to complete the book.
Chapter 27. *Reading *Ivanhoe*. Continue reading the book.
Chapter 28. Reading *The Call of the Wild*. Finish the book. Student could begin reading *Shane*. This would allow up to three weeks to complete the book.
Chapter 29. Reading *Shane*. Continue reading the book.
Chapter 30. Reading *Shane*. Finish the text. Student could begin reading A Midsummer Night's Dream. This would allow up to two weeks to complete the play.
Chapter 31. Reading *A Midsummer Night's Dream*. Finish the play.
Chapter 32. Reading "Letters" by C.S. Lewis (contained in the text).
Chapter 33. Reading "The Midnight Ride of Paul Revere" by Henry Wadsworth Longfellow (contained in the text).
Chapter 34. Reading "The Lady or the Tiger?" by Frank Stockton (contained in the text).

*This represents a large book that might be too difficult to complete in just a few weeks. You may suggest that a student simply read summaries from a library or online, or find a paraphrased text for younger readers.

Vocabulary words: There is guidance for students to systematically review their vocabulary words daily. These words are not provided to students, but pertain to vocabulary words chosen by each student reader based on their comprehension. See the student book for further instructions.

Warm-up assignments: A teacher may feel free to alter or eliminate warm-up assignments that ask a student to address an idea (i.e., book or movie) that he or she is not familiar with.

Essay/tests on Friday: The daily assignments mention outlining assigned essays, writing rough drafts for the essays, and completing their final essay drafts for Friday. This instruction is referring to the Chapter Essays/Tests that begin on page 223 in this teacher guide. A teacher may wish to have students develop the essays through the week so a student will have more time to organize his or her thoughts. If you prefer, the essay can simply be given on Friday with no prior preparation. This allows maximum flexibility for the classroom setting. Also, note that there are optional objective tests included with chapters 1, 5, 7, 10, 17, 21, 25, 27, 29, and 31.

Setting — *The Call of the Wild* (Jack London)

Chapter 1

First Thoughts

Jack London (1876–1916) lived and wrote in the last part of the 19th century and early part of the 20th century. He watched the final frontier of America — Alaska — disappear. He wrote in a style literary critics call *naturalism*. What is naturalism? *The Call of the Wild* is essentially the story of a dog named Buck. However, as the book unfolds, one notices that there is a lot more happening. Buck is invited back into his wild ancestry. In Jack London's opinion, this invitation is a metaphor for life itself.

Chapter Learning Objectives

In chapter 1 we will examine the literary concept setting and its use in Jack London's *The Call of the Wild*. We will also examine the impact of naturalism on world history.

As a result of this chapter study you will be able to . . .

1. Analyze the setting in Jack London's *The Call of the Wild*.

2. Evaluate the impact of a naturalism worldview.

Look Ahead for Friday

- Turn in a final copy of essay or take it as a test
- Optional objective test

Setting is Critical

Daily Assignment

- Warm-up: The protagonist (main character) in this novel is Buck, a dog. Describe your pet. If you don't have one, describe a pet you wish you had.
- Students will complete Concept Builder 1-A.
- Prayer journal: Students are encouraged to write in their prayer journal every day.
- Students need to review their material for the next assignment
- Students should systematically review their vocabulary words daily.

CONCEPT BUILDER 1-A

Audience

Different audiences require different writing styles. It matters to whom you are writing a piece!

Choose the audience of each passage, and circle words that tell why you chose a particular audience. Hint: clues regarding audience lie in word choice and content.

B	We conducted a single-center, randomized, controlled trial of arthroscopic surgery in patients with moderate-to-severe osteoarthritis of the knee.	A. Teachers
E	Colston tried to continue playing with the injury during the Saints' 24-20 victory over the Bucs, but finished with only three catches for 26 yards.	B. Doctors
A	What is editing? Ruth Culham of the Northwest Regional Education Laboratory separates revision (last month's column topic) from editing (spelling, grammar, capitalization, and punctuation).	C. Magazine for Women
D	My guy loves music, and he had just bought himself a new iPod. He's obsessed with the painting *The Great Wave*, and I found an iPod skin with the exact painting on it. He loved it, and now he thinks of me every time he listens to his music!	D. Teenagers
C	You want: to look bright-eyed. Hide dark circles around the eye area with an apricot-tinted color, or if you have darker skin, one that's one shade lighter than your skin tone.	E. Football Fans
F	Making the user interface for one device easy, slick, fun, and fast is a challenge. If you have multiple devices and they need to cooperate, the challenge increases dramatically. As wired and wireless communications hardware gets cheaper, the design opportunities for communicating devices become more common.	F. Computer Nerd

Lesson 2

Setting is Marginally Important

Daily Assignment

- Warm-up: Pets are our friends, and, in many ways, they have "human characteristics." But they are not human beings. Explain.
- Students will complete Concept Builder 1-B.
- Prayer journal.
- Students should outline all assigned essays for the week.

CONCEPT BUILDER 1-B

Writing Style

Compare and contrast the writing styles in the following passages:

Elements	Passage A	Passage B
Narration: Does the author let the reader see into everyone's mind? Give an example.	Yes. Shelley reveals the characters' thoughts. "There was a sense of justice in my father's upright mind which rendered it necessary that he should approve highly to love strongly."	No. London merely allows the reader to see into one character's mind. "That was why he had shied in such panic. He had felt the give under his feet and heard the crackle of a snow-hidden ice skin."
Diction: Does the author use complicated/big words? Give an example.	Yes. "He strove to shelter her, as a fair exotic is sheltered by the gardener, from every rougher wind and to surround her with all that could tend to excite pleasurable emotion in her soft and benevolent mind. Her health, and even the tranquility of her hitherto constant spirit, had been shaken by what she had gone through. During the two years that had elapsed previous to their marriage my father had gradually relinquished all his public functions; and immediately after their union they sought the pleasant climate of Italy, and the change of scene and interest attendant on a tour through that land of wonders, as a restorative for her weakened frame."	No. "He reflected awhile, rubbing his nose and cheeks, then skirted to the left, stepping gingerly and testing the footing for each step. Once clear of the danger, he took a fresh chew of tobacco and swung along at his four-mile gait."
Imagery: Does the author use a lot of descriptive words to explain things? Give an example.	Yes. "He strove to shelter her, as a fair exotic is sheltered by the gardener, from every rougher wind and to surround her with all that could tend to excite pleasurable emotion in her soft and benevolent mind."	Yes. "He reflected awhile, rubbing his nose and cheeks...."

Sample Literary Analysis

Daily Assignment

- Warm-up: Have you ever lost a pet? How did he/she die? How did you feel?
- Students will complete a daily Concept Builder 1-C.
- Prayer journal.
- Students should write rough drafts of all assigned essays.

CONCEPT
BUILDER
1-C

Building an Outline

Examine the setting in these two passages.

A. Where? *The South*

   When? *Latter part of the 20th century*

   Is the setting important? Why or why not? *While the setting adds a great deal to the story, the story itself discusses universal themes (e.g., mutability) that could be replicated in other settings.*

B. Where? *In a lab somewhere.*

   When? *Probably in the early or middle 19th century. The description of the lab implies that the scientific instruments are somewhat archaic*

   Is the setting important? Why or why not? *The theme of dissatisfaction is made more pronounced by a dingy lab, but again, the theme is not entirely dependent on the setting.*

Lesson 4

Grammar Review: Overview

Daily Assignment

- Warm-up: Buck feels great loyalty to Thornton. Loyalty is a powerful human action. Define loyalty and then describe a situation where you were loyal to someone (e.g., a friend) or something (e.g., a sports team). How did it feel to be loyal?

- Students will complete Concept Builder 1-D.

- Prayer journal.

- Review the assigned text. Keep vocabulary cards.

- This is the day that students should write, and then rewrite, the final drafts of their assigned essays.

CONCEPT BUILDER 1-D

Vocabulary

Define the following words (found in Jack London, *The Call of the Wild*) and use them in a sentence:

1. Lacerated: *To be cut off.*
   Sentence: *The soldier's leg was severely lacerated by the bomb.*

2. Primordial: *Ancient; archaic.*
   Sentence: *Buck discovered primordial urges as he answered the "call of the wild."*

3. Wizened: *Old, shriveled*
   Sentence: *The old man was wizened.*

4. Disconsolate: *Unable to be consoled or satisfied.*
   Sentence: *The disconsolate grief of the old man could not be satisfied by any kind word.*

5. Malingerer: *A lazy person acting sick to get out of work.*
   Sentence: *The malingerer hung around camp and did nothing.*

6. Bedlam: *Chaos*
   Sentence: *The wild dogs were causing bedlam in camp.*

7. Innocuously: *harmlessly*
   Sentence: *The child innocuously asked for a piece of bread.*

8. Importune: *inconvenient*
   Sentence: *The question came at an importune time.*

TRUE AND FALSE (50 POINTS)

F   In the beginning of the novel, Buck lived in rugged Minnesota.

T   In Alaska, there was a great need for hardy dogs to pull sleds.

F   Manuel sold Buck to be mean to Judge Miller.

T   Buck's initial response to cruelty was surprise.

T   Thornton was the best master, by far, that Buck had.

T   The setting was critical to this book.

T   Buck resisted the call of the wild until his master was killed.

F   Mercedes, the only woman in this book, was a very skilled tomboy who lived off the land.

T   Native Americans killed Thornton.

T   Thornton won $1,000 when Buck pulled a very heavy sled.

Chapter 1 Essay Answer

ESSAY (50 POINTS)

Read the passage from Mary Shelley's *Frankenstein* and discuss in a one-page essay how Shelley uses the setting to make her thematic points.

Summary: A "dreary night of November" sets the tone for this anti-scientific, late 19th-century romantic novel that is critical of human knowledge divorced from human subjectivity (or what Shelley and other romantics call "the heart."). As Stevenson's Dr. Jekyll, *in Dr. Jekyll and Mr. Hyde*, unintentionally creates a monster who destroys him and as Kurtz in Conrad's *Heart of Darkness* goes into the jungle and becomes uncivilized, so Dr. Frankenstein journeys into a scientific realm where he has no business. He reaps disastrous results. All these authors—but especially Shelley—use the setting to produce an ominous tone with obvious thematic impact: the monster Frankenstein is created in a dreary mansion, in an antiseptic laboratory, by an unimaginative doctor, in the dead of night. "I passed the night wretchedly," Dr. Frankenstein testifies, and so he does. This one statement of the setting, as well as anything, captures the theme of this novel: Even an innocuous flirtation with the creative abilities of nature will cause the participant to pass life wretchedly! While Shelley does not create a didactic, pedantic novel, she comes very close. She is presenting a sobering warning to all her contemporaries.

General Discussion — Worldviews

Chapter 2

First Thoughts

If you are a committed Christian believer, you will be challenged to analyze worldviews of individuals and institutions around you. You are inextricably tied to your culture, but that does not mean you can't be "in this culture" but not "of this culture." Furthermore, you will be asked to explain your own worldview and to defend it against all sorts of assaults. It is important that you pause and examine several worldviews that you will encounter. You also need to articulate your own worldview.

Chapter Learning Objectives

In chapter 2 we will write our own worldviews, and we will also analyze other worldviews in literature.

As a result of this chapter study, you will be able to . . .

1. Consider your own worldview.
2. Analyze other worldviews in literature.

Look Ahead for Friday

- Turn in a final copy of essay or take it as a test

Lesson 1

Background

Daily Assignment

- Warm-up: In the *Star Wars* movies, Ewoks enjoy the natural beauty of the forest. They are the most harmonious civilization in the whole *Star Wars* series. The Ewoks are fighting to protect the forest — not to support the revolution. What worldview do they represent?
- Students will complete Concept Builder 2-A.
- Prayer journal: Students are encouraged to write in their prayer journal every day.
- Students need to review their material for the next assignment
- Students should systematically review their vocabulary words daily.

CONCEPT BUILDER 2-A

Worldview in Art

Romanticism is a worldview that emphasizes the unusual and the subjective. Thus, romantic art is usually flamboyant and exaggerated. It is always full of bright colors and happy landscapes (e.g., water falls). Naturalism, on the other hand, emphasizes the macabre, the objective. It often portrays bleak, dreary, cold landscapes.

Draw a romantic sunset and a naturalistic sunset:

Answers will vary, but the romantic sunset might feature a waterfall or beautiful sunset, while the naturalistic sunset would contain something malevolent — like a sunset behind a wrecked village.

Lesson 2

Literary Analysis: Worldview

Daily Assignment

- Warm-up: Who is my hero/heroine? Why? What does your choice tell you about your world view?
- Students will complete Concept Builder 2-B.
- Prayer journal.
- Students should outline all assigned essays for the week.

CONCEPT BUILDER 2-B

Celebrity Worldviews

What worldview does each quote manifest? The definitions of these worldviews are found in Lesson 2.

A **Kate Gosselin:** My kids are the reason I have always done everything. My kids are the reason I laid on bed rest for 30 entire weeks. My kids are the reason that I wrote the books and it's always about them. And, I know that it looks it's all about me all the time and whatever, but what you don't see is down deep inside it's a desperate desire to provide for my kids.

A **Danny Gokey:** I get my strength from my faith in God. My goal is to be a Christian who does mainstream music. I want my music to reach out to the multitudes. I want to bring entertainment, but I want to bring encouragement and hope at the same time.

F **Zac Efron:** I don't have a Twitter, a MySpace or a Facebook or anything like that. . . . I kind of value in people not knowing where I am or what I'm doing.

E **Kara Dioguardi:** I'm one of those people who's pretty honest and kind of say what I feel. I think you're going to see me be nice at times, but I'm a little more hard on the contestants.

F **David Cook:** Whenever I feel like I need to get my ego in check, I'll call my family.

C/F **David Archuleta:** The fact that people were able to feel what I was trying to give off as I sing is one of the coolest and best feelings ever.

Lesson 3

Culture Wars: The Battle for Truth

Daily Assignment

- Warm-up: Describe an event or philosophy in current culture that is against the biblical worldview.
- Students will complete Concept Builder 2-C.
- Prayer journal.
- Students should write rough drafts of all assigned essays and speech.

CONCEPT BUILDER 2-C

Interaction with the World

Analyze the worldviews of *The Lion King* characters:

Character	Education	Religion	Relationships
Simba	Taught by his father and Rafiki. He represents generations that precede him.	Simba is raised in the religion of his father.	Simba is influenced a great deal by relationships.
Mufasa	Mufasa is Simba's father and king of the Pride lands. He represents generations that precede him.	Mufasa respects tradition and worships his ancestors.	Mufasa has many important relationships. His wife, Sarabi, is his closest confidante. His son Simba means the world to him. He even loves Scar.
Scar	Scar is educated, just like his brother Mufasa..	Scar is a cynical, self-centered realist who believes in nothing transcendent.	Scar has no friends. He uses everyone to advance his purposes.
Hyenas	The lowest creatures on the food chain!	They function in the present with no thought of tomorrow, much less any thought about metaphysical things.	The hyenas are despised by everyone.
Rafiki	Rafiki is the religious man. Probably he is self-educated and prefers heart knowledge to head knowledge.	Rafiki is the very embodiment of tradition!	Rafiki is respected by everyone.

Character	Education	Religion	Relationships
Pumba & Timon	These happy-go-lucky creatures are the embodiment of free-spirited freedom. They have no interest in education.	While Pumba and Timon are not particularly religious, they do follow a moral code.	Pumba and Timon are loved by everyone!
Zazu	Zazu is a hornbill who acts as adviser to the family. He is highly educated.	He supports the world-view and deities of his king.	Zazu is intensely loyal to the king.
Nala	Nala, like Mufasa and Simba, respects and honors education and tradition.	Nala respects traditions.	Nala is loved and respected by everyone.

Character	Worldview
Simba	Theism
Mufasa	Theism
Scar	Naturalism
Hyenas	Naturalism
Rafiki	Theism
Pumba & Timon	Theism/Romanticism
Zazu	Theism
Nala	Theism

Lesson 4

Grammar Review: Active/Passive Voice

Daily Assignment

- Warm-up: Describe one object that captures who you really are. Why did you choose that object?
- Students will complete Concept Builder 2-D.
- Prayer journal.
- Review the assigned text. Keep vocabulary cards.
- This is the day that students should write, and then rewrite, the final drafts of their assigned essay.

CONCEPT
BUILDER
2-D

My Worldview

Write your worldview: Answers will vary. These answers are examples.

A. What is the priority of the spiritual, unseen, transcendent world?

EXAMPLE: To me, the transcendent word — the Kingdom of God — is primary. I pray, "Thy will be done on earth as it is in heaven."

B. What is the essential uniqueness of humankind? Is there something different about people as compared to other living creatures?

EXAMPLE: Human beings are made in the image of God. Period. They are not one among many equal species. Humans are superior to all other species.

C. What is the objective character of truth and goodness? Is there a right thing to do? Or are all decisions based on circumstances?

EXAMPLE: The Bible is the source of objective truth. Whether I find it convenient, or not, I try to obey the Word of God.

D. Pleasure — what do you really enjoy doing? Is it moral?

EXAMPLE: I enjoy worshiping God with other Christian believers.

E. Fate — what/who really determines your life? Chance? Circumstances? God?

EXAMPLE: God is absolutely and personally involved in my life.

F. Justice — what are the consequences of our actions? Is there some sort of judgment? Do bad people suffer? Why do good people suffer?

EXAMPLE: The wages of sin is death. There is a judgment in death, after life.

Chapter 2 Test Answer

ESSAY (100 POINTS)

Write short essays discussing the worldviews in these contemporary movies.

A. *Pocahontas*

SAMPLE ANSWER: *Pocahontas* is the quintessential Romantic worshiping the benevolent outdoors. Smith would be a perfect existentialist. The materialistic, amoral English in the guise of Ratcliffe disturbs and seeks to exploit the pristine, perfect Eden. The amoral, existentialist English are like oil in water when they meet the noble, uncivilized Native Americans. The big question becomes: Who will corrupt whom? Will the Englishmen give up their corrupted civilization and embrace unspoiled romanticism? Or will the innocent Native Americans embrace corrupted, indolent civilization? The latter at first seems true. The noble savages — Native Americans — forget themselves for a while and react in self-serving ways. However, relying on their basic good natures, and relying on their dependable subjectivity, these romantics eventually see the light, and peace is maintained. Again, the agenda is a romantic agenda: peace at all costs — never mind justice or anything else. All good characters, interestingly enough, embrace a sort of theistic morality akin to the golden rule. Romantics, even naturalists, often do this. Even the pernicious Jamestown Governor Ratcliffe is a convert to moralistic romanticism. The grandmother in the tree is most disturbing and seems out of place in the movie. She represents shades of the darker sides of romanticism — its penchant to embrace Eastern religions. Students should note that modern art forms often embrace and then promote anachronistic, even opposing, worldviews simultaneously. Students must be able to discern these differences and speak truth in the face of deception.

B. *Scooby-Doo*

SAMPLE ANSWER: In this movie, like so many modern art forms, the characters wander around in an existentialist world where the feelings of the characters predominate. It is romanticism embracing moral theism: A character does what is right in his own eyes. He is free to do so as long as he does not injure anyone else. This movie celebrates individuality, as it were. With a modern self-righteousness, the group disagrees and disbands with no apparent consequences. They come together without any reconciliation — to a modern romantic and existentialist reconciliation that is too complicated a process and implies providential interference. There is no forgiveness, no admission of sin by any party. No, the characters rally around a cause and let bygones be bygones. Sincerity is more important than righteousness or justice. Humans find community when they find causes that enable each member of the community to satisfy his own self-interests. Inherent to romanticism is this sort of selfish self-centeredness. One's own perceived needs are one's Bible. Felt needs is the paramount dogma guiding all life decisions. Conversion occurs when the characters discover and then embrace this existential dogma. Everything is wonderful; all mysteries are revealed and all characters are fulfilled when this revelation is understood by all parties.

Narration — *The Call of the Wild* (Jack London)

Chapter 3

First Thoughts

The *narration* of a story is the way the author chooses to tell the story. An author intentionally uses different forms of narration, typically one of the following types. After this lesson, students should understand why an author chooses a particular narrative technique. They should also be able to write a literary analysis about the narration of any literary work.

Chapter Learning Objectives

In chapter 3 we will write our own worldviews and we will also analyze other worldviews in literature.

As a result of this chapter study you will be able to . . .

1. Define naturalism and discuss why it is not biblical.
2. Discuss the way females are presented in *The Call of the Wild.*

Look Ahead for Friday

- Turn in a final copy of essay or take it as a test

Lesson 1

Literary Analysis: Narration

Daily Assignment

- Warm-up: Pretend that you are a dog who is sleeping outside under a dripping faucet. What are you dreaming?
- Students will complete Concept Builder 3-A.
- Prayer journal: Students are encouraged to write in their prayer journal every day.
- Students need to review their material for the next assignment
- Students should systematically review their vocabulary words daily.

CONCEPT
BUILDER
3-A

Creating Narration

Create your own narration. (**Examples First-Person Narration:** I love soccer. **Omniscient Narration:** Mary and Sally thought, *I love soccer*. **Limited Omniscient Narration:** Mary thought, *I love soccer*. Sally said, "I love it, too." **Third-Person Objective:** Mary and Sally played soccer very well, and, by their actions, the reader might surmise that they loved soccer.)

ANSWER: Answers will vary. See the above examples.

Lesson 2

Chapter 1: Into the Primitive

Daily Assignment

- Warm-up: In what ways can instant messaging be harmful to writing?
- Students will complete Concept Builder 3-B.
- Prayer journal.
- Students should outline all assigned essays for the week.

CONCEPT
BUILDER
3-B

Style

You are unjustly accused of participating in a fight. Write letters to three friends: a peer, your parents, and your pastor.

I. DEAR BEST FRIEND (A PEER),
    This passage would be colloquial.

II. DEAR MOM AND DAD,
    This passage would be friendly, somewhat colloquial, but also respectful.

III. DEAR PASTOR,
    This passage would be friendly, somewhat colloquial, but also respectful.

Sample Essay: Narration

Daily Assignment

- Warm-up: Readers must judge the reliability of narrators. For example, the narrator in Edgar Allan Poe's short story "Tell Tale Heart" literarily is obviously insane as he tells the story! How reliable is that! How reliable a narrator is Buck in *The Call of the Wild*? What makes narration reliable? Unreliable?
- Students will complete a daily Concept Builder 3-C.
- Prayer journal.
- Students should write rough drafts of all assigned essays.

CONCEPT BUILDER 3-C

Naturalism in Art

A. Naturalism has realistic, often gross images.
B. Naturalism has many nature scenes but these scenes are dark, foggy, and dangerous.
C. Naturalism has a lot of confused, angry characters.
D. Naturalism creates a world where there is no God, no one in control, no benevolent force.

Rate this picture 1 (least) to 5 (greatest) in the categories above:

ANSWER: Answers will vary.

Lesson 4

Grammar Review: Spelling

Daily Assignment

- Warm-up: In first-person narration describe a memorable event (e.g., I went to the store and a man gave me a newspaper.); then, do the same thing in third-person objective narration (e.g., The man at the store gave the young person a newspaper.).

- Students will complete Concept Builder 3-D.

- Prayer journal.

- Review the assigned text. Keep vocabulary cards.

- This is the day that students should write, and then rewrite, the final drafts of their assigned essays.

CONCEPT
BUILDER
3-D

Narration in Literature

Match the following narration type with the narration examples.

A   Now this is the point...

B   The cold passed reluctantly ...

C   Scrooge knew he was dead? ...

D   "This out of all will remain ..."

Chapter 3 Test Answer

ESSAY (100 POINTS)

In a one- to two-page essay, discuss your favorite narrative in a short story or book, focusing on how the main character is developed through the narration, and why you believe this makes the character memorable.

Summary: Answers will vary.

Theme — *The Call of the Wild* (Jack London)

Chapter 4

First Thoughts

A theme is the central focus or concept the author is trying to reveal, to explore, to examine, not to be confused with a moral, or commentary it may imply. A recurring theme is a motif. Along with plot, character, setting, and style, theme is considered one of the fundamental components of fiction.

Chapter Learning Objectives

In chapter 4 we will understand the meaning of theme and discuss how it is used in literature.

As a result of this chapter study you will be able to . . .

1. Examine chapter 6, "The Love of Man," and discuss what biblical themes Buck exemplifies.
2. Evaluate how Christians should/can evaluate aberrant worldviews.

Look Ahead for Friday

- Turn in a final copy of essay or take it as a test

Lesson 1

Literary Analysis: Theme

Daily Assignment

- Warm-up: Create a short story that has a theme of immutability (never growing old).
- Students will complete Concept Builder 4-A.
- Prayer journal: Students are encouraged to write in their prayer journal every day.
- Students need to review their material for the next assignment
- Students should systematically review their vocabulary words daily.

CONCEPT
BUILDER
4-A

Theme Development

The theme is the central purpose of a literary piece. It is the central idea that an author wants to share with a reader. The author mostly uses the plot and characters to advance a theme.

In Jack London's *The Call of the Wild* an important theme is "survival of the fittest." Complete the chart below to show how London develops the theme. Find two other incidents from London's setting that advance this theme.

Setting Details	Resulting Character Trait
Buck is stolen and taken north.	He grows hard and strong.
Thornton shows Buck kindness.	Buck develops loyalty but does not misunderstand this as weakness.
Thornton is killed.	Buck answers the "call of the wild."
Theme: Survival of the Fittest	

Lesson 2

The Gift of the Magi

Daily Assignment

- Warm-up: Describe one theme in the 23rd Psalm. Next, write a poem that exhibits the same theme.

- Students will complete Concept Builder 4-B.

- Prayer journal.

- Students should outline all assigned essays for the week.

CONCEPT
BUILDER
4-B

Theme vs. Moral

A theme is not a moral. A theme is a statement of purpose of the piece. A moral is a lesson learned in the piece. **Read to find the theme and the moral of this fable.**

THEME: An elephant learns that meanness leads to consequences.

MORAL: Let this be a lesson to all that even the small and weak can join together to correct an injustice.

Lesson 3

Sample Essay: Theme

Daily Assignment

- Warm-up: What is the theme of your apartment/house? Colonial? Modern? Next describe the theme of your room. Neat? Messy?
- Students will complete Concept Builder 4-C.
- Prayer journal.
- Students should write rough drafts of all assigned essays and speech.

CONCEPT BUILDER 4-C

Themes in Movies

The theme is the central purpose of an artistic piece. It is the central idea that an artist wants to share with his viewer.

Answers will vary.

What is the central theme of these movies:

A. *Chariots of Fire*
   Endurance

B. *Ben Hur*
   Forgiveness

C. *Pocahontas*
   Love

D. *Bambi*
   Mutability

E. *Snow White and the Seven Dwarfs*
   Fidelity

Lesson 4

Grammar Review: Capitalization

Daily Assignment

- Warm-up: Sing a few bars of a song you like to your pet, and then tell the reader what the theme of this song is. Why do you like it?

- Students will complete Concept Builder 4-D.

- Prayer journal.

- Review the assigned text. Keep vocabulary cards.

- This is the day that students should write, and then rewrite, the final drafts of their assigned essay.

CONCEPT BUILDER 4-D

Capitalization Review

Correct the following sentences:

1. Our company is called For Such A Time As This.

   Our company is called For Such a Time as This.

2. "open the door now!" exclaimed the soldier.

   "Open the door now!" exclaimed the soldier.

3. I visited the washington monument.

   I visited the Washington Monument.

4. The north defeated the south in the american civil war.

   The North defeated the South in the American Civil War.

Chapter 4 Test Answer

ESSAY (100 POINTS)

In a one-page essay, state the theme of the short story "The Diamond Necklace" by the French writer, Guy de Maupassant.

Summary: Guy de Maupassant skillfully develops a theme of greed and irony. Ironically, the young lady, Matilde, spends her life, and the life of her husband, paying off a debt that she only thought she owed!

Characterization — *Joseph Narrative*

Chapter 5

First Thoughts

The Bible is the inspired, inerrant word of God. Additionally, it is a story of men and women struggling with everyday life. It is full of different types of literature, too. The following is a story, or narration, found in the first book of the Bible. Inspired by the Holy Spirit, Moses writes this wonderful story of forgiveness.

Chapter Learning Objectives

In chapter 5 we will understand the meaning of narrative and discuss how it is used in literature.

As a result of this chapter study you will be able to . . .

1. Write a list of all the wonderful characteristics that Joseph manifests (e.g., steadfastness, forgiveness, etc.) and make a similar list of the characteristics that God manifests in the same story (e.g., mercy toward Joseph in prison).

2. Write a portion of the story of Joseph from the perspective of an Egyptian historian under the employment of Pharaoh. Next, write a portion of the story from the perspective of Joseph's half-brother Judah.

Look Ahead for Friday

- Turn in a final copy of essay or take it as a test
- Optional objective test

Lesson 1

Joseph Narrative

Daily Assignment

- Warm-up: Describe an antagonist in your life. How have you handled this person?
- Students will complete Concept Builder 5-A.
- Prayer journal: Students are encouraged to write in their prayer journal every day.
- Students need to review their material for the next assignment
- Students should systematically review their vocabulary words daily.

CONCEPT
BUILDER
5-A

Active Reading

Read the Joseph narrative (Gen. 40ff)
What is the setting of this account?
ANSWER: Palestine (Israel) and Egypt during the patriarch age when Egypt held political hegemony in the Middle East.

Who is the protagonist?
ANSWER: Joseph

Who are some foils?
ANSWER: Judah and Joseph's other brothers; Pharaoh; Potiphar.

Who are the antagonists?
ANSWER: Potiphar's wife; Joseph's brothers.

How does Moses develop the protagonist?
ANSWER: Moses, the author, uses the plot to create adversities in Joseph's life, and these produce character changes that lie at the heart of this story.

Discuss some of the internal and external conflicts Joseph experiences.
ANSWER: Joseph has external conflict with his brothers. He has multiple internal conflicts: How does he remain faithful to God and serve the pagan Pharaoh? How can he forgive his evil brothers?

Imagine telling this story from Judah's perspective. How would it be different?
ANSWER: Answers will vary, but it seems obvious that Judah would discuss how selfish and self-centered his younger brother was.

Why doesn't Joseph punish his brothers?
ANSWER: Joseph has chosen to forgive them.

Why doesn't Joseph tell his brothers his true identity?
ANSWER: Initially he does this to see if his brothers have changed.

Lesson 2

Literary Analysis: Characterization

Daily Assignment

- Warm-up: Compare your family to a group of animals: who is who?
- Students will complete Concept Builder 5-B.
- Prayer journal.
- Students should outline all assigned essays for the week.

CONCEPT
BUILDER
5-B

Characterization of Joseph – Part One

Draw and label eight of the most important events that formed the character Joseph.

Dreams of domination of his brothers	*Sold to Potiphar*
Betrayal by Potiphar's wife	*Languishing in prison*
Freed from prison	*Exalted by Pharaoh*
Meets his brothers	*Reunited with his family*

Lesson 3

Characterization

Daily Assignment

- Warm-up: Who is your favorite movie actor? Movie actress? Why?
- Students will complete a daily Concept Builder 5-C.
- Prayer journal.
- Students should write rough drafts of all assigned essays.

CONCEPT
BUILDER
5-C

Characterization of Joseph – Part Two

Characters are usually presented by description and through their actions, speech, and thoughts. **Choose one incident in the life of Joseph and show how Moses, the author, reveals Joseph's character.**

Joseph's Character Development

Actions	Dialogue	Thoughts
This is the account of Joseph, a young man of 17, who was tending the flocks with his brothers, the sons of Bilhah and the sons of Zilpah, his father's wives, and he brought their father a bad report about them. *Joseph had a dream, and when he told it to his brothers, they hated him all the more.*	*He said to them, "Listen to this dream I had: We were binding sheaves of grain out in the field when suddenly my sheaf rose and stood upright, while your sheaves gathered around mine and bowed down to it."* *His brothers said to him, "Do you intend to reign over us? Will you actually rule us?"*	*Now Israel loved Joseph more than any of his other sons, because he had been born to him in his old age, and he made a richly ornamented robe for him. When his brothers saw that their father loved him more than any of them, they hated him and could not speak a kind word to him.* *And they hated him all the more because of his dream and what he had said.*

Result: *Joseph obviously is a spoiled, self-centered young man. Moses will show how he changes as the story unfolds.*

Lesson 4

Sample Literary Analysis: Play Review

Daily Assignment

- Warm-up: Who is your favorite relative? Describe him or her.
- Students will complete Concept Builder 5-D.
- Prayer journal.
- Review the assigned text. Keep vocabulary cards.
- This is the day that students should write, and then rewrite, the final drafts of their assigned essays.

CONCEPT BUILDER 5-D

Characterization: Reaction of Others

Characters are developed by reactions of others to them.

Incident	Reactions by Family	Reactions by Egyptians	Reactions by God	Resulting Characteristic in Joseph
Joseph is sold into slavery.	His father Jacob is brokenhearted. His brothers, while feeling some remorse, are grateful to be rid of him.	Potiphar bought Joseph and values his service.	God seems absent to Joseph, but Joseph continues to be faithful to His laws.	Joseph matures from a selfish young man into a growing saint of God.
Joseph refuses to disobey God with Potiphar's wife.	NA	Joseph is placed into prison.	God apparently is testing Joseph.	Joseph learns to follow God when it is convenient, and when it is not.
Joseph helps Pharaoh lead the nation in crisis.	The family indirectly benefits by Joseph's leadership. Joseph provides grain for most of the Middle East.	Joseph is revered and made a great leader.	God continues faithfully to lead Joseph. He is the same as He always was.	Joseph is still a humble follower of God. He does not give into temptation to be proud or haughty.
Joseph has a reunion with his family.	They are first terrified and then grateful.	The Egyptians are pleased because Joseph is grateful. Joseph's family is invited to join him in Egypt.	God remains the loving Father He has always been.	Joseph seems very happy.

Chapter 5 Test Answer

MATCHING (50 POINTS)

Match the characters with the role(s) they assume. Some characters will fulfill more than one role. Be prepared to defend your answer.

A   Joseph

C   Jacob

B/C Potiphar's wife

C   Pharaoh

C   The baker

B/C Joseph's brothers

A. Protagonist

B. Antagonist

C. Foil

Match the following:

B   Judah struggles with his feelings about selling Joseph into captivity.

A   Joseph physically struggles with his brothers when they put him into the pit.

B   Jacob worries about sending Benjamin to Egypt.

A   Jacob announces that his brothers are thieves.

A. External Conflict

B. Internal Conflict

Chapter 5 Essay Answer

ESSAY (50 POINTS)

Write a one-page essay discussing characterization in the short story "Luck of the Roaring Camp," by Bret Harte.

Summary: (Students should develop their essay around the following characterization points) Harte develops the character of the baby by relating reactions of colorful foils in the short story. At the same time, the foils themselves reveal their peculiarities which add to the humorous tone of the short story.

Plot — *Joseph Narrative*

Chapter 6

First Thoughts

The plot includes the events of the story, in the order the story gives them. A typical plot has five parts: *Exposition, Rising Action, Crisis* or *Climax, Falling Action,* and *Resolution.* The plot is the story itself. A simple example is *Jack and the Bean Stalk,* which exhibits all the elements. First, we meet Jack and his family (exposition). Then we see a crisis coming — Jack is desperately poor (rising action). Next, we reach the climax — when the giant chases Jack to and then down the vine. Then we sense the action is falling (after the giant is dead) and there is a resolution (Jack and his family live happily ever after).

Chapter Learning Objectives

In chapter 6 we explore the literary device plot. We see how Moses develops the account of the life of Joseph.

As a result of this chapter study you will be able to . . .

1. Examine the account of how this biblical plot unfolded.
2. Develop and understand how plot moves a story from start to finish.

Look Ahead for Friday
- Turn in a final copy of essay or take it as a test

Lesson 1

Play Review—Plot

Daily Assignment

- Warm-up: Summarize your favorite novel, and state why you liked it so much. What is its climax?
- Students will complete Concept Builder 6-A.
- Prayer journal: Students are encouraged to write in their prayer journal every day.
- Students need to review their material for the next assignment
- Students should systematically review their vocabulary words daily.

CONCEPT
BUILDER
6-A

Plot Practice

Discuss any book you have read, and identify the exposition (introductory information), rising action, climax, denouement (falling action), and resolution.

My choice is Mark Twain's *The Adventures of Huckleberry Finn.*

Exposition

All the principal characters are introduced: Huck Finn, Huck's father, Jim, Tom Sawyer.

Rising Action

Huck escapes from his abusive father with the runaway slave Jim.

Climax

Huck determines to disobey the law and to help Jim escape.

Denouement

Jim is captured, and Huck and his friend Tom Sawyer help him escape.

Resolution

Jim is released from slavery.

Lesson 2

Grammar Review: Commas

Daily Assignment

- Warm-up: What part of your life would you change, if you could?
- Students will complete Concept Builder 6-B.
- Prayer journal.
- Students should outline all assigned essays for the week.

CONCEPT
BUILDER
6-B

Plot Analysis of a Movie

Discuss any movie that you have seen and identify the exposition (introductory information), rising action, climax, denouement (falling action), and resolution.

Discuss any movie that you have seen and identify the exposition, rising action, climax, denouement, and resolution. Answers will vary. Here is an example from the movie *Chariots of Fire*:

Exposition
The protagonist and other characters are introduced.

Rising Action
We see them preparing for the Olympics.

Climax
There is a crisis when Eric finds he cannot run on Sunday.

Denouement
He and his peers win many medals.

Resolution
The story ends in a flashback sequence.

Lesson 3

Plot: "The Frog-Prince"

Daily Assignment

- Warm-up: Summarize your favorite movie and state why you liked it so much. What is its climax?
- Students will complete Concept Builder 6-C.
- Prayer journal.
- Students should write rough drafts of all assigned essays and speech.

CONCEPT
BUILDER
6-C

Literary Plot

Match each component of this story with the literary component of the plot.

Summary of *The Runaway Bunny* by Margaret Wise Brown.

D   The little bunny finally understands that he cannot escape the pursuing love of his mother.

A. Exposition (introductory material)

E   The little bunny happily accepts a carrot and decides to stay at home permanently.

B. Rising Action (unfolding action)

A   The reader learns that the principal characters are a baby bunny and his mom. We also learn that the young bunny is planning to run away.

C. Climax (the most exciting part)

B   The little bunny tries to run away from his mom.

D. Denouement (the falling action)

C   The reader learns that no matter where the bunny runs, the mommy bunny pursues and catches him.

E. Resolution (the conclusion)

Lesson 4

Student Essay

Daily Assignment

- Warm-up: Everyone has a story. Share one of the saddest parts of your story. Did this event occur in the rising action or falling action in your life?

- Students will complete Concept Builder 6-D.

- Prayer journal.

- Review the assigned text. Keep vocabulary cards.

- This is the day that students should write, and then rewrite, the final drafts of their assigned essay.

CONCEPT BUILDER 6-D

Completing a Story

Complete this story by filling in the plot in your own words.

EXPOSITION (INTRODUCTORY INFORMATION)

September 11, 1975, was a particularly warm, promising day even in the South where fall oftentimes is lost between tepid, late summer afternoons and frosty winter mornings. My heart was beaming too, for on this day I was to begin a two-day trip to Boston, where within the month I was to begin my seminary studies.

RISING ACTION

Answers will vary. The student will create his own story.

CLIMAX

Answers will vary.

FALLING ACTION

But I never forgot this bridge, because against its rain-wasted side, my poor compact car crumbled like a cheap, flimsy pop can. At the same time, my dreams were similarly shattered. Before that day was to end I was to experience horror as I had never known. Besides breaking my hand in two places, I had a severed right foot, compound multiple fractures in my right femur, and a painful fractured right hip. And, by the time this ordeal ended, I had decided to forget the ministry. I had no intentions of trusting my life to a God who would throw me against the side of that concrete bridge on Highway 1. It would take me another half a decade to finally finish my seminary work.

RESOLUTION

Answers will vary.

ESSAY (100 POINTS)

Write a one-page essay in which you discuss the plot development of a favorite movie, book, or play. In your answer, refer to the rising action, climax, falling action, and resolution.

Summary: *Answers will vary.*

Tone: Humor — *The Adventures of Tom Sawyer* (Mark Twain)

Chapter 7

First Thoughts

Perhaps no book captures the American idea of boyhood more than this novel. Partly autobiographical — Twain grew up on the Mississippi River — this book transcends its time and location. Not counting *The Gilded Age*, which was co-authored with Charles Dudley Warner, *The Adventures of Tom Sawyer* was Mark Twain's first novel. By the time Mark Twain died, it had become an American classic, and it remains perhaps the best loved of all his books among general readers.

Chapter Learning Objectives

In chapter 7 we explore the tone of Mark Twain's novel, and we analyze the way he creates humor.

As a result of this chapter study you will be able to . . .

1. Discuss when/if a lie is acceptable.
2. Chapter 8 in *Tom Sawyer* is a parody of a romantic novel. Explain.

Look Ahead for Friday

- Turn in a final copy of essay or take it as a test
- Optional objective test

Lesson 1

Literary Analysis: Humor/Tone

Daily Assignment

- Warm-up: Describe someone who is really funny — who makes you laugh. What makes that person funny?
- Students will complete Concept Builder 7-A.
- Prayer journal: Students are encouraged to write in their prayer journal every day.
- Students need to review their material for the next assignment
- Students should systematically review their vocabulary words daily.

CONCEPT BUILDER 7-A

Tone

Tone is the feeling that a writer creates for the reader. He/she uses several techniques. Use the chart below to identify the principal mood Twain creates and to list the different elements that he uses to create that mood/ tone.

Mood: *Humor*

ELEMENT	EXAMPLE
Figurative Language	*"Hang the boy, can't I never learn anything? Ain't he played me tricks enough like that for me to be looking out for him by this time? But old fools is the biggest fools there is. Can't learn an old dog new tricks, as the saying is. . . ."*
Imagery	*The old lady pulled her spectacles down and looked over them about the room; then she put them up and looked out under them. She seldom or never looked through them for so small a thing as a boy; they were her state pair, the pride of her heart, and were built for "style," not service — she could have seen through a pair of stove-lids just as well. She looked perplexed for a moment, and then said, not fiercely, but still loud enough for*
Descriptions	*The old lady reached out her hand and felt Tom's shirt, and said:* *"But you ain't too warm now, though." And it flattered her to reflect that she had discovered that the shirt was dry without anybody knowing that that was what she had in her mind. But in spite of her, Tom knew where the wind lay, now. So he forestalled what might be the next move*

ELEMENT	EXAMPLE
Dialogue	*"TOM!"* *No answer.* *"TOM!"* *No answer.* *"What's gone with that boy, I wonder? You TOM!"* *No answer.*
Sound Devices (slang, et al.)	*"By jingo! for two cents I will do it."*
Situational Irony (humorous situations)	*"Tom, it was middling warm in school, warn't it?"* *"Yes'm."* *"Powerful warm, warn't it?"* *"Yes'm."* *"Didn't you want to go in a-swimming, Tom?"* *A bit of a scare shot through Tom — a touch of uncomfortable suspicion. He searched Aunt Polly's face, but it told him nothing. So he said:* *"No'm — well, not very much."* *The old lady reached out her hand and felt Tom's shirt, and said:* *"But you ain't too warm now, though." And it flattered her to reflect that she had discovered that the shirt was dry without anybody knowing that that was what she had* *in her mind. But in spite of her, Tom knew where the wind lay, now. So he forestalled what might be the next move:* *"Some of us pumped on our heads — mine's damp yet. See?"* *Aunt Polly was vexed to think she had overlooked that bit of circumstantial evidence, and missed a trick. Then she had a new inspiration:* *"Tom, you didn't have to undo your shirt collar where I sewed it, to pump on your head, did you? Unbutton your jacket!"* *The trouble vanished out of Tom's face. He opened his jacket. His shirt collar was securely sewed.* *"Bother! Well, go 'long with you. I'd made sure you'd played hookey and been a-swimming. But I forgive ye, Tom. I reckon you're a kind of a singed cat, as the saying is — better'n you look. This time."* *She was half sorry her sagacity had miscarried, and half glad that Tom had stumbled into obedient conduct for once.*

Lesson 2

Humor from *The Adventures of Tom Sawyer*

Daily Assignment

- Warm-up: Describe your favorite comedian. Why do you like him/her?
- Students will complete Concept Builder 7-B.
- Prayer journal.
- Students should outline all assigned essays for the week.

CONCEPT BUILDER 7-B

Active Reading

Read the excerpt from chapter one in *Tom Sawyer* by Mark Twain, and then answer the following questions:

Why does Twain begin his book with so much dialogue?

Dialogue is a perfect way to introduce humor. It is also a great way to show character traits.

Who is the protagonist?

Tom Sawyer

What is the narrative technique?

Omniscient Narration, but Twain prefers to give most narration through Tom's perspective.

From the first page or two, what can you infer about Tom Sawyer's personality?

He is a mischievous but moral young man.

Sample Essay: Tone in *The Screwtape Letters*

Daily Assignment

- Warm-up: Tell your favorite joke. Analyze why it is humorous.

- Students will complete Concept Builder 7-C.

- Prayer journal.

- Students should write rough drafts of all assigned essays and speech.

CONCEPT
BUILDER
7-C

Changing the Tone

Tone or mood is the feeling that a writer creates for the reader. He/she often uses the plot to develop the mood. For instance, change the following incident into a sad/serious incident.

The scene would be far more serious if Tom really had a legitimate excuse when Aunt Polly finds him.

Lesson 4

Grammar Review: Commas

Daily Assignment

- Warm-up: Describe an incident that would be humorous to one person and not to someone else.
- Students will complete Concept Builder 7-D.
- Prayer journal.
- Review the assigned text. Keep vocabulary cards.
- This is the day that students should write, and then rewrite, the final drafts of their assigned essay.

CONCEPT BUILDER 7-D

The Author's Voice

Literary critics sometimes refer to mood as an "author's voice." Voice is a way an author allows a reader to discern the human personalities in the author's work. For example, if I wanted to show the reader that a character was a teenager I could have the character say, "Hey, dude, what is happening man?" How does Twain develop voice?

Complete the following diagram, considering how Twain develops voice. Write your responses on top of the circles.

Mood/Style:

The mood is humorous.

Language/Diction:

Twain uses colloquialisms and slang to develop this humor

Characterization:

Tom is an affable, innocent, but intelligent young man. This adds to the mood.

Chapter 7 Test Answer

MULTIPLE CHOICE (25 POINTS)

C The author of Tom Sawyer is (A) Bret Harte, (B) Huck Finn, (C) Samuel Clemens, (D) William Faulkner.

B Tom and Huck go to the graveyard to (A) find Injun Joe (B) rid themselves of warts (C) find a dead cat (D) scare Aunt Polly.

A Tom got in trouble in school for (A) lying about Becky's torn page (B) cheating on a test (C) talking too much in class (D) pretending he was lost on the Mississippi River.

C Tom and Huck ultimately returned from Jackson Island because (A) Huck was bitten by a snake (B) Tom was sick (C) they were homesick (D) they were hungry.

D Injun Joe was to die in the cave because (A) the sheriff caught him (B) he was lost (C) Tom shot him (D) his way out was blocked.

Chapter 7 Essay Answer

ESSAY (75 POINTS)

Write a one-page essay in which you discuss how humor is presented in the short story "The Ransom of Red Chief," by O. Henry.

Summary: First-person narration is a popular narrative technique for humorous writers. The narrator is intimately involved in the action; he is not a neutral observer. His being involved increases the possibilities of dramatic irony.

Red Chief, while exhibiting some unimaginative archetype traits, nonetheless invites the reader to laugh.

The primary mode of humor is dramatic irony: it is the kidnappers who are held captive by the victim!

The collaborated letter is hilarious! Full of hyperbole!

Allegory — *Idylls of the King*
(Alfred Lord Tennyson)

Chapter 8

First Thoughts

You will recognize immediately the storyline in *Idylls of the King*. This book, which is really a very long narrative poem, is another version of the King Arthur legend. Yes, you will recognize King Arthur, Guinevere, Sir Lancelot, and the other knights of the Round Table. The poem is hard to read at times, but it is worth the effort. Alfred Lord Tennyson is one of the best English poets of the Victorian Age.

Chapter Learning Objectives

In chapter 8 we analyze the use of allegory in *Idylls of the King*.

As a result of this chapter study you will be able to . . .

1. Discuss symbolism in *Idylls of the King*.

2. Analyze Tennyson's faith journey.

3. Evaluate Tennyson's view of heaven.

Look Ahead for Friday

- Turn in a final copy of essay or take it as a test

Lesson 1

Literary Analysis: Allegory

Daily Assignment

- Warm-up: What is your favorite book? Why?

- Students will complete Concept Builder 8-A.

- Prayer journal: Students are encouraged to write in their prayer journal every day.

- Students need to review their material for the next assignment

- Students should systematically review their vocabulary words daily.

CONCEPT BUILDER 8-A

Active Reading

Read this excerpt of *Idylls of the King* by Lord Alfred Tennyson, and answer the following questions.

Part I Excerpt

1. Describe King Arthur. Who does he symbolize?
ANSWER: Answers will vary.

2. What is the narrative point of view? Why do you think Tennyson chose this point of view?
ANSWER: Limited omniscient narration. He wished to tell the story from Arthur's point of view.

3. What is the setting? Is it important? In other words, could this story happen anywhere?
ANSWER: Camelot. The story captures universal, timeless themes. In that sense, yes, it could occur anywhere anytime.

Lesson 2

Allegory in *The Scarlet Letter*

Daily Assignment

- Warm-up: What is your favorite car? Why?
- Students will complete Concept Builder 8-B.
- Prayer journal.
- Students should outline all assigned essays for the week.

CONCEPT BUILDER 8-B

Allegory in *Idylls of the King*

An allegory is full of symbolism. Note the symbols in *Idylls of the King*.

Character	What he/she represents
King Arthur	Christ-like figure
Mordred	A Judas Iscariot figure.
Ivanhoe	Peter or one of the other disciples.
Guinevere	A figure somewhat like Mary

Characterization

Daily Assignment

- Warm-up: What do you want to do/be when you grow up? Why?

- Students will complete a daily Concept Builder 8-C.

- Prayer journal.

- Students should write rough drafts of all assigned essays.

CONCEPT
BUILDER
8-C

Paragraphs

One of the central components of prose selection is the paragraph. It does not matter how long a paragraph is. Length is not important as long as the paragraph contains a sentence or sentences unified around one central, controlling idea.

Rewrite the paragraph in your own words.

Huckleberry Finn was one of the earliest novels where the issue of motivation and self are paramount. We have come a long way, baby! Kenneth J. Gergen in his book *The Saturated Self: Dilemmas of Identity in Contemporary Life* (HarperCollins, 1991) argues that self-motivation has appeared at the end of this century as a sort of selfishness that is very destructive to Christianity. Huck Finn also has a mean dad. As Huckleberry regularly relativizes his situation on the banks of the Mississippi, likewise Christians are making their faith into another relative system of truth.

Lesson 4

Student Essay: Excalibur

Daily Assignment

- Warm-up: If you could be in one movie, what movie would that be? Which character would you be?
- Students will complete Concept Builder 8-D.
- Prayer journal.
- Review the assigned text. Keep vocabulary cards.
- This is the day that students should write, and then rewrite, the final drafts of their assigned essays.

CONCEPT
BUILDER
8-D

Poetic Devices

Alliteration is the repetition of consonant sounds at the beginning of words.

Assonance is the repetition of vowel sounds.

Consonance is the repetition of consonant sounds in the middle and at the end of words.

Repetition is the recurrence of words and phrases.

Show examples of each below, in your own words.

Poetic Devices	Examples
Alliteration	*And with a shameful swiftness:*
Assonance	*"O King," she cried, "and I will tell thee: few, Few, but all brave, all of one mind with him;"*
Consonance	*And Arthur, passing thence to battle, felt Travail, and throes and agonies of the life,*
Repetition	*For first Aurelius lived and fought and died, And after him King Uther fought and died,*

ESSAY (100 POINTS)

In a one-page essay, describe the use of symbolism in the following powerful scene from Victor Hugo's *Les Miserables.*

Summary: (Some symbolism represented in *Les Miserables* follows. Your student may find other instances.) This is one of the most powerful, and symbolic passages in Western literature. The bishop represents Christ. The bishop's house-keepers represent Jesus' 12 disciples. Jean Valjean would be Judas. However, the story digresses at this point. As 30 pieces of silver were paid to Judas for betraying Jesus, silver "saved" another man's soul. "Do not forget, never forget, that you have promised to use this money in becoming an honest man."

Characterization — *Idylls of the King* (Alfred Lord Tennyson)

Chapter 9

First Thoughts

Idylls of the King, published between 1856 and 1885, is a cycle of 12 narrative poems by the English poet Alfred, Lord Tennyson. The character Arthur attempts and fails to ameliorate mankind and create a perfect kingdom, from his coming to power to his death at the hands of the traitor Mordred. Tennyson uses several characters to develop this mysterious, mythical figure. The failure of Arthur to raise others to the same level as himself ultimately presages a tragic ending.

Chapter Learning Objectives

In chapter 9 we examine Tennyson's characters, who so effectively develop the character of Arthur.

As a result of this chapter study you will be able to . . .

1. Compare and contrast Guinevere and Elaine, and finally, discuss the wonderful foil Lancelot.

2. Compare and contrast King Arthur with King David. Consider their strengths and weaknesses and kinds of leadership.

3. Describe the historical King Arthur and how his story evolved over time.

Look Ahead for Friday

- Turn in a final copy of essay or take it as a test

Lesson 1

Sample Essay: Characterization

Daily Assignment

- Warm-up: Often God uses an antagonist in our lives to make us more like Him. Describe such a situation in your own life.
- Students will complete Concept Builder 9-A.
- Prayer journal: Students are encouraged to write in their prayer journal every day.
- Students need to review their material for the next assignment
- Students should systematically review their vocabulary words daily.

CONCEPT
BUILDER
9-A

Characterization of Arthur

Tennyson uses narration, character reaction, and the setting to develop Arthur. Note the narration and character reaction in a summary as was done with the setting.

Setting	And thus the land of Cameliard was waste, Thick with wet woods, and many a beast therein,/ And none or few to scare or chase the beast; So that wild dog, and wolf and boar and bear Came night and day, and rooted in the fields, And wallowed in the gardens of the King.	*The land was in chaos until Arthur came and brought order.*
Narration	And Arthur, passing thence to battle, felt Travail, and throes and agonies of the life, Desiring to be joined with Guinevere; And thinking as he rode, "Her father said That there between the man and beast they die. Shall I not lift her from this land of beasts Up to my throne, and side by side with me?"	*Arthur, the unselfish hero, is thinking of his beloved Guinevere.*
Character Reaction	And Arthur yet had done no deed of arms, But heard the call, and came: and Guinevere Stood by the castle walls to watch him pass;	*We see our hero from the eyes of Guinevere.*

Lesson 2

Characterization of Animals

Daily Assignment

- Warm-up: Describe the most abhorrent (i.e., the worst) villain you known.
- Students will complete Concept Builder 9-B.
- Prayer journal.
- Students should outline all assigned essays for the week.

CONCEPT
BUILDER
9-B

Epic Poetry

Epic poetry is poetry that celebrates the exploits of a national figure. It is often meant to be sung. Identify the **antagonist** (opponent of the protagonist) and **crisis** in this epic poem.

Protagonist	Antagonist	Crisis
Casey	Opposing baseball team	Casey must get a hit!

Lesson 3

Grammar Review: Paragraphs

Daily Assignment

- Warm-up: Compare yourself to one of the characters in *Idylls Of The King*. Why did you choose that person?
- Students will complete Concept Builder 9-C.
- Prayer journal.
- Students should write rough drafts of all assigned essays and speech.

CONCEPT BUILDER 9-C

Epic Heroes

Epic heroes are larger than life.

Underline words that describe Arthur.

Brave	Tentative	Cowardly	Honest	Loyal	Strong
Aggressive	Handsome	Smart	Immoral	Sensitive	Weak
Humble	Selfish	Selfless	Unpredictable	Overconfident	Outgoing

Underline words that describe Casey.

Brave	Tentative	Cowardly	Honest	Loyal	Strong
Aggressive	Handsome	Smart	Immoral	Sensitive	Weak
Humble	Selfish	Selfless	Unpredictable	Overconfident	Outgoing

Underline words that describe Samson (in the Bible).

Brave	Tentative	Cowardly	Honest	Loyal	Strong
Aggressive	Handsome	Smart	Immoral	Sensitive	Weak
Humble	Selfish	Selfless	Unpredictable	Overconfident	Outgoing

Lesson 4

Student Essay

Daily Assignment

- Warm-up: Discuss two or three foils in your life. Why have these people been so vital to your development?
- Students will complete Concept Builder 9-D.
- Prayer journal.
- Review the assigned text. Keep vocabulary cards.
- This is the day that students should write, and then rewrite, the final drafts of their assigned essay.

CONCEPT BUILDER 9-D

Epic Hero Exploits

Inevitably epic heroes conquer hardships, slay dragons, and accomplish heroic deeds. In fact, every hero has to overcome one or two obstacles or he/she will not be great.

List the obstacles that face these heroes.

Hero/Heroine	Obstacles He/She Faces
King Arthur	*Mordred and other enemies.*
Spider-Man	*Many villains, super strength, and others.*
Queen Esther	*She had to persuade her husband/king to save her people.*
My Mom	*Answers will vary*
My Dad	*Answers will vary*
A Friend	*Answers will vary*

ESSAY (100 POINTS)

In a one-page essay, discuss the way the author creates memorable characters in the passage.

Summary: The personalities of all the characters are replicated in the character of the land in which they live. The land is wild, unpredictable, and unforgiving. So are its owners. For instance, Helen defies convention. Like the weather, she will not be controlled. Another way the author creates memorable characters is by the use of a young narrator. His responses are age-appropriate, ingenious, and candid. This enhances the more unique aspects of each character. Next, the author develops his characters by the way that others in the story — notably the narrator — react to her. Finally, his characters are sometimes archetypal. Does Mammy Lee come across as a unique person, or is she an archetype who belongs in a movie like *Gone with the Wind*?

Plot — *Treasure Island* (Robert Louis Stevenson)

Chapter 10

First Thoughts

Stevenson wrote *Treasure Island* for his stepson in 1881. He said, "If this doesn't fetch the kids, why, they have gone rotten since my day." It's a tale of pirates, a treasure map, a mutiny, and a one-legged sea cook. *Treasure Island* remains one of literature's best-loved adventure stories. The heroes and villains of the classic tale — Long John Silver, Jim Hawkins, Dr. Livesey, Billy Bones, Squire Trelawney, and Ben Gunn — are some of the most famous literary characters in American literature. In short, this novel is a must-read for every American youth!

Chapter Learning Objectives

In chapter 10 we analyze one of the premier adventure novels in the English language.

As a result of this chapter study you will be able to . . .

1. Evaluate the just or unjust reward that Long John Silver receives.

2. Discuss the excessive use of coincidence in this novel.

Look Ahead for Friday

- Turn in a final copy of essay or take it as a test
- Optional objective test

Lesson 1

Literary Analysis: Plot

Daily Assignment

- Warm-up: If your life were a "novel," where would the climax occur? Describe this incident.
- Students will complete Concept Builder 10-A.
- Prayer journal: Students are encouraged to write in their prayer journal every day.
- Students need to review their material for the next assignment
- Students should systematically review their vocabulary words daily.

CONCEPT
BUILDER
10-A

Active Reading

Treasure Island by Robert Louis Stevenson
Chapter 1 — "The Old Sea-dog at the Admiral Benbow"

Stevenson does not give the reader the name of this strange visitor (until later). Why?

ANSWER: A nameless visitor adds more suspense to the plot, and suspense is obviously Stevenson's goal.

Imagery is a word that describes descriptions that authors use to bring their subject alive. Circle three examples.

ANSWER: "I remember him as if it were yesterday, as he came plodding to the inn door." I remember him as if it were yesterday, as he came plodding to the inn door, his sea-chest following behind him in a hand-barrow — a tall, strong, heavy, nut-brown man, his tarry pigtail falling over the shoulder of his soiled blue coat, his hands ragged and scarred, with black, broken nails, and the sabre cut across one cheek, a dirty, livid white. I remember him looking round the cover and whistling to himself as he did so, and then breaking out in that old sea-song that he sang so often afterwards: "Fifteen men on the dead man's chest — Yo-ho-ho, and a bottle of rum!" in the high, old tottering voice that seemed to have been tuned and broken at the capstan bars. Then he rapped on the door with a bit of stick like a handspike that he carried, and when my father appeared, called roughly for a glass of rum. This, when it was brought to him, he drank slowly, like a connoisseur, lingering on the taste and still looking about him at the cliffs and up at our signboard.

Lesson 2

Grammar Review: Write in Positive Terms

Daily Assignment

- Warm-up: Write a story that begins with the following passage. Be sure you include exposition, rising action, a climax, denouement (falling action), and resolution. My mother's father, James Jesse Bayne — I call him Big Daddy — ran away from his two-room, Louisiana pine barren home when he was eight. For the next seven years he lived in woods and swamps in the wild Delta bottoms. Living on the outskirts of early 20th-century poor southern towns, he experienced poverty that was sublime in its intensity. Southern cuisine and lifestyle were the epitome of conservation and economy.

  Practically nothing was discarded from any animal: intestines, gizzards, stomachs — it all was eaten. There was precious little left for hoboes like Big Daddy, who was forced to eat crawdads and red-bellied brim. There was not much that was big about Big Daddy. At 16 his blond — almost white — hair and blue eyes oversaw a body that was not symmetrical. For instance, his left arm was at least two inches longer than his right.

- Students will complete Concept Builder 10-B.

- Prayer journal.

- Students should outline all assigned essays for the week.

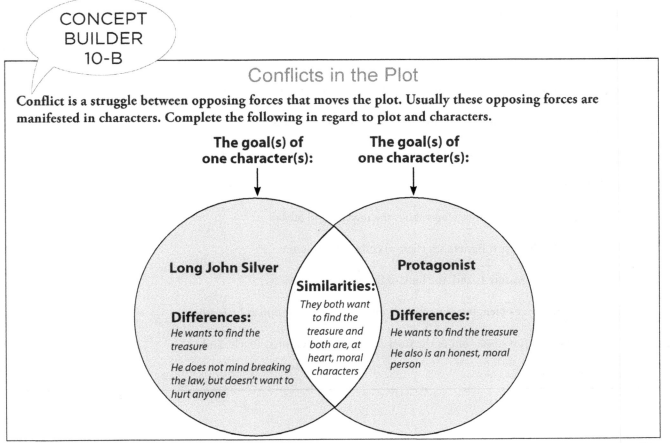

CONCEPT BUILDER 10-B

Conflicts in the Plot

Conflict is a struggle between opposing forces that moves the plot. Usually these opposing forces are manifested in characters. Complete the following in regard to plot and characters.

The goal(s) of one character(s):

The goal(s) of one character(s):

Long John Silver

Differences:
He wants to find the treasure

He does not mind breaking the law, but doesn't want to hurt anyone

Similarities:
They both want to find the treasure and both are, at heart, moral characters

Protagonist

Differences:
He wants to find the treasure

He also is an honest, moral person

Lesson 3

Choice of Words

Daily Assignment

- Warm-up: Draw a picture then write a story that is based on your picture. Be sure you include exposition, rising action, a climax, denouement (falling action), and resolution.
- Students will complete a daily Concept Builder 10-C.
- Prayer journal.
- Students should write rough drafts of all assigned essays.

CONCEPT BUILDER 10-C

Sequencing the Plot — Part 1

The sequence is the order of events in a plot. It is never coincidental; every author has a purpose in sequencing his events. Number the events as they occur in the book.

1 An old drunken seaman named Billy Bones becomes a long-term lodger at the Admiral Benbow Inn.

10 After several other events, the treasure is divided amongst Trelawney and his loyal men …

7 Hiding in the woods, Jim sees Silver murder Tom, a crewman loyal to Smollett …

8 In the meanwhile, Trelawney, Livesey, and their men surprise and overpower …

3 Jim Hawkins comes to the house of local landlord Squire Trelawney and his …

4 Despite Captain Smollett's misgivings about the mission and Silver's …

2   Jim and his mother open Bones's sea chest to collect the amount …

5 When they reach Treasure Island, the bulk of Silver's men go ashore …

6 Jim lands with Silver's men, but runs away from them almost as soon as he is ashore.

9 During the night, Jim sneaks out of the stockade, takes Ben Gunn's coracle, and …

http://en.wikipedia.org/wiki/Treasure_Island

Lesson 4

How *Treasure Island* Was Written

Daily Assignment

- Warm-up: Look back at the rising action in your personal story. Discuss ways that God watched over you and therefore was a part of this rising action.
- Students will complete Concept Builder 10-D.
- Prayer journal.
- Review the assigned text. Keep vocabulary cards.
- This is the day that students should write, and then rewrite, the final drafts of their assigned essays.

CONCEPT
BUILDER
10-D

Sequencing the Plot — Part 2

The sequence is the order of events in a plot. It is never coincidental; every author has a purpose in sequencing his events. Look at the sequence of events as they emerge in *Treasure Island*. Now, put the different components in the plot: Rising, Action, Exposition, Climax, Falling Action (Denouement), Resolution.

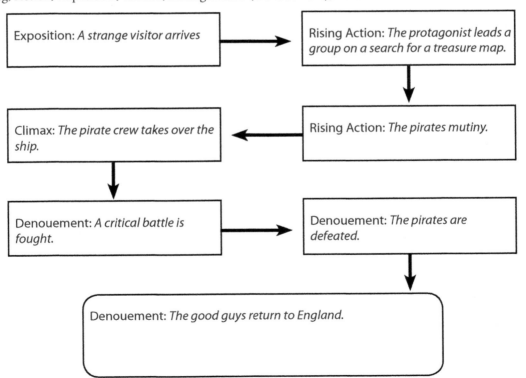

Chapter 10 Test Answer

MULTIPLE CHOICE (50 POINTS)

A While at the Admiral Benbow, Billy Bones fears (A) a one-legged man (B) the police (C) a tax-collector (D) pneumonia.

A The protagonist of this novel is (A) Jim (B) Long John Silver (C) Billy Bones (D) Blackbeard.

C The black spot means that the bearer (A) has won the lottery (B) has been drafted (C) is marked to die (D) will soon assume is place on board a ship.

B Israel Hands is killed by (A) Long John (B) Jim (C) Mary Sue (D) Dr. Livesey.

D At the end, Long John (A) returns to England to stand trial (B) dies (C) marries a young lady (D) deserts.

Chapter 10 Essay Answer

ESSAY (50 POINTS)

In a one-page essay, discuss the way H.G. Wells introduces his protagonist in *The Invisible Man*.

Summary: Quite intentionally, Wells introduces his character on a dreary night, in an enclosed stuffy house. He reveals his character through narration with a rather unspectacular, ordinary, polite woman, Mrs. Hall. Using this foil (i.e., Mrs. Hall) he can slowly reveal his protagonist — as if he were unwinding the cloth off the character for the reader. Mrs. Halls' innocent musings about what happened to what she thought was a suffering man were more prophetic than she knew. He was not suffering physically, but he was suffering in his heart. Later, he will suffer in both ways.

Suspense — *Treasure Island*
(Robert Louis Stevenson)

Chapter 11

First Thoughts

Perhaps no book has more adventure tales than Stevenson's *Treasure Island*. It is full of suspense. Readers are often sitting on the edge of their seats! The tone of a literary piece is the mood or feeling that it evokes in the reader. One important tone or mood is suspense.

Chapter Learning Objectives

In chapter 11 we will analyze how Stevenson produces suspense in Treasure Island.

As a result of this chapter study you will be able to . . .

1. Determine how Stevenson creates suspense in *Treasure Island*.

2. Analyze the worldview of *Treasure Island*.

3. Compare and contrast the way suspense is created in *Treasure Island* with the way suspense is created in *Kidnapped*.

Look Ahead for Friday

- Turn in a final copy of essay or take it as a test

Lesson 1

Literary Example of Suspense

Daily Assignment

- Warm-up: When is fear OK? And when is fear bad? What is the difference between fear and suspense?
- Students will complete Concept Builder 11-A.
- Prayer journal: Students are encouraged to write in their prayer journal every day.
- Students need to review their material for the next assignment
- Students should systematically review their vocabulary words daily.

CONCEPT
BUILDER
11-A

Suspense

Draw a suspenseful picture of a stormy day. Then draw a warm, happy picture of a stormy day.

Answer will vary.

Lesson 2

Grammar Review: Possessives

Daily Assignment

- Warm-up: Describe a suspenseful book you read. What made it suspenseful?
- Students will complete Concept Builder 11-B.
- Prayer journal.
- Students should outline all assigned essays for the week.

CONCEPT
BUILDER
11-B

Suspense 1

Show how Stevenson builds suspense in the first few chapters of his book using different literary elements. Fill in the circles with incidents from the story.

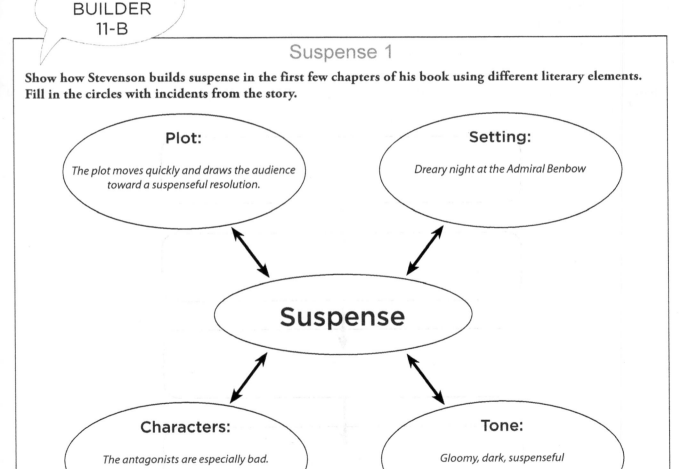

Plot:
The plot moves quickly and draws the audience toward a suspenseful resolution.

Setting:
Dreary night at the Admiral Benbow

Suspense

Characters:
The antagonists are especially bad.

Tone:
Gloomy, dark, suspenseful

Lesson 3

Suspense in "Riki Tiki Tavi"
by Rudyard Kipling

Daily Assignment

- Warm-up: Describe a suspenseful movie. What made it suspenseful?
- Students will complete a daily Concept Builder 11-C.
- Prayer journal.
- Students should write rough drafts of all assigned essays.

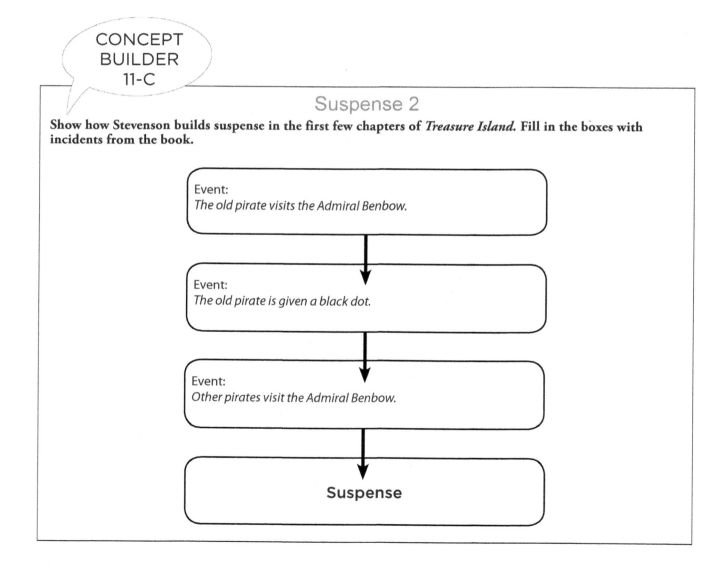

CONCEPT
BUILDER
11-C

Suspense 2

Show how Stevenson builds suspense in the first few chapters of *Treasure Island*. Fill in the boxes with incidents from the book.

Event:
The old pirate visits the Admiral Benbow.

Event:
The old pirate is given a black dot.

Event:
Other pirates visit the Admiral Benbow.

Suspense

Lesson 4

Student Essay

Daily Assignment

- Warm-up: What makes certain animals scary? Like a cobra? Or a raven? Describe the scariest animal you know.

- Students will complete Concept Builder 11-D.

- Prayer journal.

- Review the assigned text. Keep vocabulary cards.

- This is the day that students should write, and then rewrite, the final drafts of their assigned essays.

CONCEPT BUILDER 11-D

Predicting and Foreshadowing

Most authors are quite intentional about the way they structure their literary piece. A clever reader, however, will discern the outcome/resolution long before the literary piece ends. Find as many hints as possible in *Treasure Island* (if possible, before you finish reading it) and offer an informed prediction.

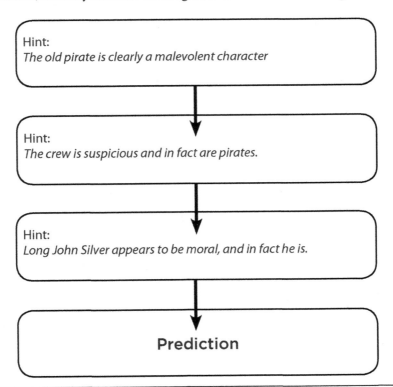

Hint:
The old pirate is clearly a malevolent character

↓

Hint:
The crew is suspicious and in fact are pirates.

↓

Hint:
Long John Silver appears to be moral, and in fact he is.

↓

Prediction

ESSAY (100 POINTS)

In a one-page essay, discuss the way H.G. Wells creates suspense in this chapter of his novel, *War of the Worlds*.

Summary: Darkness always invites suspense. The combination of revelation and secret keeps the reader guessing. The reader, like the characters in the story, is fed information piecemeal. The truth is slowly and methodically revealed. Wells slowly reveals the details of the emerging Martians. They appear pretty scary—snake-like creatures—but the reader has no idea how dangerous. Nonetheless, what is more sinister than the appearance of a snake-like creature? Finally, Wells uses first-person narration so that the reader will be present at the vital moment. In fact, to make sure that the reader is personally involved, he has a young boy fall in the hole next to the alien space craft.

Narration — *How Green Was My Valley* (Richard Llewellyn)

Chapter 12

First Thoughts

This unpretentious novel is the story of Huw Morgan, a Welsh boy growing up in the coal fields. Tragedy, humor, courage, and strength permeate this remarkable novel. Richard Llewellyn's 1939 international best-selling novel *How Green Was My Valley* stands the test of time as a literary classic. Set in a Welsh coal mining village in the last quarter of the 19th century, its themes of spiritual honesty opposed to physical yearning and bondage are developed in a language that combines Fitzgerald's richness and Steinbeck's clarity. The author delights readers with incisive ways of observing everyday life that make them seem timeless. This characteristic helps make a writing transcend generations.

Chapter Learning Objectives

In chapter 12 we will analyze narration and the way it is used in *How Green Was My Valley*.

As a result of this chapter study you will be able to . . .

1. Closely examine Huw's family and discuss how the family members exhibit Judeo-Christian characteristics toward one another.

2. Analyze how the pastor foil functions.

Look Ahead for Friday

- Turn in a final copy of essay or take it as a test

Lesson 1

Literary Analysis: Narration

Daily Assignment

- Warm-up: Describe your earliest memory. How reliable is this memory?
- Students will complete Concept Builder 12-A.
- Prayer journal: Students are encouraged to write in their prayer journal every day.
- Students need to review their material for the next assignment
- Students should systematically review their vocabulary words daily.

CONCEPT BUILDER 12-A

Elements of a Story

Analyze the following elements of the novel *How Green Was My Valley.*

Elements	Yes/No	Because . . .
Characters Do the characters seem real?	Yes	*They experience real-life dramas.*
Narration Is Huw a credible narrator?	Yes	*He is an intelligent, reliable observer.*
Setting Is the setting important? Does it seem real?	Yes	*The juxtaposition of the beauty of a Welsh village and the ugly coal mines is one metaphor for the theme of the novel: mutability.*
Plot Does the story flow logically? Does it flow well?	Yes	*While the novel is a flashback, the author carefully develops a logically developed story.*
Theme Is there a theme?	Yes	*Mutability, inter-generation love.*

Lesson 2

Sample Essay: Narration

Daily Assignment

- Warm-up: Using metaphors and words that a four-year-old will understand, explain how rain clouds are formed.
- Students will complete Concept Builder 12-B.
- Prayer journal.
- Students should outline all assigned essays for the week.

CONCEPT BUILDER 12-B

Forming Conclusions

Analyze the conclusion of the novel *How Green Was My Valley.*

Elements	Yes/No	Because . . .
In spite of the fact that his hometown can be ugly and brutal, Huw obviously loves his hometown.	Yes	*Because the people he loves live there.*
Huw is in a loving, supportive family.	Yes	*All the characters are well-adjusted and supportive of the family unit.*
The coal mine brings both life and death to Huw's community.	Yes	*While the mine brings income to the family, it also kills some fathers and brings destruction on the landscape.*
While Huw is not overtly a Christian, his actions and attitudes clearly show that he is a theist (or someone who acts out of a moral code).	Yes	*Huw obviously respects his father and is honest.*

Lesson 3

Grammar Review: Parallelism

Daily Assignment

- Warm-up: Describe a relative or friend who has been very important to your formation as a person.
- Students will complete a daily Concept Builder 12-C.
- Prayer journal.
- Students should write rough drafts of all assigned essays.

CONCEPT
BUILDER
12-C

Generalizations

To make a generalization about a literary work is to form an analytical opinion based upon facts and observations in the story. What generalizations from *How Green Was My Valley* can you conclude from the following facts/observations?

Facts/Observations	
Facts/Observations Huw remembers father and brothers when they came home from the mines on Saturday night.	*The very intensity of the language, the vividness of the details, clearly shows that Huw cared deeply for his father. In fact, Huw loved his family very much. Even mundane events like getting off work at the factory on Saturday night intruded themselves into Huw's memory.*
Facts/Observations There was trouble brewing at the mines. The men talked of unions and organizing, and the owners were angry.	*There is a potential for harm for his father and brothers. Huw is very concerned. There is an ominous tone in this narrative.*
Facts/Observations When he learned that his brother Ivor was to marry, he was sorry to lose his brother; but from the first moment Huw saw Ivor's Bronwen, he loved her.	*Huw felt secure in his family's love. He was able to extend that love to Outsiders — even when it meant, in effect, that he might lose some family members in the process.*

Generalization
Huw loved his father a great deal.

Lesson 4

Student Essay

Daily Assignment

- Warm-up: Describe the place you want to live in the future. Why do you choose this place?
- Students will complete Concept Builder 12-D.
- Prayer journal.
- Review the assigned text. Keep vocabulary cards.
- This is the day that students should write, and then rewrite, the final drafts of their assigned essays.

CONCEPT
BUILDER
12-D

Narrative Techniques

Analyze the narrative technique of the novel *How Green Was My Valley,* **as well as the use of other narrative techniques in books you have read.**

Narrative Technique	Advantage/Disadvantage	Example
First Person Narration: The narrator tells the story.	The reader is drawn into the character and into the story very quickly. The narrator can use dialogue to reveal the character's thoughts. This is a way to have the reader feel empathy toward one particular character. First- person narration is also a great way to exhibit colloquial language in order to produce humor (e.g., *The Adventures of Tom Sawyer* by Mark Twain). One obvious disadvantage is that the narrator must be reliable, or the reader will question the veracity of the narrator's story (e.g., *A Separate Peace* by John Knowles) Huw is a pretty reliable first-person narrator: "Strange that the mind will forget so much of what only this moment has passed, and yet hold clear and bright the memory of what happened years ago; of men and women long since dead." — Huw Morgan, *How Green Was My Valley*	I really enjoyed hitting the baseball. After I hit the ball, it flew to Mark. (The reader is invited into the mind of the narrator, who is telling the story in first person.)
Omniscient Narration: The author uses all the characters to tell the story.	*This narrative technique gives the author the most power. He/she may develop the world of the reader at the author's leisure. Authors who want to make the plot primary prefer this technique. This technique works very well in short story formats (e.g., "The Gift of the Magi," O. Henry) where prose economy is important, but it may hurt larger novel pieces where characterization is more important. For example, omniscient narration in* War and Peace *by Leo Tolstoy probably adds 300 pages to the novel. Omniscient narration forces Tolstoy to describe in great detail personality. Tolstoy cannot use the consciousness or even dialogue to develop the plot. He is forced to use omniscient narration.*	David really enjoyed hitting the baseball. As the baseball flew to Mark, he thought about the last time he was hit by a baseball.
Limited Omniscient Narration: The author uses one or two characters to tell the story.	*This narrative technique allows the author to tell the story through the mind of a character, but to do so more subtly. Modern authors prefer this technique over first-person narration. The disadvantages are that the reader sometimes struggles to understand the motivation of other "foil" characters. For instance, in Earnest Hemingway's* A Farewell to Arms *the protagonist, Frederick Henry, is a whining naturalist. His romantic friends are inadequately developed (in this author's opinion) by Hemingway.*	David really enjoyed hitting the ball. The ball was hit to Mark.
Third Person Objective: The author (not the narrator) tells the story.	*It is difficult to find examples of this narration. It is popular in journalism and other types of impersonal writing — which, generally speaking, is the nemesis of the fiction genre.*	David hit the baseball. Mark was hit by the baseball.

ESSAY (100 POINTS)

In a one-page essay, discuss how reliable the narrator is in this passage from Daniel Defoe's *Robinson Crusoe*. Next, rewrite the passage from Friday's perspective.

Summary: Crusoe is a typical 17th-century man who struggles with racism and parochialism. Perhaps more enlightened than most, Crusoe is nevertheless fairly reliable. Among white Europeans, virtually no one championed the civil rights of any minorities. For Defoe to do so, through his character Robinson Crusoe, would be contrived beyond belief and far ahead of his time.

Answers will vary concerning Friday's perspective of this event. Friday presumably accepted his station in life. Of course, Defoe creates Friday, who has no notion of what it means to be a minority person.

Theme — *Alice in Wonderland* (Lewis Carroll)

Chapter 13

First Thoughts

Walt Disney returned the precocious Alice to the American psyche in the 1960s, but he hardly did Carroll's brilliant fantasy justice. On one level, *Alice in Wonderland* is a children's story; on another level it is a scathing criticism of Victorian England. As you read Carroll's novel, try to read it at both levels.

Chapter Learning Objectives

In chapter 13 we will analyze themes in *Alice in Wonderland*.

As a result of this chapter study you will be able to . . .

1. Some define maturity as learning to delay gratification. Using this definition, find biblical characters who were mature and immature.

2. Find examples of puns and other word plays in *Alice in Wonderland* and explain why Carroll uses them in his book.

Look Ahead for Friday

- Turn in a final copy of essay or take it as a test

Lesson 1

Literary Analysis: Theme

Daily Assignment

- Warm-up: If you were directing a movie about Alice, what major actress would you have play Alice? Why did you make this choice?

- Students will complete Concept Builder 13-A.

- Prayer journal: Students are encouraged to write in their prayer journal every day.

- Students need to review their material for the next assignment

- Students should systematically review their vocabulary words daily.

CONCEPT
BUILDER
13-A

Active Reading

Read chapter 1 of *Alice in Wonderland* ("Down the Rabbit-Hole") by Lewis Carroll, and then answer the following questions.

1. What is the narrative technique? What advantages does this offer Carroll?
ANSWER: Limited Omniscient. He is able to use Alice's mind to show how she matures as a character.

2. Who is the protagonist? How is she created?
ANSWER: Alice. She is an innocent young girl who loses a lot of her innocence as the novel progresses.

3. What is the setting? Is it believable?
ANSWER: A rabbit hole/fantasy land. This fantasy world engenders the same human characteristics that are universally present.

4. Give two examples of imagery.
ANSWER: "However, this bottle was NOT marked 'poison,' so Alice ventured to taste it, and finding it very nice, (it had, in fact, a sort of mixed flavour of cherry-tart, custard, pine-apple, roast turkey, toffee, and hot buttered toast) she very soon finished it off" and "and she tried her best to climb up one of the legs of the table, but it was too slippery. . . ."

5. Even though this is a fantasy, can you identify with Alice?
ANSWER: Most readers can. Her struggles to overcome adversity are substantial and part of the universal human condition.

Lesson 2

Sample Essay: Theme

Daily Assignment

- Warm-up: Alice is on a great adventure. What is the best adventure you have had?
- Students will complete Concept Builder 13-B.
- Prayer journal.
- Students should outline all assigned essays for the week.

CONCEPT BUILDER 13-B

Elements of a Story

Analyze the following elements of the novel *Alice in Wonderland*.

Elements	Yes/No	Because . . .
Characters Do the characters seem real?	Yes	Even though this is a fantasy, it is also a parody. The essence of parody is that the author pokes fun at a real issue by use of fantastic characters. For example, Gulliver's Travels.
Narration Is the narration credible (reliable, believable)?	Yes	Alice's innocence make her observations fresh and informative.
Setting Is the setting important? Does it seem real?	Yes	On one hand, the fantasy world of the rabbit hole gives the author all sorts of possibilities. On the other hand, the author could have used other settings to develop the same themes.
Plot Does the story flow logically? Does it flow well?	Yes	The novel feels like the protagonist is on an episodic adventure with every story unrelated to the previous story.
Theme Is there a theme?	Yes	The author develops the theme of hypocrisy. Through the protagonist's journey, the author shows how dishonest and facile components of Alice's world are.

Lesson 3

Grammar Review:
Keep Related Words Together

Daily Assignment

- Warm-up: If you were directing a movie about Alice, what person in your family would you have play Alice? Why did you make this choice?

- Students will complete a daily Concept Builder 13-C.

- Prayer journal.

- Students should write rough drafts of all assigned essays.

CONCEPT BUILDER 13-C

Characters: Static or Dynamic?

A static character stays the same. A dynamic character changes. Does Alice change? How?

Character	Alice	Queen
Protagonist, antagonist, foil	Protagonist	Antagonist
Static or dynamic?	Dynamic	Static
If the character changes, how?	Alice matures.	NA
Why does he/she change?	As Alice faces new obstacles, she matures.	She does not change.

Lesson 4

Student Essay

Daily Assignment

- Warm-up: What has been the hardest thing about growing up?
- Students will complete Concept Builder 13-D.
- Prayer journal.
- Review the assigned text. Keep vocabulary cards.
- This is the day that students should write, and then rewrite, the final drafts of their assigned essays.

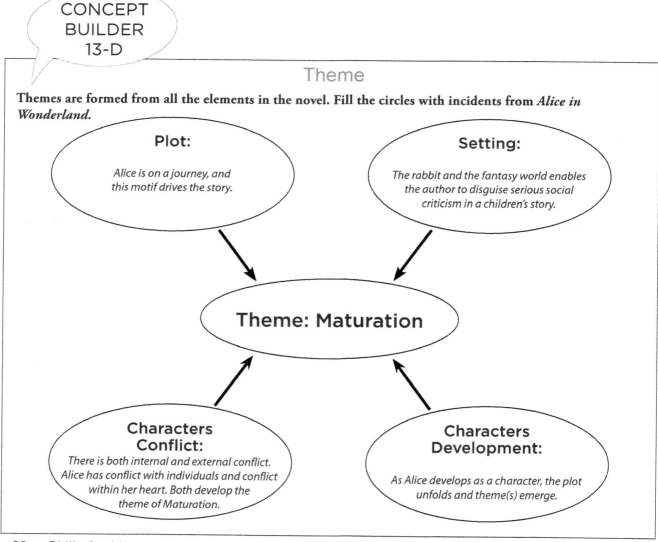

CONCEPT
BUILDER
13-D

Theme

Themes are formed from all the elements in the novel. Fill the circles with incidents from *Alice in Wonderland*.

Plot:

Alice is on a journey, and this motif drives the story.

Setting:

The rabbit and the fantasy world enables the author to disguise serious social criticism in a children's story.

Theme: Maturation

Characters Conflict:

There is both internal and external conflict. Alice has conflict with individuals and conflict within her heart. Both develop the theme of Maturation.

Characters Development:

As Alice develops as a character, the plot unfolds and theme(s) emerge.

Chapter 13 Test Answer

ESSAY (100 POINTS)

Behind this story about a colorful character, Roshanna, is a powerful theme. In a one-page essay, discuss what that theme is.

Summary: The story of Roshanna is the story of the American urban church. In spite of the fact that America has become a predominately urban society, churches in North America do not appear to be prepared to deal with particular issues. Two particularly troublesome problems have to do with race and poverty. The author of this piece shows, through human relationships, the complexity and depth of these problems. Students could further develop the issues of race and poverty in urban churches.

Parody — *Alice in Wonderland* (Lewis Carroll)

Chapter 14

First Thoughts

Amadeus, a movie based on a Broadway play about the famous composer Mozart, takes parody to new heights. A parody pokes fun at society and/or individuals in society. In this case, Mozart constantly pokes fun at Salieri, who is jealous of Mozart's genius and is offended by his coarseness and superficiality. Frustrated by his own mediocrity, Salieri tries to thwart Amadeus's career, but only succeeds in destroying himself. Some parodies are quite sobering. *The Floating Opera* (1956), John Barth's parody of modern life, invites the reader to seriously consider whether life has any meaning at all (Barth advances the worldview called absurdism). Entire books are parodies (e.g., *Don Quixote*, Cervantes, and *Alice in Wonderland*, Lewis Carroll).

Chapter Learning Objectives

In chapter 14 we will analyze the use of parody in *Alice in Wonderland*.

As a result of this chapter study you will be able to . . .

1. Explore what the Bible has to say about morality.
2. Compare George Orwell's *Animal Farm* with *Alice in Wonderland*.

Look Ahead for Friday

- Turn in a final copy of essay or take it as a test

Lesson 1

Literary Analysis: Parody

Daily Assignment

- Warm-up: What actress would you choose to play the Queen of Hearts?
- Students will complete Concept Builder 14-A.
- Prayer journal: Students are encouraged to write in their prayer journal every day.
- Students need to review their material for the next assignment
- Students should systematically review their vocabulary words daily.

CONCEPT BUILDER 14-A

Characterization

Characterization is the way an author develops a character in his literary work. Offer evidence from the text to show how Carroll develops Alice as a character.

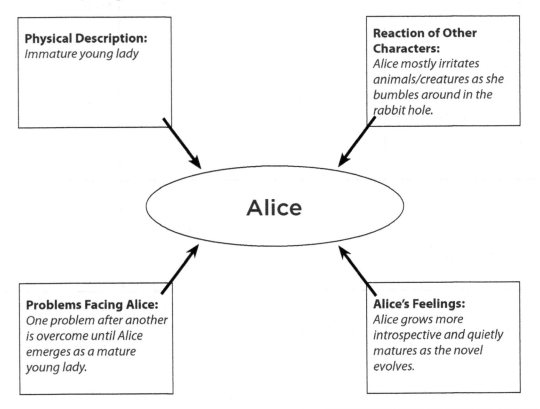

Physical Description:
Immature young lady

Reaction of Other Characters:
Alice mostly irritates animals/creatures as she bumbles around in the rabbit hole.

Alice

Problems Facing Alice:
One problem after another is overcome until Alice emerges as a mature young lady.

Alice's Feelings:
Alice grows more introspective and quietly matures as the novel evolves.

Lesson 2

Grammar Review: Irregardless

Daily Assignment

- Warm-up: Describe a situation when someone inappropriately made fun of someone else.
- Students will complete Concept Builder 14-B.
- Prayer journal.
- Students should outline all assigned essays for the week.

CONCEPT
BUILDER
14-B

Episodes

This novel is episodic — Carroll takes the reader from episode to episode. As Alice wanders in her imaginary world, she learns new lessons that help her develop as a character. Normally, this development occurs as she experiences internal conflict.

Elements	Internal Conflict	Outcome/ Behavioral Change
Alice is bored with sitting on the riverbank with her sister, who is reading a book. Suddenly she sees a white rabbit, wearing a coat and carrying a watch, run past, lamenting running late. She follows it down a rabbit hole and falls very slowly down a tunnel lined with curious objects.	*Alice is both naive and inquisitive–both immature traits.*	*Alice begins her long road to maturity.*
Alice finds a box under the table in which there is a cake with the words "EAT ME" on it. She eats it and the cake makes Alice grow so tall that her head hits the ceiling. She cries.	*Alice is frustrated and unhappy with her circumstances.*	*She learns that things may be difficult but she can still find her way out of a dilemma.*
The Cheshire Cat appears in a tree, directing her to the March Hare's house.	*He disappears but his grin remains behind to float on its own in the air, prompting Alice to remark that she has often seen a cat without a grin but never a grin without a cat. This disconcerting event causes some confusion, but Alice, at this point, moves on quickly.*	*Alice, like most mature people, has learned to adjust to new situations.*

Lesson 3

An Example of Parody

Daily Assignment

- Warm-up: Contrast the *The Chronicles of Narnia* and *Alice in Wonderland*. How is the fantasy component different?
- Students will complete a daily Concept Builder 14-C.
- Prayer journal.
- Students should write rough drafts of all assigned essays.

Parody

A parody pokes fun at an individual, institution, or society at large. In this case, Carroll is poking fun at Victorian England.

Complete the following chart. (Answers will vary. Students may need to consult an outside source. The following are a few options.)

Incident/Elements	Textual Evidence
Bill the Lizard may be a play on the name of Benjamin Disraeli.	This occurs when Alice is stuck in one of the rooms of the White Rabbit's house.
Victorian children were expected to behave at all times. As Marjorie and C.H.B. Quennell point out in their book A History of Everyday Things in England, "In practice this meant that instant obedience to every order, respectful manners and punctuality were expected as a matter of course from every member of the family. Argument and 'answering back' were never permitted, and indeed, they were seldom attempted" (103). Many of the rules put before Victorian children must have seemed somewhat arbitrary.	*When Alice is at the trial of the Knave of Hearts, Carroll parodies this sort of rule and the expected behavior by having Alice "talk back" to the king.*
The Queen of Hearts is presumptuous and dangerous and represents Queen Victoria.	*The Queen of Hearts is a foul-tempered monarch, that Carroll himself pictured as "a blind fury," and who is quick to decree death sentences at the slightest offense. Her most famous line, one which she repeats often, is "Off with their heads!"*
Parodies of Victorian songs/poems.	*Twinkle, twinkle, little star, How I wonder what you are! Up above the world so high, Like a diamond in the sky. — June Taylor Twinkle, twinkle, little bat How I wonder what you're at! Up above the world you fly Like a tea-tray in the sky. — the Hatter*
The Lobster Quadrille that Alice encounters is a parody of the quadrille, a dance that was used to open nearly every fashionable ball at the time that Alice's adventures was written and published.	*The Mock Turtle and Gryphon's mad romp.*

Lesson 4

Student Essay

Daily Assignment

- Warm-up: Did you like *Alice In Wonderland*? Why or why not?
- Students will complete Concept Builder 14-D.
- Prayer journal.
- Review the assigned text. Keep vocabulary cards.
- This is the day that students should write, and then rewrite, the final drafts of their assigned essays.

Setting

The setting is very important to this novel. Fill in the empty circles with supporting details from the text.

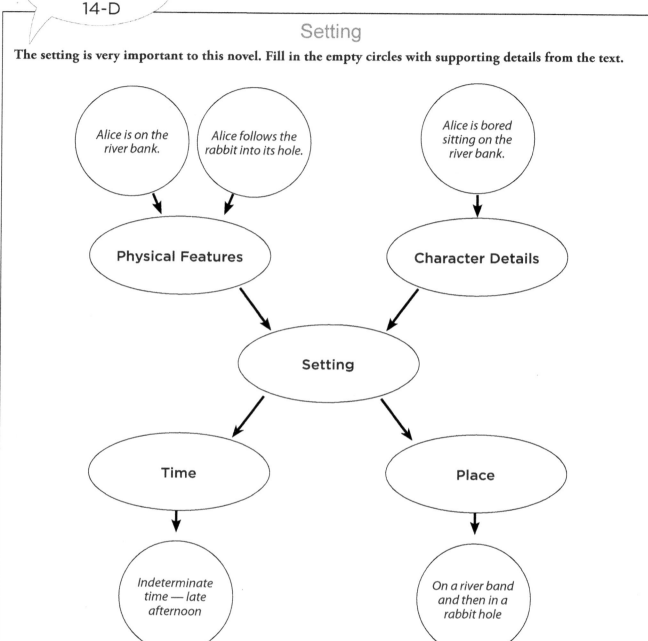

Alice is on the river bank.

Alice follows the rabbit into its hole.

Alice is bored sitting on the river bank.

Physical Features

Character Details

Setting

Time

Place

Indeterminate time — late afternoon

On a river band and then in a rabbit hole

Chapter 14 Test Answer

ESSAY (100 POINTS)

Write a one-page Summary that is a parody of *Tom Sawyer*. Present him as a spoiled, selfish boy who is so full of himself that he cannot see the humor of his situation. In other words, you are being asked to write a parody of a parody. This writing technique is in contrast to Twain's *Tom Sawyer*, who is full of insights into human characters.

Summary: Answers will vary. The answer could be something like this . . .

Hello, my name is Tom Sawyer. Yeah, you spell Tom with a "T," moron!

What are my earliest memories? Well, being with a bunch of losers for one — for instance, take Aunt Polly. Wow! What a sanctimonious — to all you dopes out there that means "falsely noble" — woman Aunt Polly is.

Dialogue — "Oracle of the Dog" (G.K. Chesterton)

Chapter 15

First Thoughts

If C.S. Lewis were the greatest apologist of the 20th century, G.K. Chesterton was perhaps the greatest of the 19th century. He was also a great fiction writer, an example of a sonorous marriage of consummate writing skill and pious Christianity. The task that Chesterton undertook — to influence and hopefully convert secular culture through skillful art — is one that belongs to this generation more than ever. Chesterton once lamented that Christians are like Englishmen who visit France. These Englishmen, Chesterton argued, spoke slowly and with elucidation. They were shocked when they realized that the French did not understand them. The French would never understand English — no matter how slowly and effectively the Englishmen spoke. The only language the French understood was French. Likewise, Christians, Chesterton continued, spoke in Christian language to people who didn't know the language. Until Christians speak in secular language, the secular world will not understand them. Think about it.

Chapter Learning Objectives

In chapter 15 we will analyze the use of dialogue in G.K. Chesterton's "The Oracle of the Dog."

As a result of this chapter study you will be able to . . .

1. Ascertain how Chesterton uses dialogue to advance his plot and develop his characters.

2. Analyze how far Christians can go to be "accepted," when sharing their faith with unbelievers, before they compromise their witness

3. Find examples of coincidence in "Oracle of the Dog."

Look Ahead for Friday

*   Turn in a final copy of essay or take it as a test

Lesson 1

Literary Analysis: Dialogue

Daily Assignment

- Warm-up: Try to persuade your parents to allow you to attend a church party that ends beyond your curfew.
- Students will complete Concept Builder 15-A.
- Prayer journal: Students are encouraged to write in their prayer journal every day.
- Students need to review their material for the next assignment
- Students should systematically review their vocabulary words daily.

CONCEPT
BUILDER
15-A

Dialogue

Dialogue is used by a writer to advance the plot and to develop characters. Read this excerpt from *The Red Badge of Courage* (chapter 1) by Steven Crane, and then answer the following questions.

1. How does the dialogue advance the plot?
ANSWER: The conversations that the young private (i.e., Henry Fleming) has and the conversations he overhears, tell the reader important information.

2. What is the narrative point of view? Why does Crane choose this approach?
ANSWER: Omniscient narration, but in a way that still allows the reader to draw his own conclusions. The naturalist Crane would prefer to let the story unfold in a "natural" way, but no doubt finds it impossible without occasionally allowing the reader a chance to see into the mind of a character or two.

Lesson 2

"The Oracle of the Dog"

Daily Assignment

- Warm-up: Imagine what a dog would say as he waits for his master to take him for a walk.
- Students will complete Concept Builder 15-B.
- Prayer journal.
- Students should outline all assigned essays for the week.

CONCEPT BUILDER 15-B

Visualizing

Descriptions in "The Oracle of the Dog" help the readers visualize the action as it unfolds in the plot. While there is very little action, the reader is asked to follow very closely the resolution of the mystery. Detail what the plot is. Next, what is the plot? Where does the action occur? What are some of the actions that are occurring?

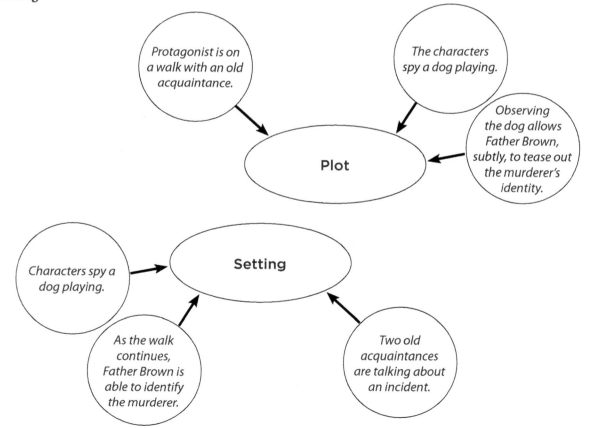

Protagonist is on a walk with an old acquaintance.

The characters spy a dog playing.

Observing the dog allows Father Brown, subtly, to tease out the murderer's identity.

Plot

Characters spy a dog playing.

Setting

As the walk continues, Father Brown is able to identify the murderer.

Two old acquaintances are talking about an incident.

Lesson 3

Grammar Review: Different From

Daily Assignment

- Warm-up: Write a conversation between a grandfather and his grandson about what they will do during the day.
- Students will complete Concept Builder 15-C.
- Prayer journal.
- Students should write rough drafts of all assigned essays and speech.

CONCEPT
BUILDER
15-C

Dialogue: Develop the Characters

Dialogue is used by a writer to advance the plot and to develop characters. Read this excerpt from _The Adventures of Tom Sawyer_ (chapter 1) by Mark Twain, and then answer the following questions.

1. What does this dialogue tell you about Tom?

ANSWER: Tom is a charming, creative, precocious child who loves to be humorous with his aunt. His colloquialisms merely add to his charm.

2. What does the dialogue tell you about Aunt Polly?

ANSWER: On the outside she seems rough, but on the inside she is as good as gold.

Student Essay

Daily Assignment

- Warm-up: Write an imaginary conversation that a three- and four-year-old might have about Sunday School.
- Students will complete Concept Builder 15-D.
- Prayer journal.
- Review the assigned text. Keep vocabulary cards.
- This is the day that students should write, and then rewrite, the final drafts of their assigned essay.

CONCEPT BUILDER 15-D

Dialogue: Develop the Characters

Dialogue is used by a writer to advance the plot and to develop characters. Read this excerpt from *The Time Machine* (chapter 3) by H.G. Wells, and then answer the following question.

Wells tries his best to capture the mixture of feelings the Time Traveler experiences. Discuss some of these feelings.

ANSWER: Here are some examples: I am afraid I cannot convey the peculiar sensations of time travelling. They are excessively unpleasant. There is a feeling exactly like that one has upon a switchback — of a helpless headlong motion! I felt the same horrible anticipation, too, of an imminent smash. As I put on pace, night followed day like the flapping of a black wing. The dim suggestion of the laboratory seemed presently to fall away from me, and I saw the sun hopping swiftly across the sky, leaping it every minute, and every minute marking a day. I supposed the laboratory had been destroyed and I had come into the open air. I had a dim impression of scaffolding, but I was already going too fast to be conscious of any moving things. The slowest snail that ever crawled dashed by too fast for me. The twinkling succession of darkness and light was excessively painful to the eye.

Chapter 15 Test Answer

ESSAY (100 POINTS)

In *Little Women*, Louisa May Alcott is a master at describing characters through dialogue.

In a one-page essay, using chapter 1, discuss how Alcott uses dialogue to describe characters.

Summary: Alcott uses dialogue exclusively to tell the reader in subtle, and not so subtle, ways who her characters are. From the first, for instance, the reader knows that Jo is the assertive, vivacious, and intelligent sister. She suggests the unusual, and her activities are often on the edge of propriety. Jo has no unspoken thought! Beth is clearly the sensible sister — she keeps the peace. Beth also speaks for her parents. Her dialogue presents her as a "surrogate" parent. She is a foil to Jo. Amy and Meg usually merely follow the crowd. Thus, with virtually no description of the characters — the reader has no idea of their age or appearance — the reader nonetheless feels that he knows them. Through dialogue the reader now knows that Jo is a tomboy and Amy is a scatterbrain. Meg is the eldest daughter — again, dialogue, not third-person narration, provides this information for the reader.

Humor — *The Screwtape Letters* (C.S. Lewis)

Chapter 16

First Thoughts

The Screwtape Letters is fiction, but it seems very real. The issues confronted in this book occur in everyday lives. The book contains 31 letters from Screwtape, the devil, to his nephew, Wormwood, a young demon. Screwtape is writing friendly advice to his nephew concerning how to obtain the soul of a young man.

Chapter Learning Objectives

In chapter 16 we will analyze the way C.S. Lewis develops humor in *The Screwtape Letters*.

As a result of this chapter study you will be able to . . .

1. Understand the difference between humor and satire.

2. Compare a passage from *The Voyage of the Dawn Treader* (Narnia Chronicles by C.S. Lewis) to John 14:1–7.

3. Discuss how a Christian believer overcomes and resists evil temptations.

Look Ahead for Friday

-   Turn in a final copy of essay
-   Take Weekly Test

Lesson 1

Sample Essay: Humor

Daily Assignment

- Warm-up: What is the primary challenge you face as you grow in Christ?
- Students will complete Concept Builder 16-A.
- Prayer journal: Students are encouraged to write in their prayer journal every day.
- Students need to review their material for the next assignment
- Students should systematically review their vocabulary words daily.

CONCEPT
BUILDER
16-A

Humor

Read the text below and answer the following questions.

1. How is characterization used to develop humor?
ANSWER: This woman is obviously a strong-willed individual: My mother, who walked three miles a day and regularly ate chicken gizzards fried in old lard shrugged her shoulders and forgot about the whole thing. In fact, even after Geritol and BC Powders failed, she refused to visit her doctor. To question a doctor-friend's diagnosis was worse than a serious illness — it was downright unfriendly, something my mother manifestly refused to be.

2. How is plot used to develop humor?
ANSWER: On one level this is a tragic event: the woman is obviously very sick, fatally sick. On another level, it is a humorous event. The introduction of colorful characters like Dr. Johnny Joe and his behavior during the operation offer the reader comic relief from the very serious plot.

Lesson 2

Grammar Review: Colloquialisms

Daily Assignment

- Warm-up: Recite any grammatical "rules" that you have memorized.
- Students will complete Concept Builder 16-B.
- Prayer journal.
- Students should outline all assigned essays for the week.

CONCEPT
BUILDER
16-B

Humor: Dramatic Irony

Dramatic irony occurs when a reader has special knowledge that the characters do not have. Circle examples of dramatic irony in the text below.

1. The main character is Mammaw. Yet, she is not even present! How is this dramatic irony?

ANSWER: The Mammaw character has a ubiquitous presence to the narrator. Her peculiarities are manifested through the consciousness of the narrator and through his dialogue.

2. The garden is compared to the author's grandmother. Why is this humorous?

ANSWER: In her own way, Mammaw was very much like this garden: "A southern garden was both afflicted and blessed by a ten-month growing season. It was constantly battling interloping Johnson grass and ravenous rodents. As a result, while northern flowers, shrubs, and perennials sported vivid colors and vigorous stems vitalized by cool summer evenings and short growing seasons, southern Arkansas begonias and roses had to endure endlessly long, hot summer days. Their paleness was the result of too much sun, not too little. However, commitment to task assured ardent redolence if not inspired accretion." She was old fashioned but winsome in her aberrant behavior.

Lesson 3

Grammar Review: Different From

Daily Assignment

- Warm-up: Is there really a devil? How do you know?
- Students will complete Concept Builder 16-C.
- Prayer journal.
- Students should write rough drafts of all assigned essays and speech.

CONCEPT
BUILDER
16-C

Humor: Situational Irony

Situational irony occurs when a character (or the reader) is surprised by what happens. Answer the questions below and explain why this situation is so ironical/humorous.

1. What is the narrative technique?
ANSWER: Omniscient narration

2. How does the author create humor using a snake?
ANSWER: Snakes were both the friends and mortal enemies of my mother's family. It is ironical, and humorous, that a snake is used to kill other undesirable snakes!

3. Is the reader surprised by what happens? Is Big Daddy? Big Momma? Why? What is the outcome?
ANSWER: Yes. Is Big Daddy? Yes, very surprised. Big Momma? It is not clear but the reader may surmise that she is surprised too.

Lesson 4

Student Essay

Daily Assignment

- Warm-up: What is the most effective way to overcome sin?
- Students will complete Concept Builder 16-D.
- Prayer journal.
- Review the assigned text. Keep vocabulary cards.
- This is the day that students should write, and then rewrite, the final drafts of their assigned essay.

CONCEPT BUILDER 16-D

Humor: Exaggeration & Personification

Technically speaking, humor is a cognitive (of the mind) experience that produces laughter. It comes in many different forms. The following is a humorous poem.

Exaggeration	*An old spoon/Bent, gouged/Polished to an evil Glitter.*
Personification	*Now, it is a living/Thing: ready/To scratch a name/On a prison wall*

ESSAY (100 POINTS)

In Chapter One of Charles Dickens' *A Christmas Carol*, the reader is presented a memorable figure, Ebenezer Scrooge. In the first few pages, Scrooge comes alive as Dickens introduces him to the reader in a mock-serious tone. In a one-page essay, discuss how Dickens uses tone to present Ebenezer Scrooge.

Summary: The master of understatement, Dickens introduces Ebenezer Scrooge in a tongue-in-cheek manner. Regardless of Scrooge's money and power, Marley had died and so would Scrooge someday. Dickens reminds the reader of this fact as he reminds Scrooge.

Dickens presents Scrooge as a typical grouch. This familiar archetype comfortably invites the reader to laugh and to cry when the reader reads this passage. Scrooge is pathetic but the reader laughs and cries at the same time. He is the quintessential villain, one who is very familiar to the Victorian English audience.

The scene with the nephew is a typical Dickens approach to a serious subject. It is both serious and humor. The good-natured nephew lets the reader know that Scrooge's bark is worse than his bite. However, it is tragic that Scrooge has wasted all this time and abused the family he did not appreciate.

Tone: Propaganda — *Uncle Tom's Cabin* (Harriet Beecher Stowe)

Chapter 17

First Thoughts

Isabella Jones Beecher gave her sister-in-law Harriet Beecher Stowe the idea to write *Uncle Tom's Cabin*. Isabella was outraged by Congress' decision to pass the Fugitive Slave Law (1850) that gave southern slave owners the right to reclaim runaway slaves in northern states. It was bad enough that Southerners participated in slavery, but now they were forcing Northerners to participate, too. Thinking about what she could do to protest this new outrage, Isabella Beecher sent a letter to her sister-in-law, Harriet Beecher Stowe, a housewife with six children who occasionally wrote for magazines. "If I could use a pen as you can," she wrote, "I would write something that would make this whole nation feel what an accursed thing slavery is." As Charles Stowe tells the story, his mother read the letter aloud to her children in their parlor in Brunswick, Maine. She rose from her chair and "with an expression on her face that stamped itself on the mind of her child, said: "I will write something. I will if I live." The "something" was *Uncle Tom's Cabin*. The book inspired the north and inflamed the south. Abraham Lincoln once claimed that Stowe and her little book did more to cause the Civil War than any other single person or thing.

Chapter Learning Objectives

In chapter 17 we will examine the use of tone in Harriet Beecher Stowe's *Uncle Tom's Cabin*.

As a result of this chapter study you will be able to . . .

1. Analyze the use of propaganda in *Uncle Tom's Cabin*.

2. Use arguments that Harriet Beecher Stowe advances in *Uncle Tom's Cabin*. After reading it, summarize Pastor Freeman's main arguments and, using Scripture, write a rebuttal.

3. Evaluate arguments offered by Stowe concerning the emancipation of slaves.

Look Ahead for Friday

- Turn in a final copy of essay or take it as a test

- Optional objective test

Lesson 1

Propaganda (Student Essay)

Daily Assignment

- Warm-up: Harriet Beecher Stowe argued persuasively, but some argue, dishonestly to advance her position. Does a just cause justify "stretching the truth"?
- Students will complete Concept Builder 17-A.
- Prayer journal: Students are encouraged to write in their prayer journal every day.
- Students need to review their material for the next assignment
- Students should systematically review their vocabulary words daily.

CONCEPT
BUILDER
17-A

Characterization

Read chapter 1 ("In Which the Reader Is Introduced to a Man of Humanity") from *Uncle Tom's Cabin* by H.B. Stowe, and then answer the following questions.

1. Describe Mr. Shelby. Is he the protagonist? Or Uncle Tom?

ANSWER: His companion, Mr. Shelby, had the appearance of a gentleman; and the arrangements of the house, and the general air of the housekeeping, indicated easy, and even opulent circumstances. As we before stated, the two were in the midst of an earnest conversation. He is not the protagonist, and is an important foil. Whether Uncle Tom is the protagonist or not is debatable. Perhaps. Many would see Eliza as the protagonist.

2. Some African-Americans have been offended by the Uncle Tom character. They argue that he is more of an unflattering stereotype than a real person. What do you think?

ANSWER: Answers will vary.

3. Eliza is a powerful woman in American literature. She was willing to break the law to keep her family together. What are your feelings about that?

ANSWER: To this reader, it is necessary, at times, to break the law if it violates God's law.

Lesson 2

Grammar Review: Misused Words

Daily Assignment

- Warm-up: What would you do if you were Arthur Shelby? Did he do the right thing?
- Students will complete Concept Builder 17-B.
- Prayer journal.
- Students should outline all assigned essays for the week.

Character Conflict

Uncle Tom's Cabin is full of colorful characters with all sorts of conflict. Describe the ones listed below.

Character	Conflict	Internal/External	Result
Little Eva	Uncle Tom is sold and placed on a riverboat, which sets sail down the Mississippi River. While on board, Tom meets and befriends a young white girl named Eva. When Eva falls into the river, Tom saves her. In gratitude, Eva's father, Augustine St. Clare, buys Tom from the slave trader and takes him with the family to their home in New Orleans. During this time, Tom and Eva begin to relate to one another because of their mutual Christian faith.	Little Eva is conflicted about Uncle Tom's loss of his family but very glad that he is her property/ friend (internal conflict).	Eventually Eva understands the evils of slavery, and, after her untimely death, Uncle Tom is freed. However, this changes later and he is sold to the villainous Simon Legree.
Uncle Tom	*Uncle Tom is sold away from his family.*	*Uncle Tom does not want to leave his family, but he does not know what to do (internal conflict). Next, he has conflict with his new owner Simon Legree (external conflict). Later, he has to forgive people who have been cruel to him (internal conflict).*	*Even though he is forced to spend several years away from his family, eventually he is freed or so it appears. However, this is not to be. Tom is sold to the evil Simon Legree.*
Eliza Harris	*Eliza learns that her son Harry is being sold away from her.*	*She feels bad about leaving her mistress (internal conflict), but she leaves anyway (external conflict).*	*Eventually she meets her husband and escapes to freedom.*
Simon Legree	*He is a despicable man.*	*He feels virtually no internal conflict because he has no conscience.*	*The reader is unsure of his fate, but the author implies that Legree has virtually no hope of redemption.*
Arthur Shelby	*Shelby is forced to sell his slaves to cover some debts.*	*He feels bad about this but feels he has to do so anyway (internal conflict).*	*He decides to sell Uncle Tom and Harry.*

Lesson 3

On the Influence of *Uncle Tom's Cabin*

Daily Assignment

- Warm-up: Many of us feel that some legal issues are immoral (i.e., against God's laws). How does one disobey civil laws in a way that honors God?

- Students will complete Concept Builder 17-C.

- Prayer journal.

- Students should write rough drafts of all assigned essays and speech.

CONCEPT BUILDER 17-C

Persuasion

Uncle Tom's Cabin **is a great classic — well written and one of a kind. But it is also trying to convince people to support a political position (i.e., anti-slavery). Discuss how Stowe does this by presenting a problem, complicating matters, and offering an outcome.**

Problem

A slaveholder has to solve a problem: he needs money so he has to sell some slaves. This problem becomes an opportunity for Stowe to show her readers how harmful slavery is both to the slaves and to the slave owners.

Complicating Matters

He loves his slaves, and he does not wish to separate them from loved ones.

Outcome

Ultimately, Tom dies for his mistake, but Eliza successfully escapes.

Lesson 4

Critics Corner

Daily Assignment

- Warm-up: Can a powerless victim really be guilty of prejudice? For instance, could Eliza be prejudiced against white people? Explain your answer.
- Students will complete Concept Builder 17-D.
- Prayer journal.
- Review the assigned text. Keep vocabulary cards.
- This is the day that students should write, and then rewrite, the final drafts of their assigned essay.

CONCEPT BUILDER 17-D

Persuasive Technique

Examine the following from *Uncle Tom's Cabin* and complete the example from each.

Persuasive Techniques		Example
Plot	*Separating slave families did happen; however, it was not common.*	*Shelby has to sell Uncle Tom and Harry.*
Character(s)	*Almost all characters are stereotypes or stock characters (i.e., they represent a type rather than an individual).*	*Shelby is a typical, benevolent slave owner. Legree is a typical, cruel slave owner. Uncle Tom represents the popular view of gentle, satisfied slaves.*
Setting	*The South is a perfect setting to make a political statement about slavery.*	*Stowe does not give any examples of slaves owners who might reflect more favorably on this institution (an institution this reader finds abhorrent).*

Chapter 17 Test Answer

OBJECTIVE QUESTIONS (50 POINTS)

C Arthur Shelby is willing to break up slave families because (A) he is a cruel man (B) he is tired of farming (C) he is heavily in debt (D) he divorces his wife.

A One of the slaves sold is (A) Harry (B) Mary (C) Eliza (D) Arthur.

A Eliza flees to freedom by crossing the frozen (A) Ohio River (B) Mississippi River (C) Raritan River (D) Susquehanna River.

D Tom is sold to a vicious slaveholder named (A) Homer Jones B) Arthur Shelby (C) Robert E. Lee (D) Simon Legree.

C Tom Loker is a changed man after (A) being freed (B) getting married (C) being healed by Quakers (D) returning to Africa.

Chapter 17 Essay Answer

ESSAY (50 POINTS)

In a one-page essay, discuss why the following passage is propaganda. It was written by Nazi leaders during World War II.

Summary: The author implies that the Americans and British originated air attacks on civilians when, in fact, Germany initiated this approach on Rotterdam, Leningrad, and London. The implication is that Germany was being attacked by England and America. The fact is, Germany attacked France, England, Russia, and Poland first, and declared war against the United States. The author slyly speaks of Germany as being synonymous with Europe. He tries to tie the interests of Europe with those of Germany, as if they are the same. Propaganda inevitably takes part of the truth and exaggerates or twists it to advance a position. In this case, the author wishes to demonize his enemies and extol his friends.

Allegory — *Uncle Tom's Cabin*
(Harriet Beecher Stowe)

Chapter 18

First Thoughts

Uncle Tom is more than propaganda — it is a religious tract. Harriet Beecher Stowe, a very committed Christian herself, sought to share the gospel with unbelievers. As a matter of fact, some scholars argue that she is more concerned about conversion than abolition. In that sense, this piece of fiction is allegorical, or symbolizes something.

Chapter Learning Objectives

In chapter 18 we will examine the use of allegory in Harriet Beecher Stowe's *Uncle Tom's Cabin*.

As a result of this chapter study you will be able to . . .

1. Discuss the use of allegory in *Uncle Tom's Cabin*. Discuss how Stowe symbolizes the Christian motifs of journey, entrance into the promised land, sin, and others.

2. Evaluate Stowe's mixture of evangelism and social justice.

3. Compare and contrast this novel with John Bunyan's *Pilgrim's Progress*.

Look Ahead for Friday

- Turn in a final copy of essay or take it as a test

Allegory

Daily Assignment

- Warm-up: Forgiveness is important, but how do we forgive someone but at the same time hold him/her accountable for his/her bad choices?

- Students will complete Concept Builder 18-A.

- Prayer journal: Students are encouraged to write in their prayer journal every day.

- Students need to review their material for the next assignment

- Students should systematically review their vocabulary words daily.

CONCEPT BUILDER 18-A

Brochure to Represent My Life

Create a brochure to represent your life.

ANSWER: Answers will vary.

Lesson 2

Uncle Tom's Cabin: On the Meaning of Little Eva

Daily Assignment

- Warm-up: Forgiveness is central to our mental health. Describe an incident where you forgave someone who did not deserve to be forgiven or who never asked to be forgiven.

- Students will complete Concept Builder 18-B.

- Prayer journal.

- Students should outline all assigned essays for the week.

CONCEPT BUILDER 18-B

A Book to Represent My Life

Complete this one-page cover of a book that represents your life.

ANSWER: Answers will vary.

Lesson 3

Grammar Review: Misused Words

Daily Assignment

- Warm-up: There is a theory that says we mature as we learn to accept necessary suffering. Describe one incident of necessary suffering that helped you grow in Christ.
- Students will complete a daily Concept Builder 18-C.
- Prayer journal.
- Students should write rough drafts of all assigned essays.

CONCEPT BUILDER 18-C

Biblical Symbolism

Uncle Tom's Cabin is full of biblical symbolism. Give examples of each of these.

Biblical Story	*Uncle Tom* Allegory
The Exodus Narrative: Let my People Go!	*Eliza seeks to escape to the Promised Land to find freedom and succor.*
The Exodus Narrative: Fleeing from Pharaoh!	*Simon Legree is the Pharaoh figure. The Ohio River would be the Red Sea.*
The Good Samaritan	*Northerners (e.g., Quakers) who help Eliza and her husband escape are good Samaritans.*

Lesson 4

Student Essay

Daily Assignment

- Warm-up: There is a theory that says we mature as persons as we face and overcome obstacles. Describe one obstacle you have faced and how it helped you grow as a person.
- Students will complete Concept Builder 18-D.
- Prayer journal.
- Review the assigned text. Keep vocabulary cards.
- This is the day that students should write, and then rewrite, the final drafts of their assigned essays.

CONCEPT BUILDER 18-D

Character: Change & Motivation

Complete the chart below.

Character	Eliza	Uncle Tom	Little Eva
Protagonist (or one of the main characters), Antagonist, Foil	Protagonist	Foil	Foil
Dynamic (changes)/ Static (stays the same)	*Dynamic*	*Static*	*Dynamic*
Motivation(s)	*Eliza wants to escape.*	*Uncle Tom tries to remain calm and moral in an immoral world.*	*Eva changes from a passive slave owner child, to an anti-slavery proponent.*

ESSAY (100 POINTS)

Write a one-page allegory of your Christian life.

Summary: Answers will vary. The student may choose to compare a trip to a mall, or to grandmother's house, as an allegory of the Christian life. (The essay should include some conversion experience, trials and tribulations, victories, and hope for a triumphant ending!)

Character Development — *Anne Frank: The Diary of a Young Girl* (Anne Frank)

Chapter 19

First Thoughts

Anne Frank's diary is one of the most famous nonfiction novels ever written. Born on June 12, 1929, Anne Frank was a German-Jewish teenager who went into hiding during the Nazi occupation of the Netherlands. In spite of the fact that Anne's father was a World War I German war veteran, Anne and her family fled from Germany in the middle 30s to escape persecution of the Jewish people. When the Nazis conquered Holland in 1940, Anne and her family had nowhere else to run. At first things went fairly well. Finally, however, in 1942 the Nazis started deporting Jewish people to death camps in the east. She and her family, along with four others, spent 25 months during World War II in rooms above her father's former office in Amsterdam. "So much has happened it's as if the whole world had suddenly turned upside down," Anne wrote in her diary on June 8, 1942. Betrayed by friends to the Nazis, Anne, her family, and the others living with them were arrested and deported to Nazi concentration camps. Seven months after she was arrested, Anne Frank died of typhus in March of 1945 at Bergen-Belsen concentration camp. She was 15 years old. Anne's father was the only family member who survived this terrible time in history.

Chapter Learning Objectives

In chapter 19 we will examine the use of characterization in *The Diary of Anne Frank*.

As a result of this chapter study you will be able to . . .

1. Using the perspective that Anne is a maturing young lady, discuss her views on boys, fate, loneliness, war, and parents. Show how she matures as a character.

2. Apply the biblical approach to Anne's words.

3. Pretend that Anne Frank did not die; pretend that she survived.

Look Ahead for Friday

- Turn in a final copy of essay or take it as a test

Lesson 1

Background

Daily Assignment

- Warm-up: On Saturday, July 15, 1944 Anne Frank made a remarkable entry in her diary. Anne was 15 years old then and, with her family and others, had been hiding in an attic room for more than two years. Three weeks after this entry the hiding place was found and the Nazis sent all the inhabitants to concentration camps. Seven months later Anne died in the camp at Bergen-Belsen. That day she wrote: "It's really a wonder that I haven't dropped all my ideals, because they seem so absurd and impossible to carry out. Yet I keep them, because in spite of everything, I still believe that people are really good at heart. I simply can't build up my hopes on a foundation consisting of confusion, misery, and death. I see the world gradually being turned into wilderness. I hear the ever approaching thunder, which will destroy us too. I can feel the suffering of millions and yet, if I look up into the heavens, I think that it will all come right, that this cruelty too will end, and that peace and tranquility will return again." Respond to this quote. Is Anne right?

- Students will complete Concept Builder 19-A.

- Prayer journal: Students are encouraged to write in their prayer journal every day.

- Students need to review their material for the next assignment

- Students should systematically review their vocabulary words daily.

CONCEPT BUILDER 19-A

Anti-Semitism

The characters in *The Diary of Anne Frank* are dealing with one primary social conflict: the Holocaust. Discuss how each deals with this conflict in the chart below.

Character	Anne	Anne's Mom & Dad	Peter
Issue: Anti-Semitism	Anne does not speak about this subject very much.	They are aware of this injustice but do not feel that Anne understands enough to explore with them the deeper justice issues involved. Besides, they do not want to scare her.	Peter seems to accept anti-Semitism as a reality, as it were, in Dutch society.

Lesson 2

Sample Characterization Essay

Daily Assignment

- Warm-up: After the Nazi invasion of the Netherlands in May 1940, the Dutch people were immediately faced with the question of choice: how to respond to the Nazi occupation. Tens of thousands of Dutch people followed Hitler, and millions more looked the other way. The Nazis needed Dutch collaborators to carry out their orders. What would have influenced someone to become a collaborator?

- Students will complete Concept Builder 19-B.

- Prayer journal.

- Students should outline all assigned essays for the week.

CONCEPT BUILDER 19-B

Anne's Autobiographical Incident

Complete the chart below.

Hiding in the Annex

Anne's family was hiding from imminent death and they knew it. That colored the entire book. There is a foreboding presence of death in the novel — yet, in spite of this, Anne is able to live a fairly normal life.

Incidents

Anne felt ambivalence toward shy and awkward Peter van Pels. Eventually, though, she recognized a kinship with him and the two entered an innocent romance. She received her first kiss from him, but her feelings toward him began to cool as she questioned whether her feelings for him were genuine, or resulted from their shared confinement.

Anne struggled with her relationship with her mother but felt great friendship with her father.

Concerning Whom?

Peter, her father, and her mother.

Anne's Response?

Anne felt ambivalence toward Peter, disliked her mom, and deeply loved her father; however, the adolescent Anne's response is completely normal and one should understand that she loved her mom, too.

Lesson 3

Sample Characterization Essay

Daily Assignment

- Warm-up: Otto Frank, Anne's father, took out some of the negative comments Anne made about her mother and a number of the other residents of the Secret Annex. He believed that Anne would have wanted him to do so. Do you think he was correct?
- Students will complete a daily Concept Builder 19-C.
- Prayer journal.
- Students should write rough drafts of all assigned essays.

> CONCEPT
> BUILDER
> 19-C

Forming Conclusions

Complete the chart below.

Conclusion	Yes/No	Because . . .
In spite of living in austere, harsh surroundings, Anne still manages to be happy.	Yes	She had terrific courage and optimism.
Anne falls in love with a young man.	Yes	Like most adolescent girls, Anne is exploring her feelings toward people of another gender. It is completely innocent.
Anne loves her father more than she loves her mother.	Not really.	The fact that she argues with her mom a lot does not mean that she does not love her.

Lesson 4

Grammar Review: Misused Words

Daily Assignment

- Warm-up: Most Germans claim that they did not know about the Holocaust (as it was occurring). Do you believe them? Who is responsible for the murder of 6 million people?

- Students will complete Concept Builder 19-D.

- Prayer journal.

- Review the assigned text. Keep vocabulary cards.

- This is the day that students should write, and then rewrite, the final drafts of their assigned essays.

CONCEPT
BUILDER
19-D

My Autobiographical Incident

Identify and describe an incident that changed your life.

ANSWER: Answers will vary.

ESSAY (100 POINTS)

Write a one-page essay discussing the development of a character in one of your favorite novels. Support your development by using specific references from the novel.

Summary: Answers will vary with the novel that is chosen. However, students should support their statements with specifics about characterization from the novel they choose

Setting — *Anne Frank: The Diary of a Young Girl* (Anne Frank)

Chapter 20

First Thoughts

Without a doubt, the setting is critical to *Anne Frank: The Diary of a Young Girl*. The setting set the perimeter and tone for the entire literary piece. Certainly the story would have been entirely different if it were not written in World War II and had not occurred in a small apartment above a business.

Chapter Learning Objectives

In chapter 20 we will examine the use of setting in *The Diary of Anne Frank*.

As a result of this chapter study you will be able to . . .

1. Discuss the importance of setting to *Anne Frank: The Diary of a Young Girl*.

2. Analyze how Esther saved the Jewish nation from a terrible holocaust.

3. Compare and contrast ways the setting of *The Call of the Wild* by Jack London develops Buck and the way Anne Frank's setting affects her. Why is the setting critical to both books?

Look Ahead for Friday

- Turn in a final copy of essay or take it as a test

Lesson 1

Setting

Daily Assignment

- Warm-up: Why do bad things happen to good people?
- Students will complete Concept Builder 20-A.
- Prayer journal: Students are encouraged to write in their prayer journal every day.
- Students need to review their material for the next assignment
- Students should systematically review their vocabulary words daily.

CONCEPT
BUILDER
20-A

Elements of a Story

Analyze the following elements of *The Diary of Anne Frank.*

Elements	Yes/No	Because . . .
Characters Do the characters seem real?	Yes	*The characters manifest universal human characteristics with which it is easy for the reader to identify.*
Narration Is Anne a credible narrator?	Yes	*The characters manifest universal human characteristics with which it is easy for the reader to identify.*
Setting Is the setting important? Does it seem real?	Yes	*The Annex is vividly described.*
Plot Does the story flow logically? Does it flow well?	Yes	*Although the story is prose non- fiction, the episodic approach rings true.*
Theme Is there a theme?	Yes	*Indomitable courage in the most austere conditions.*

Lesson 2

Sample Essay: Setting

Daily Assignment

- Warm-up: You are Jewish, 14, and on a train with Anne to Auschwitz Concentration Camp. What are you thinking? What are your first impressions of this concentration camp?
- Students will complete Concept Builder 20-B.
- Prayer journal.
- Students should outline all assigned essays for the week.

CONCEPT
BUILDER
20-B

Plot Development

Fill these boxes concerning the plot of Anne's account.

Exposition

Anne's family realizes that they must go into hiding or risk deportation to work camps or worse.

Rising Action

Several personal crises emerge: her feelings toward Peter and feelings toward her mother.

Climax

There is no climax in this non-fiction piece — there are high moments in her relationship with Peter.

Falling Action

Anne begins, at the end of the stay, to understand more and more of life. April 5, 1944: "And if I don't have the talent to write books or newspaper articles, I can always write for myself. But I want to achieve more than that. I can't imagine living like Mother, Mrs. van Daan and all the women who go about their work and are then forgotten. I need to have something besides a husband and children to devote myself to! . . . I want to be useful or bring enjoyment to all people, even those I've never met. I want to go on living even after my death! And that's why I'm so grateful to God for having given me this gift, which I can use to develop myself and to express all that's inside me! When I write I can shake off all my cares. My sorrow disappears, my spirits are revived!"

Resolution

Anne and her friends and family are discovered and deported. Most of them will die in concentration camps.

Lesson 3

Grammar Review: Writer in the Background

Daily Assignment

- Warm-up: The following are portions of Anne's diary that her father removed. "What has their marriage become? ... It isn't an ideal marriage. Father is not in love. He kisses her as he kisses us (children). ... He sometimes looks at her teasingly and mockingly but never lovingly. ... She loves him as she loves no other and it is difficult to see this kind of love always unanswered." Why would he remove these? Do parents who love each other sometimes fight? Why?

- Students will complete a daily Concept Builder 20-C.

- Prayer journal.

- Students should write rough drafts of all assigned essays.

CONCEPT
BUILDER
20-C

Sequencing

Place these events in the order in which they occur in *The Diary of Anne Frank.*

1 On the morning of Monday, July 6, 1942, the family moved into the hiding place.

5 Some time later, after first dismissing the shy and awkward Peter van Pels, she recognized a kinship with him and the two became close friends.

3 After sharing her room with Pfeffer, she found him to be insufferable and resented his intrusion, and she clashed with Auguste van Pels, whom she regarded as foolish.

7 Anne's closest friendship was with Bep Voskuijl, "the young typist . . . the two of them often stood whispering in the corner."

6 She received her first kiss from Peter, but her infatuation with him began to wane as she questioned whether her feelings for him were genuine.

8 On the morning of August 4, 1944, the Annex was stormed by the German Security Police (Grüüne Polizei) following a tip-off from an informer who was never identified.

2 On July 13, the Franks were joined by the van Pels family: Hermann, Auguste, and 16-year-old Peter, and then in November by Fritz Pfeffer, a dentist and friend of the family.

4 She regarded Hermann van Pels and Fritz Pfeffer as selfish, particularly in regard to the amount of food they consumed.

Lesson 4

Student Essay:
The Setting in *The Diary Of Anne Frank*

Daily Assignment

- Warm-up: Anne wrote this about her mom. "If she had just one aspect of an understanding mother, either tenderness or friendliness or patience or anything else, I would keep trying to approach her. But this unfeeling nature, these mocking ways. To love that becomes more impossible each day." Do you really think Anne meant this? Do you think she would have removed those words later? Do you think or write some things that you later regret? Why do we do things like that?

- Students will complete Concept Builder 20-D.

- Prayer journal.

- Review the assigned text. Keep vocabulary cards.

- This is the day that students should write, and then rewrite, the final drafts of their assigned essays.

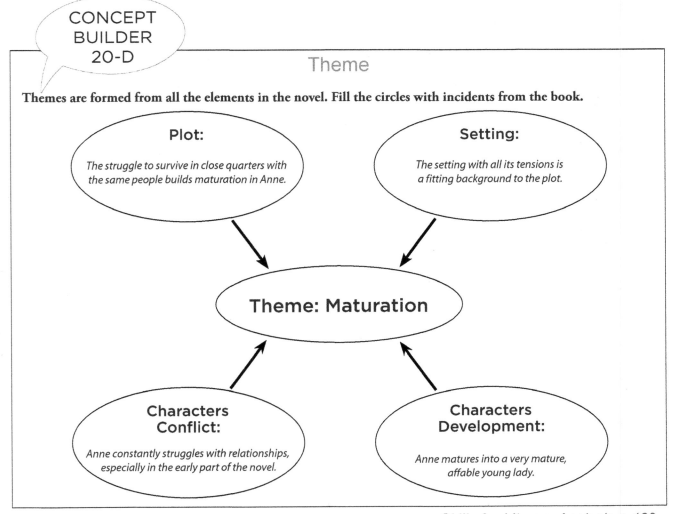

CONCEPT BUILDER 20-D

Theme

Themes are formed from all the elements in the novel. Fill the circles with incidents from the book.

Plot:
The struggle to survive in close quarters with the same people builds maturation in Anne.

Setting:
The setting with all its tensions is a fitting background to the plot.

Theme: Maturation

Characters Conflict:
Anne constantly struggles with relationships, especially in the early part of the novel.

Characters Development:
Anne matures into a very mature, affable young lady.

ESSAY (100 POINTS)

In a one-page essay, discuss the importance of setting to the short story "An Occurrence at Owl Creek Bridge" by Ambrose Bierce.

Summary: The fact that this short story occurs in the American Civil War is important, but not critical. It could have occurred in any war.

Fear, stream of consciousness, and other emotions in this short story are universal and timeless.

Plot — *Silas Marner* (George Eliot)

Chapter 21

First Thoughts

This short novel is the story of how a young, unloved child restores faith and hope to a brokenhearted recluse. This old man had been rejected by society and then rejected society himself. George Eliot, whose real name was Mary Ann Evans, wrote *Silas Marner*. In her day, Evans/Eliot was the most popular writer in England — more popular even than Charles Dickens. Her writings exhibit theism (but certainly not Christian theism).

Chapter Learning Objectives

In chapter 21 we will examine the use of coincidence in *Silas Marner* by George Eliot.

   As a result of this chapter study you will be able to . . .

1. Analyze the use of coincidence.

2. Discuss the way George Eliot describes organized religion.

3. Research Eliot's (Evan's) life. Compare and contrast her own childhood to Eppie's childhood.

Look Ahead for Friday

   *   Turn in a final copy of essay or take it as a test

   *   Optional objective test

Plot: Coincidence

Daily Assignment

- Warm-up: Eppie is raised by Silas. But Silas is an old, single, eccentric man. Is he the best father for Eppie? Or would Eppie's biological father be a better father? Offer evidence to support your answer.

- Students will complete Concept Builder 21-A.

- Prayer journal: Students are encouraged to write in their prayer journal every day.

- Students need to review their material for the next assignment

- Students should systematically review their vocabulary words daily.

CONCEPT
BUILDER
21-A

Active Reading

Read this excerpt from *Silas Marner* (chapter 1) by George Eliot, and then answer the following question.

What sort of town is Raveloe? Why is this setting important?

ANSWER: Raveloe is a town in transition from the cottage (home-based) industries of which Silas is a part and the emerging industrial revolution. There is great economic dislocation and uneasiness. Thus, the setting is very important to this novel. It sets the scene for the unjust charges and betrayal that emerge.

Lesson 2

Grammar Review: Overworked Words

Daily Assignment

- Warm-up: The story of Silas Marner's life has a mythic dimension to it. Silas undergoes a spiritual journey that is a variation on the great religious myth of Western culture. In the Christian myth, man is expelled from a garden, saved by the birth of the Christ-child, and promised a life in bliss in the heavenly city of Jerusalem described in the Book of Revelation. Silas travels a similar path from expulsion to redemption, but the symbolism is reversed. He is expelled from a city, saved by a child, and ends up in a garden (as seen in the final chapter when Eppie and Aaron grow a garden just outside his cottage). In the course of this journey, which occupies over thirty years of Silas's life, he travels from a stern, Bible-centered Calvinistic religion, in which the central concern is the "Assurance of salvation," to a more tolerant, nondogmatic version of Christianity in which the emphasis falls not on the idea of salvation but on tolerance and solidarity with others in a cooperative human community —Brian Aubrey. Agree or disagree with this comment.

- Students will complete Concept Builder 21-B.

- Prayer journal.

- Students should outline all assigned essays for the week.

CONCEPT
BUILDER
21-B

Coincidence

Coincidence plays a large part in the plot. In fact, the plot would not progress at all without coincidence.

Complete the following chart.

Example of Coincidence	Purpose	Is it necessary? Why?
"He [Dunstan] knocked loudly, rather enjoying the idea that the old fellow would be frightened by sudden noise. He heard no movement in reply: all was silence in the cottage. . . . Dunstan knocked still more loudly, and, without pausing for a reply, pushed his fingers through the latch-hole, intending to shake the door and pull the latch-string up and down, not doubting that the door was fastened. But, to his surprise, at this double motion the door opened, and he found himself in front of a bright fire, which lit up every corner of the cottage — the bed, the loom, the three chairs, and the table — and showed him that Marner was not there." (32–33; ch. 4)	*Eliot wanted to have Dunstan commit an injustice against Silas so that, later, Dunstan would die and Eliot could make a moral statement.*	*Probably, because it was the only way Eliot could advance the plot. Besides, it is quite plausible that such an event might occur.*
"Suddenly, as the child rolled downward on its mother's knees, its eyes were caught by a bright glancing light on the white ground, and, with the ready transition of infancy, it was immediately absorbed in watching the bright living thing running towards it, yet never arriving. . . . It came from a bright place; and the little one, rising on its legs, toddled through the snow . . . toddled on to the open door of Silas Marner's cottage, and right up to the warm Hearth." (94; ch. 12)	*Eliot wanted to tie Silas' gold to Eppie's hair. These are critical symbols (i.e., redemption) in this novel.*	*Actually this reader thinks it is an ingenious and entirely credible way to make the connection. Very subtle.*
"Slowly the demon [opium] was working his will, and cold and weariness were his helpers. Soon she [Molly] felt nothing but a supreme immediate longing that curtained off all futurity — the longing to lie down and sleep. "Mammy!" the little one cried again and again, stretching itself forward so as to almost escape from Silas's arms, before he himself was aware that there was something more that the bush before — that there was a human body, with the head sunk low in the furze, and half-covered with snow." (94, 97; ch. 12)	*This scene is more problematic. Eliot strays very close to the melodramatic.*	*This reader understands that the poor Molly has to die, and she has to die somewhere in proximity to Silas' house, but I wonder if this scene is not a little bit heavy handed.*

Lesson 3

Coincidence in *Uncle Tom's Cabin*

Daily Assignment

- Warm-up: What does this quote mean? "...the past becomes dreamy because its symbols have all vanished, and the present too is dreamy because it is linked with no memories." —*Silas Marner*, Chapter 1.

- Students will complete a daily Concept Builder 21-C.

- Prayer journal.

- Students should write rough drafts of all assigned essays.

CONCEPT
BUILDER
21-C

Forming Conclusions

As he or she reads a text, every reader forms conclusion. What conclusions did you form about the novel *Silas Marner*?

ANSWER: Answers will vary.

Lesson 4

Student Essay: Coincidence

Daily Assignment

- Warm-up: What does this quote mean? "As the child's mind was growing into knowledge, his mind was growing into memory: as her life unfolded, his soul, long stupefied in a cold narrow prison, was unfolding too, and trembling gradually into full consciousness."— *Silas Marner*, Chapter 14.

- Students will complete Concept Builder 21-D.

- Prayer journal.

- Review the assigned text. Keep vocabulary cards.

- This is the day that students should write, and then rewrite, the final drafts of their assigned essays.

CONCEPT
BUILDER
21-D

Plot Development

Every prose fiction work has a story, or plot. These include exposition, rising action, climax, falling action, and resolution. Complete this chart. For example, in Margaret Wise Brown's children's classic *The Runaway Bunny*, the exposition occurs when the reader learns that the principal characters are a baby bunny and his mom. We also learn that the young bunny is planning to run away. During the rising action we see that no matter where the bunny runs, the mommy bunny pursues and catches him. The climax occurs when the little bunny realizes that he cannot run away from his mom. The falling action occurs rather quickly, as the little bunny finally understands that he cannot escape the pursuing love of his mother. Finally, the resolution occurs when the little bunny happily accepts a carrot and decides to stay at home permanently.

Exposition: Introduction of Characters and Initial Action

Silas Marner is a member of a small Christian congregation in Lantern Yard, England, who is accused of stealing the congregation's funds while sitting with a very ill elder of the group. Two clues are given against him: a pocket-knife and the discovery of the bag formerly containing the money in his own house. Silas says that he last used the knife to cut some string for his friend William, who leads the campaign against him. Silas is unjustly convicted and the woman he was to marry breaks the engagement and later marries his former best friend, William. The reader wonders if William made up the charges to get Silas's girl. With his life shattered and his heart broken, he leaves Lantern Yard.

Rising Action: Initial and Subsequent Incidences That Advance the Plot

Silas then settles near the village of Raveloe, where he lives as a recluse. He is further damaged when the reprobate Dunstan Cass, a younger son of Squire Cass, the town's leading landowner, steals his money. The loss of his gold drives Silas into a deep gloom, although a number of the villagers endeavor to help him. Soon, however, an orphaned child comes to Raveloe. She was not known by the people there, but she is really the child of Godfrey Cass, the eldest son of the local squire. Her mother, Molly, is secretly married to Godfrey, but is also of low birth and addicted to opium. On a winter's night, Molly tries to make her way into town with the child to prove that she is Godfrey's wife. On the way she sits down to rest amid the snow. Molly dies. Her child wanders from her mother's still body into Silas's house. Upon discovering the child, Silas follows her tracks in the snow and discovers Molly. Silas decides to keep the child and names her Eppie, after his deceased mother and sister, Hephzibah.

Climax: The Turning Point

Eppie changes his life completely. Symbolically, Silas loses his material gold to theft, only to have it replaced by the golden-haired Eppie.

Falling Action: Subsequent Incidences That Offer Some Resolution

Meanwhile, the irresponsible father of Eppie, Godfrey Cass, is now free to marry his new love, Nancy, concealing his relationship with Mollie from Nancy. Eppie grows up and is an absolute delight to everyone. She brings Silas back into human community. Later in the book, Dunstan Cass is found at the bottom of the pond in front of Silas's house with his gold and it is restored to Silas. Godfrey confesses to his wife, Nancy, that the dead woman was his first wife and that Eppie is his child.

Resolution: The Concluding Resolution of the Plot

The couple, who are childless, go to Silas and reveal this to him, asking that Silas give Eppie up to their care. However, the decision falls to Eppie, who has no desire to be raised as a gentleman's daughter if it means forsaking Silas. At the end, Eppie marries a local boy, Aaron, son of Dolly Winthrop, and both of them move into Silas's newly enlarged house, courtesy of Godfrey.

Chapter 21 Test Answer

OBJECTIVE TEST (50 POINTS)

B   Silas Marner is a (A) preacher (B) weaver (C) miller (D) policeman.

A   He is an outsider, the object of suspicion because (A) of his special skills and the fact that he has come to Raveloe from elsewhere (B) he is learning disabled (C) he is rich (D) he is poor.

D   He is driven from the town because (A) he has terminal cancer (B) someone gave him some money (C) he won the lottery (D) someone falsely accused him of theft and excommunicated him.

C   Eppie's biological father is (A) Dunster (B) Silas (C) Godfrey (D) George.

B   Eppie decides to (A) live with her biological father (B) stay with Silas (C) move to another town (D) to marry David.

Chapter 21 Essay Answer

ESSAY (50 POINTS)

In Book III, chapter 13 of *A Tale of Two Cities*, by Charles Dickens, one of the most famous coincidences in world literature occurs. The protagonist, aristocrat Charles Darnay, is in a French prison waiting to be executed the next day. An acquaintance, who looks a lot like Darnay, enters the prison to visit Darnay.

Determine whether or not this coincidence is necessary to the plot of this book. Support your argument with instances from the excerpt.

Summary: There are several coincidences in this novel; however, none were so extraordinary as this one in the prison immediately before Darnay is to be killed. This coincidence is indeed appropriate. Why?

1. The author made it clear from the beginning of the novel that these two men looked remarkably similar.

2. This coincidence was the most economical way to end this novel.

3. While the incident is coincidental, it is not otherwise contrived. In other words, Dickens does offer more credible scenes to support this one. For example, it is entirely likely that an expatriate French aristocrat would be condemned to die in the French Revolution.

Tone: Irony and Sentimentality — *Silas Marner* (George Eliot)

Chapter 22

First Thoughts

This short novel is the story of redemption, salvation, and restoration without a Christian framework for those laudable events. Silas Marner is restored to his joy and fortune in spite of his Christian faith — not because of his Christian faith. He is no Hester Prynne (in *The Scarlet Letter*) staying connected to the community no matter what the shortcomings of this community may be. He is no Huw (in *How Green Was My Valley*) who rejects any pretense of unforgiveness. Within the perimeters of his perceived injustice, Silas creates a naturalistic world within his secular but still morally theistic ethical system. In other words, Silas keeps the good works aspect of theism while rejecting the God who made these good works possible. This presages even more disturbing developments for the future works of literature.

Chapter Learning Objectives

In chapter 22 we will examine the use of irony and sentimentality (tone) in *Silas Marner* by George Eliot.

As a result of this chapter study you will be able to . . .

1. Decide if Eliot used too much sentimentality
2. Compare a biblical figure to Godfrey Cass. Then, discuss Godfrey's weaknesses.
3. Analyze the way Eliot uses irony.
4. Compare the use of sentimentality in this novel with *Pride and Prejudice* by Jane Austen.

Look Ahead for Friday

- Turn in a final copy of essay or take it as a test

Lesson 1

Irony and Sentimentality

Daily Assignment

- Warm-up: What actors and actresses would you choose to play the characters in *Silas Marner*?
- Students will complete Concept Builder 22-A.
- Prayer journal: Students are encouraged to write in their prayer journal every day.
- Students need to review their material for the next assignment
- Students should systematically review their vocabulary words daily.

CONCEPT
BUILDER
22-A

Active Reading

In *Silas Marner* by George Eliot, compare and contrast how Silas's views on religion and children changed before and after he was accused of stealing.

Before he was accused of stealing

Religion	Children
Silas Marner is a member of a small Christian congregation in Lantern Yard. It is the center of his very uneventful life.	*Silas is shy and always uncomfortable around children. He more or less ignores them.*

After he was accused of stealing

Religion	Children
Silas totally rejects his faith until Eppie enters his life.	*After Eppie arrived he was friendly and outgoing (at least in Marner standards!).*

Lesson 2

Grammar Review: Periods for Commas

Daily Assignment

- Warm-up: Rewrite the ending of *Silas Marner*. This time, have Eppie choose her biological father.
- Students will complete Concept Builder 22-B.
- Prayer journal.
- Students should outline all assigned essays for the week.

CONCEPT
BUILDER
22-B

Elements of a Story

Analyze the following elements of the novel *Silas Marner* by George Eliot.

Elements	Yes/No	Because . . .
Characters Do the characters seem real?	*Mostly*	*Some of the characters appear to be archetypes (i.e., type or stock characters) more than real people (e.g., Dunstan and Molly).*
Narration Is Silas a credible narrator?	*Yes*	*He is a bundle of different emotions. His personality rings true with this reader.*
Setting Is the setting important? Does it seem real?	*Not really.*	*The universal themes of this novel could be developed in most any setting.*
Plot Does the story flow logically? Does it flow well?	*Yes but . . .*	*There is an inordinate amount of coincidence.*
Theme Is there a theme?	*Yes*	*Redemption*

Lesson 3

Sentimentality in the Prodigal Son

Daily Assignment

- Warm-up: How is the Church treated in this novel? Why is Eliot so critical? Is this an accurate portrayal of the Church?
- Students will complete a daily Concept Builder 22-C.
- Prayer journal.
- Students should write rough drafts of all assigned essays.

CONCEPT
BUILDER
22-C

Irony

Irony is the contrast between what is expected and what actually happens. In situational irony, the character expects one thing to happen and another thing happens. In dramatic irony, the reader knows more about a situation or a character than the characters does. Here are some examples of irony from the novel *Silas Marner* by George Eliot. Decide whether the examples are situational or dramatic irony.

Situation	Situational Irony	Dramatic Irony
Silas's best friend betrays him.	Yes	No
Silas thinks he has lost everything when his gold disappears, but later he finds that he has gained the world with Eppie.	Yes	No
The squire thinks he "dodges a bullet" when his mistress dies, only to find that he lost the best thing he had (i.e., Eppie).	Yes	Yes
Silas expects Eppie to choose her birth father over her adopted father. But she does not do that.	No	Yes
That which was meant for bad for Silas turns out to be the best thing that could happen to him.	No	Yes

Lesson 4

Student Essay: Sentimentality

Daily Assignment

- Warm-up: Do you think Americans would want to see a movie made on this book? Why or why not?
- Students will complete Concept Builder 22-D.
- Prayer journal.
- Review the assigned text. Keep vocabulary cards.
- This is the day that students should write, and then rewrite, the final drafts of their assigned essays.

CONCEPT BUILDER 22-D

Sentimentality

Sentimentality is an author's technique used to evoke empathy and emotion from a reader. Many critics think that it is unnecessary. What do you think?

Example of Sentimentality	Purpose	Is it necessary? Why?
"Silas Marner was lulling the child. She was perfectly quiet now, but not asleep — only soothed by sweet porridge and warmth into that wide-gazing calm which makes us older human beings, with our inward turmoil, feel a certain awe in the presence of a little child, such as we feel before some quiet majesty or beauty in the earth or sky — before a steady glowing planet, or a full-flowered eglantine, or the bending trees over a silent pathway." (99; ch. 13)	*To show the reader how profound this event was to the protagonist.*	*Because this event, is used by Eliot to develop her theme, It was necessary to evoke deep emotion in the reader.*
"Thank you, ma'am — thank you, sir, for your offers — they're very great, and far above my wish. For I should have no delight i' life any more if I was forced to go away from my father, and knew he was sitting at home, a-thinking of me and feeling lonely We've been used to be happy together every day, and I can't think o' no happiness without him. And he says he'd nobody i' the world till I was sent to him, and he'd have nothing when I was gone. And he's took care of me and loved me from the first, and I'll cleave to him as long as he lives, and nobody shall ever come in between him and me." (143; ch. 19)	*This is the final crisis moment in the novel: will Eppie choose Silas or her birth father?*	*Given the profundity of the event, this reader finds it to be necessary. However, it is somewhat melodramatic — even for a Victorian British novel.*

ESSAY (100 POINTS)

Continuing with the story of Charles Darnay and Sydney Carton, in a one-page essay, examine the final chapter of *The Tale of Two Cities* and argue for or against your opinion of whether the ending is sentimental.

Summary: Answers will vary — but it certainly is a sentimental passage, and perhaps Dickens goes too far. The passage is unnecessary and distracting. What Carton did was heroic enough without the dramatics.

Theme — *Silas Marner* (George Eliot)

Chapter 23

First Thoughts

A great story includes characters, plot, and other literary components. It also has profound and eternal meeting. Its meaning, or theme, should transcend time and location.

Chapter Learning Objectives

In chapter 23 we will examine several themes in *Silas Marner* by George Eliot.

As a result of this chapter study you will be able to . . .

1. Discuss several themes in *Silas Marner* and show how George Eliot (i.e., Evans) uses plot, setting, and characterization to develop them.

2. Explore redemption. This is an important theme in Silas Marner. Using copious textual examples, discuss the biblical understanding of redemption.

3. Compare a character in *Silas Marner* to a biblical character.

Look Ahead for Friday

- Turn in a final copy of essay or take it as a test

Lesson 1

Student Essay: Theme

Daily Assignment

- Warm-up: Poor Silas learns that he cannot change the past. No one can. Yet, when we are born again, we experience a sort of rewriting of our history. Explain.

- Students will complete Concept Builder 23-A.

- Prayer journal: Students are encouraged to write in their prayer journal every day.

- Students need to review their material for the next assignment

- Students should systematically review their vocabulary words daily.

CONCEPT BUILDER 23-A

Author Bias

Eliot clearly had biased views toward certain subjects, and she communicated these views in her writing. Complete the following chart to show how she did this in her text.

Subject	Eliot's View	Textual Examples
Religion	*It is obvious to this reader that Mary Ann Evans (George Eliot) was biased against organized religion. In fact, in her own life, she made some bad choices that the Church did not support.*	*The Lantern Yard Church (probably a Plymouth Brethren Church) is presented in a very poor light indeed.*
Rich People	*In all the Eliot books that this reader has read, rich people are always presented in a dim light Most of them are selfish and self-serving.*	*The Cass family is a great example of the bankrupt British aristocracy (according to Eliot).*
The Industrial Revolution	*Eliot appears to be somewhat neutral on this topic, more or less admitting that it is inevitable Contrast this to Thomas Hardy and The Mayer of Casterbridge.*	*The opening comments discuss the displaced aspect of Lantern Yard. Plus, the poor situation that Godfrey faces evidences the loss of gentry wealth and the rise of a wealthy middle class. In a sense, Silas Marner is representative of that wealthy, hard-working, frugal, emerging middle class.*

Lesson 2

Themes: Sacrificial Love and Wisdom

Daily Assignment

- Warm-up: Mary Ann Evans, the author of *Silas Marner*, rejected her faith. Give an example of how this affected the way she wrote her novel.
- Students will complete Concept Builder 22-B.
- Prayer journal.
- Students should outline all assigned essays for the week.

CONCEPT BUILDER 23-B

My Own Bias

Our own biases determine our views on a subject. Complete the following chart.

ANSWER: Answers will vary.

Lesson 3

Grammar Review: Consistency

Daily Assignment

- Warm-up: It seems like everyone gets what he deserves in this novel. Explain.
- Students will complete Concept Builder 23-C.
- Prayer journal.
- Students should write rough drafts of all assigned essays and speech.

CONCEPT
BUILDER
23-C

Family History

Eliot has a new family! Tell me about your family.

ANSWER: Answers will vary.

Lesson 4

Student Essay

Daily Assignment

- Warm-up: The home is a central motif in this novel. Discuss your home and why it is important to you.
- Students will complete Concept Builder 23-D.
- Prayer journal.
- Review the assigned text. Keep vocabulary cards.
- This is the day that students should write, and then rewrite, the final drafts of their assigned essay.

CONCEPT BUILDER 23-D

Comparison/Contrast

Eliot clearly had biased views toward certain subjects, and she communicates these views in her writing. Likewise, Llwellyn, in his book *How Green Was My Valley*, also has certain bias/opinions. Compare these views and opinions. Complete the following chart.

Subject	Eliot	Llewellyn
Religion	*Eliot rejected traditional religion and the church while embracing a watered down, subjective, Judeo-Christian morality.*	*While Llewellyn saw the limits of the Church, he in no way rejected the church.*
Rich People	*Eliot generally does not like rich people.*	*Llewellyn, through his protagonist, Huw, shows great respect to the owners of the mill.*
The Industrial Revolution	*Eliot is ambivalent.*	*Llewellyn resents some of the casualties of the industrial revolution (e.g., Huw's dad). He portrays that vividly in his descriptions of the slag piles.*

ESSAY (100 POINTS)

Write a one-page essay in which you discuss at least two themes in this portion of the short novel *His New Mittens* by Stephen Crane.

Summary: Some themes include:

> Growing up — the young man is experiencing the trauma of childhood taunting. Obedience — the child obeyed his mother in spite of temptation. Cruelty — more serious is the sense of cruelty about this naturalistic world that sobers the youth (and the reader!).

Précis — "The Religious Life of the Negro" (Booker T. Washington)

Chapter 24

First Thoughts

Booker T. Washington is one of the greatest Americans of the 19th century. Born a slave, Washington became a famous humanitarian, scholar, and teacher. Washington advanced the controversial position that African Americans should accept their social status while striving to advance themselves economically and morally.

Chapter Learning Objectives

In chapter 24 we will write a précis of "The Religious Life of the Negro" by Booker T. Washington.

As a result of this chapter study you will be able to . . .

1. Write a précis of "The Religious Life of the Negro" by Booker T. Washington.

2. Discuss Christian values Washington advanced in this essay even though he was not overtly writing a Christian essay.

3. Evaluate if Washington was too soft on prejudice in his essay.

Look Ahead for Friday

- Turn in a final copy of essay or take it as a test

Lesson 1

Précis Writing

Daily Assignment

- Warm-up: By the last years of his life, Washington had moved away from many of his accommodationist policies. Speaking out with a new frankness, Washington attacked racism. In 1915 he joined ranks with former critics to protest the stereotypical portrayal of blacks in a new movie, "Birth of a Nation." Some months later he died at age 59. A man who overcame near-impossible odds himself, Booker T. Washington is best remembered for helping black Americans rise up from the economic slavery that held them down long after they were legally free citizens (National Park Service). Have you ever changed your mind about something? Why?

- Students will complete Concept Builder 24-A.

- Prayer journal: Students are encouraged to write in their prayer journal every day.

- Students need to review their material for the next assignment

- Students should systematically review their vocabulary words daily.

CONCEPT
BUILDER
24-A

Active Reading

Read this excerpt from "The Religious Life of the Negro" by Booker T. Washington, and then answer the following questions:

1. What is Washington's view of the indigenous (native) African religions?
ANSWER: Not only are they wrong, they can be a terrible detraction to his present community.

2. What is Washington's views of the Church?
ANSWER: The Church is a laudable center of African American life.

Lesson 2

"The Raven"

Daily Assignment

- Warm-up: Why do you think many Civil Rights leaders are pastors?
- Students will complete Concept Builder 24-B.
- Prayer journal.
- Students should outline all assigned essays for the week.

CONCEPT
BUILDER
24-B

Comparing Views

Compare/contrast these two views with your own views.

ANSWER: Answers will vary.

Lesson 3

Discerning Fundamental Metaphors
of a Literary Piece

Daily Assignment

- Warm-up: Washington, born a slave, had every reason to be angry at his white captors, yet, there is no evidence that he had any rancor in his heart. Why?

- Students will complete Concept Builder 24-C.

- Prayer journal.

- Students should write rough drafts of all assigned essays and speech.

CONCEPT
BUILDER
24-C

Persuasive Appeal

Complete the chart below based on Washington's views, historical insights, and your own views.

Argument:
Religion was very important to African-Americans.

Thesis Statement:
To many slaves, and then freed African Americans, religion was vitally important because it was a very personal way to express feelings and hope in a way that others could not deny.

Reasons and Evidence

Slave owners encouraged Christianity among the slaves because they saw it as a way to control them. After Emancipation, African Americans continued to keep their faith, and especially their Church, at the center of their lives. Their leaders, for instance, emerged from the Church (e.g., Martin Luther King Jr.).

Counter-arguments

More radical African Americans (e.g., Malcolm X) rejected the Church and Christianity because it was "white."

Response to Counter-arguments

That is a short-sighted view. Anglos actually are a minority among Christians. South Korea alone has more Christians than the USA.

Lesson 4

Grammar Review: Specific, Definite Language

Daily Assignment

- Warm-up: Some critics argue that Washington "sold out" to whites and did not advance the cause of his people enough. What do you think?

- Students will complete Concept Builder 24-D.

- Prayer journal.

- Review the assigned text. Keep vocabulary cards.

- This is the day that students should write, and then rewrite, the final drafts of their assigned essay.

CONCEPT
BUILDER
24-D

Persuasive Essay

Booker T. Washington was a great American. However, within the African American community, some were critical of him. In particular, he wrote an essay, "The Religious Life of the African American Negro," where he argued that African Americans should accept their social position (segregation) for the greater good of educational and religious advancement. In other words, Washington seemed to suggest that African Americans should accept racial prejudice as inevitable (at least for now) and simply go on and live their lives the best way that they could. Agree or disagree with Booker T. Washington.

ANSWER: Answers will vary.

ESSAY (100 POINTS)

Write a précis (75–150 words) of the following essay.

Summary: Using the basic tenants of the Enlightenment, the author argues that homeschooling is more than an educational movement. He argues that it is a social revolution with wonderful opportunities arising for arguably "post"-Christian America.

Characterization — *Anne of Green Gables* (L. Maude Montgomery)

Chapter 25

First Thoughts

Maude Montgomery was born at Clifton, Prince Edward Island, Canada, in November of 1874. When her mother died, Montgomery was in an orphanage for a while — but that was the extent of any similarity between her life and Anne Shirley's. Her father remarried and Mrs. Montgomery grew up with her father and her stepmother in Prince Edward Island. In 1911, she married Rev. Ewen Macdonald and moved to Ontario, where she raised three children. Marrying at age 37, Mrs. Montgomery had already established herself as a published author. She published her first book, *Anne of Green Gables*, in 1908 and continued to write prolifically. She died in 1942 and was buried at Prince Edward Island.

Chapter Learning Objectives

In chapter 25 we will discuss characterization in *Anne of Green Gables* by Maude Montgomery.

As a result of this chapter study you will be able to . . .

1. Use copious references from the text to discuss the way Maude Montgomery develops her protagonist Anne Shirley.

2. Discuss how the author of the Book of Job creates his main character (i.e., Job).

3. *Anne of Green Gables* is replete with rich characters. Discuss how Montgomery uses at least three characters (or foils) to develop Anne.

Look Ahead for Friday

*   Turn in a final copy of essay or take it as a test
*   Optional objective test

Lesson 1

Characterization

Daily Assignment

- Warm-up: How does Montgomery make Anne so charming?

- Students will complete Concept Builder 25-A.

- Prayer journal: Students are encouraged to write in their prayer journal every day.

- Students need to review their material for the next assignment

- Students should systematically review their vocabulary words daily.

CONCEPT
BUILDER
25-A

Active Reading

Read this excerpt from *Anne of Green Gables* (chapter 1) by Lucy Maud Montgomery, and then answer the following questions:

1. What is the narrative point of view?

ANSWER: Omniscient Narration

2. Describe Rachel.

ANSWER: Rachel is a cantankerous middle-aged neighbor who, nonetheless, has a great heart.

3. Describe Matthew.

ANSWER: Matthew is Marilla's quiet, shy brother.

Lesson 2

Characterization in the Bible: Ahab

Daily Assignment

- Warm-up: Do you think this novel is a children's novel, or can it be enjoyed by readers of all ages? Explain.
- Students will complete Concept Builder 25-B.
- Prayer journal.
- Students should outline all assigned essays for the week.

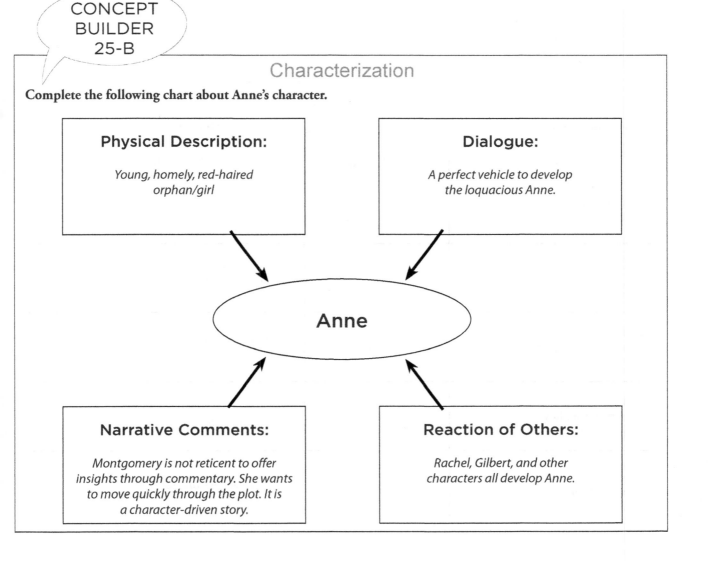

Lesson 3

Grammar Review: Quotations

Daily Assignment

- Warm-up: Do you have a best friend? Describe him or her?
- Students will complete Concept Builder 25-C.
- Prayer journal.
- Students should write rough drafts of all assigned essays and speech.

CONCEPT
BUILDER
25-C

Elements of a Story

Analyze the following elements of the novel *Anne of Green Gables* by Lucy Maud Montgomery.

Elements	Yes/No	Because . . .
Characters Do the characters seem real?	Yes	*They all seem like the people we would meet in our neighborhood.*
Narration Is Anne a credible narrator?	Yes	*Anne has both strengths and weaknesses.*
Setting Is the setting important? Does it seem real?	No	*While Prince Edward Island is beautiful, it could be replaced.*
Plot Does the story flow logically? Does it flow well?	Yes	*While the story is episodic, to this reader, it moves along quite well.*
Theme Is there a theme?	Yes	*Love, forgiveness, and redemption*

Lesson 4

Student Essay

Daily Assignment

- Warm-up: Do you identify with Anne? Why or why not?
- Students will complete Concept Builder 25-D.
- Prayer journal.
- Review the assigned text. Keep vocabulary cards.
- This is the day that students should write, and then rewrite, the final drafts of their assigned essay.

CONCEPT
BUILDER
25-D

Plot Development

Complete the following based on the plot of *Anne of Green Gables.*

Exposition

Anne arrives at her new home.

Rising Action

Each episode has rising action. The first crisis was when Anne and Diana drank alcoholic wine by mistake.

Climax

Anne and Diana are discovered, and it appears Anne has lost a friend.

Falling Action

There seems to be no resolution.

Resolution

Another crisis arises, and Anne saves Diana's sister's life.

Chapter 25 Test Answer

OBJECTIVE TEST (50 POINTS)

A   Anne is (A) an orphan girl (B) a wealthy heiress (C) an accomplished circus rider (D) a relative to Matthew.

C   Matthew arrives at the train station to pick up (A) a package (B) a girl (C) a boy (D) a horse.

D   Anne's favorite childhood friend is (A) Marilla (B) Matthew (C) Deanna (D) Diana.

A   Initially, Anne did not like a boy whose name is (A) Gilbert (B) Martin (C) Matthew (D) David.

B   After Matthew dies, Anne decides to stay at Green Gables to help Marilla because (A) Marilla is poor (B) Marilla is going blind (C) Marilla is lonely (D) Anne is homesick.

Chapter 25 Essay Answer

ESSAY (50 POINTS)

In 75–150 words, discuss how the author creates his character in the following essay.

Summary: The father is naturally proud of his sons; however, he has other things on his mind: he is dying. This quite ordinary man has become extraordinary because of life's situations and because of his faith in Christ.

Theme — *Anne of Green Gables*
(L. Maude Montgomery)

Chapter 26

First Thoughts

A great story includes characters, plot, and other literary components. It also has profound and eternal meaning. Its meaning, or theme, should transcend time and location. The following paper demonstrates one theme in Joseph Conrad's *Heart of Darkness*. In this book, the thoughtful protagonist Marlow is looking for the idealistic Kurtz who has disappeared while trying to enlighten the natives in Africa.

Chapter Learning Objectives

In chapter 26 we will discuss themes in *Anne of Green Gables* by Maude Montgomery.

As a result of this chapter study you will be able to . . .

1. Using a number of textual examples on the important theme of adoption in *Anne of Green Gables*, discuss the biblical understanding of adoption.

2. As *Anne of Green Gables* unfolds, the characters change in significant and permanent ways. Discuss these changes in the following characters: Anne, Marilla, Matthew, Gilbert, and Rachel.

Look Ahead for Friday

- Turn in a final copy of essay or take it as a test

Lesson 1

Sample Essay: Theme

Daily Assignment

- Warm-up: Anne is not perfect. For one thing, she struggles with anger. Do you have a problem with anger? How do you handle it?

- Students will complete Concept Builder 26-A.

- Prayer journal: Students are encouraged to write in their prayer journal every day.

- Students need to review their material for the next assignment

- Students should systematically review their vocabulary words daily.

CONCEPT BUILDER 26-A

Making Judgments

Readers really should make judgments about what they read. Read the following issues and make your judgments based on the text.

ANSWER: Answers will vary.

Lesson 2

Theme: Affirming Love

Daily Assignment

- Warm-up: Anne remains eternally optimistic and thinks cheerfully about her future. Can you think of some-one you know like that?

- Students will complete Concept Builder 26-B.

- Prayer journal.

- Students should outline all assigned essays for the week.

CONCEPT
BUILDER
26-B

Characterization of Anne

Characters are developed by reactions of others to them. In the following chart, discuss how Anne develops as a character.

Creation of Anne as a Character

Reaction to Marilla and Matthew

In Anne's relationship with her adopted parents, for the first time in her life she finds sustaining unconditional love. This transforms her as a character. In fact, no other relationship(s) are as important.

Reaction of Rachel and other adults

While Rachel's relationship with Anne begins poorly, ultimately the experience of reconciliation with another adult makes a great impact on Anne. Again, she experiences redemption and sustaining love, and these change her considerably. Plus, she experiences forgiveness from someone she has wronged. Anne's teacher, and other adults, reinforce these characteristics.

Reaction of Diana and other children

Finding peer friends is a great breakthrough for Anne. Most of her relationships with young people were with care-giving roles she had with children. In particular, Anne's relationship with Gilbert is an interesting one. Throughout this novel, and subsequent novels, Montgomery uses Gilbert to build the sort of young woman who emerges at the end of her classic(s).

Lesson 3

Grammar Review: Using Unnecessary Words

Daily Assignment

- Warm-up: Striving to make Matthew and Marilla proud, Anne devotes herself to her studies wholeheartedly and earns the prestigious Avery Scholarship, which grants her enough money to attend a four-year college the following fall. When Anne learns that Marilla is likely to go blind, she decides to stay at Green Gables and teach nearby so that she can care for Marilla, giving up her aspirations for a four-year degree. Did Anne do the right thing? Can you think of another solution?

- Students will complete Concept Builder 26-C.

- Prayer journal.

- Students should write rough drafts of all assigned essays and speech.

Sequencing the Plot

The sequence is the order of events in a plot. It is never coincidental; every author has a purpose in sequencing his events. What is the sequence of events as they emerge in *Anne of Green Gables*?

Event 1

Marilla and Matthew Cuthbert, unmarried middle-aged siblings who live together at Green Gables, a farm in the town of Avonlea, on Prince Edward Island, decide to adopt a boy from an orphan asylum in Nova Scotia as a helper on their farm. But the person whom they adopt turns out to be Anne Shirley.

Event 2

After some mishaps, Anne takes much joy in life, and adapts quickly, thriving in the environment of Prince Edward Island. She is something of a chatterbox, and drives the prim, duty-driven Marilla to distraction, although shy Matthew falls for her immediately.

Event 3

Anne enters school and makes friends and enemies.

Event 4

Other adventures include her games with her friendship group (Diana, Jane, and Ruby), her rivalries with the Pye sisters (Gertie and Josie), and her domestic mistakes such as dyeing her hair green.

Event 5

Anne, along with Gilbert, Ruby, Josie, Jane, and several other students, eventually goes to the Queen's Academy and obtains a teaching license in one year, in addition to winning the Avery Prize in English, which allows her to pursue a B.A. at Redmond College.

Event 6

The book ends with Matthew's death. Anne shows her devotion to Marilla and Green Gables by deciding to stay at home and help Marilla, whose eyesight is diminishing. To show his friendship, Gilbert Blythe gives up his teaching position in the Avonlea School to work at White Sands School instead, thus enabling Anne to teach at the Avonlea School and stay at Green Gables all through the week. After this kind act, Anne and Gilbert become friends.

Resolution

Lesson 4

Student Essay

Daily Assignment

- Warm-up: Later when Gilbert hears of Anne's decision to stay home with Marilla, he gives up his post as the teacher at Avonlea school so Anne can teach there and be closer to Marilla. Did Gilbert do the right thing? Can you think of another solution?
- Students will complete Concept Builder 26-D.
- Prayer journal.
- Review the assigned text. Keep vocabulary cards.
- This is the day that students should write, and then rewrite, the final drafts of their assigned essay.

CONCEPT BUILDER 26-D

Making Inferences

An inference is a conclusion or Summary drawn from information. What inferences can you draw from this book?

Title: *Anne of Green Gables*

Details from the story	What I know from reading or experience	Inference
After some mishaps, Anne takes much joy in life, and adapts quickly, thriving in the environment of Prince Edward Island. She is something of a chatterbox, and drives the prim, duty-driven Marilla to distraction, although shy Matthew falls for her immediately.	*My little sister is like Anne and I know that she means well. Montgomery obviously is fond of her protagonist, too.*	*Clearly, Anne will do just fine. She will develop into a winsome, wholesome character.*
The book ends with Matthew's death. Anne shows her devotion to Marilla and Green Gables by deciding to stay at home and help Marilla, whose eyesight is diminishing. To show his friendship, Gilbert Blythe gives up his teaching position in the Avonlea School to work at White Sands School instead, thus enabling Anne to teach at the Avonlea School and stay at Green Gables all through the week. After this kind act, Anne and Gilbert become friends.	*I have had childhood enemies who later became good friends. We can see Gilbert and Anne growing closer together.*	*I wonder if romance is in the air?*

ESSAY (100 POINTS)

Write a 75–150 word essay discussing the theme in the following essay.

Summary: The young Christian learns that God is with him, even in the valley of the shadow of death. He comes to understand that brokenness is not necessarily a bad thing; in fact, what is learned through brokenness can become a valuable part of the Christian life.

Plot — *Ivanhoe* (Sir Walter Scott)

Chapter 27

First Thoughts

Walter Scott was born in 1771 in Edinburgh, Scotland. He was one of Scotland's most popular adventure novelists. He began his writing career by writing long narrative poems (as Alfred Lord Tennyson had done). His "The Lay of the Last Minstrel" (1805) and "The Lady of the Lake" (1810) were extremely popular throughout Scotland and the English-speaking world. However, by around 1813, Lord Byron had overtaken him in popularity and with literary success as a narrative poet, and Scott turned to novels to rejuvenate his career (and to replenish his pocketbook). His *Waverly* (1814), a historical novel set during the Scottish Rebellion of 1745, became a huge success, and Scott began a long career as a historical novelist.

Chapter Learning Objectives

In chapter 27 we will discuss the plot in *Ivanhoe* by Sir Walter Scott.

As a result of this chapter study you will be able to . . .

1. Discuss the plot of *Ivanhoe*. In your discussion reference the structure of the plot: rising action, climax, falling action.

2. Examine Ivanhoe and other literary figures (e.g., *Beowulf*) who exhibit Christ-like tendencies. On the other hand, they are war-like. Discuss the ways that Ivanhoe is Christ-like and the ways that he is not.

3. Write a 3,000-word adventure story.

Look Ahead for Friday

- Turn in a final copy of essay or take it as a test
- Optional objective test

Lesson 1

Sample Essay: Plot

Daily Assignment

- Warm-up: Compare and contrast Rowena and Rebecca in *Ivanhoe*.
- Students will complete Concept Builder 27-A.
- Prayer journal: Students are encouraged to write in their prayer journal every day.
- Students need to review their material for the next assignment
- Students should systematically review their vocabulary words daily.

CONCEPT
BUILDER
27-A

Active Reading

Read this excerpt from *Ivanhoe* (chapter 1) by Sir Walter Scott, and then answer the following questions:

1. What is the setting? Is it important?

ANSWER: England during the Crusades. It is important because one would only find knights and fair maidens during this time. At the same time, the novel captures many universal, timeless themes.

2. What is the narrative point of view?

ANSWER: Omniscient narration.

3. What is a central conflict in the plot?

ANSWER: The Norman conquerors are despotic rulers of the conquered Saxons. While the story is episodic, the protagonist, Ivanhoe, fights one battle after another for justice and goodness.

Lesson 2

Plot

Daily Assignment

- Warm-up: Many of the characters in *Ivanhoe* enter the plot disguised. Why does Scott do that?
- Students will complete Concept Builder 27-B.
- Prayer journal.
- Students should outline all assigned essays for the week.

CONCEPT
BUILDER
27-B

Symbolism

Ivanhoe **is full of adventure and is a historical romance; however, Ivanhoe does represent virtue and goodness. Draw symbols that represent the words below.**

ANSWER: Answers will vary.

Lesson 3

Grammar Review: Document Design

Daily Assignment

- Warm-up: When you think about "knights and damsels in distress," what do you think? What is your earliest impression of these events?

- Students will complete a daily Concept Builder 27-C.

- Prayer journal.

- Students should write rough drafts of all assigned essays.

CONCEPT
BUILDER
27-C

Elements of a Story

Analyze the following elements of the novel *Ivanhoe* by Sir Walter Scott.

Elements	Yes/No	Because . . .
Characters Do the characters seem real?	No	Most of the characters are "type" characters or archetypes. They represent a personality or worldview rather than a human being.
Setting Is the setting important? Does it seem real?	Yes	Twelfth-century England is a time one would expect to find knights and jousting matches.
Plot Does the story flow logically? Does it flow well?	Somewhat	It is an episodic tale and this reader had a hard time keeping all the names of the characters in mind and also found it to be difficult to follow all the plot turns.
Theme Is there a theme?	Yes	Loyalty, perseverance.

Lesson 4

Student Essay: Plot in *Ivanhoe*

Daily Assignment

- Warm-up: Many readers enjoy Scott's story but are distracted by his wordy style. What do you think?

- Students will complete Concept Builder 27-D.

- Prayer journal.

- Review the assigned text. Keep vocabulary cards.

- This is the day that students should write, and then rewrite, the final drafts of their assigned essays.

CONCEPT BUILDER 27-D

Journey Motif

A motif is a theme or tone that permeates a literary work. The central motif of this novel is the journey motif. Ivanhoe is on a journey home, and then a journey from place to place.

Create an imaginary journey from your home to another location. On that journey, identify landmarks that you will pass along this journey, and imagine what dangers will seek to keep you from your destination. If necessary, pretend!

ANSWER: Answers will vary.

Chapter 27 Test Answer

OBJECTIVE TEST (50 POINTS)

D Ivanhoe has recently returned from (A) wars in France (B) exploring China (C) conquering Spain (D) participating in the Crusades.

A He is disguised as (A) a religious pilgrim (B) a black knight (C) an old man (D) as an army captain.

C King Richard is (A) dead (B) in England (C) in an Austrian prison (D) fighting in Palestine.

B King John is (A) Richard's father (B) Richard's brother (C) Richard's cousin (D) no relation of Richard's.

C The black knight is really (A) Ivanhoe (B) King John (C) King Richard (D) Rowena.

Chapter 27 Essay Answer

ESSAY (50 POINTS)

Write a two-page story exhibiting all the elements of a sound plot (rising action, climax, falling action, resolution).

Summary: Answers will vary

Worldviews of Protagonist — *Ivanhoe* (Sir Walter Scott)

Chapter 28

First Thoughts

Many of Walter Scott's works were historical romances about his homeland, but his best and most famous novel, 1819's *Ivanhoe*, had nothing to do with Scotland at all. Set in England in the last years of the 12th century, *Ivanhoe* tells the story of a noble knight involved with King Richard I — known to history as "Richard the Lion-Hearted" — and his return to England from the Crusades. This Ivanhoe, not to be confused with the Ivanhoe in the King Arthur legends, is a quintessential hero.

Chapter Learning Objectives

In chapter 28 we will discuss the worldview in *Ivanhoe* by Sir Walter Scott.

As a result of this chapter study you will be able to . . .

1. Discuss how Scott uses the plot and characters to communicate his worldview in *Ivanhoe*.

2. Compare the way Scott presents women (one-dimensional and somewhat shallow) with the way the virtuous woman is presented in Proverbs 31.

3. Evaluate if Christians should read literature that has aberrant worldviews.

Look Ahead for Friday

- Turn in a final copy of essay or take it as a test

Lesson 1

Sample Essay: Worldview

Daily Assignment

- Warm-up: If you had to play a character in a movie based on *Ivanhoe*, which one would you choose? Why?
- Students will complete Concept Builder 28-A.
- Prayer journal: Students are encouraged to write in their prayer journal every day.
- Students need to review their material for the next assignment
- Students should systematically review their vocabulary words daily.

CONCEPT BUILDER 28-A

Active Reading - Imagery

Read "The Walrus and The Carpenter" from *Alice in Wonderland* by Lewis Carroll, and then answer the questions below:

ANSWER: Answers will vary.

Lesson 2

Worldview Model

Daily Assignment

- Warm-up: Did you like the ending of Ivanhoe? If not, write a more satisfying ending. If you liked the ending, why did you like it?

- Students will complete Concept Builder 28-B.

- Prayer journal.

- Students should outline all assigned essays for the week.

CONCEPT BUILDER 28-B

The Antagonist

There are several antagonists (foils opposed to the protagonist) in *Ivanhoe*. Check the categories that apply to these and other antagonists in movies and books.

ANSWER: Answers will vary.

Lesson 3

Grammar Review: Misused Words

Daily Assignment

- Warm-up: Would *Ivanhoe* make a good movie? Why or why not?
- Students will complete a daily Concept Builder 28-C.
- Prayer journal.
- Students should write rough drafts of all assigned essays.

CONCEPT BUILDER 28-C

Author's Worldview

Sir Walter Scott, through his plot and characters, communicates a particular world view. Compare that world view with your world view by answering yes or no to the following statements.

ANSWER: Answers will vary.

Lesson 4

Student Essay: Worldview in *Ivanhoe*

Daily Assignment

- Warm-up: Some critics argue that there are too many characters in *Ivanhoe*. Agree or disagree and explain your answer.
- Students will complete Concept Builder 28-D.
- Prayer journal.
- Review the assigned text. Keep vocabulary cards.
- This is the day that students should write, and then rewrite, the final drafts of their assigned essays.

CONCEPT BUILDER 28-D

Making Moral Decisions

Characters in *Ivanhoe* are constantly asked to make moral decisions. Likewise, we as believers have to make moral decisions, too. Complete the chart below.

Moral Dilemma	What will I do?	Why?
A student in Sunday school tells a racial joke that is inappropriate. What will you do?	*I will ask him to stop. If he does not, I will tell someone in authority.*	*I will follow Matthew 18, but the behavior must stop.*
In World War II, some Christians hid Jewish people from their German captors, even though it was against the law. What would you do?	*I will hide Jewish people. In my opinion, we are not required to obey laws that violate the Bible.*	*At the same time, like Daniel in the Bible, I would try to overcome evil with good. If confronted, like Corrie ten Boon, I would honor my Lord by telling the truth and by standing up for His principles.*
You buy a notebook in a store. The cashier gives you back too much change. What will you do?	*I absolutely will return the change.*	*Stealing is in violation of the Ten Commandments.*

ESSAY (100 POINTS)

Read the following poem by T.S. Eliot, and in a one-page essay, discuss its worldview.

Summary: Eliot's poem is a clever metaphor contrasting a hippopotamus to the Church. The worldview is Christian theism. Eliot converted to Christianity at the end of his life and wrote some of the most powerful theistic poetry in the 20th century.

Tone: Suspense — *Shane* (Jack Warner Schaefer)

Chapter 29

First Thoughts

Shane is one of the most popular movies and books of the 20th century. On one level, Shane is a superb cowboy-and-Indians story. On another level, this tale of the mysterious stranger who rides in from the distant hills and rides off again, is a stock archetype story (prototype or representative), replicated in several different genres and narratives. The protagonist is desperate to escape his past. The gunfighter Shane changes into the farmer Shane at a little farmstead, where he is befriended by the farmer's young son. However, the scheming cattle barons make his escape impossible. Mystery man Shane helps the farmers stand up to the cowboy bullies sent by the ranchers. Matters get out of hand when the head rancher, frustrated by Shane's presence and mettle, calls in a ruthless gunman from nearby Cheyenne to bring matters to a head. Shane is more than a match. This archetypal story is a powerful well-written piece of fiction for several reasons. While the storyline is common and predictable — the brave gunfighter saves the sedentary farmer and his family — the characters are well-developed and complicated. Shane wants to retire and cannot. Joe is a hard-working farmer who is really brave — even though his son does not know it until the end of the novel. Shane's relationship with the wife is subtle and skillfully developed by the author. All these conspire to make this novel a well-written piece of fiction.

Chapter Learning Objectives

In chapter 29 we will examine the way Jack Schaefer creates suspense in *Shane*.

As a result of this chapter study you will be able to . . .

1. Discuss how Schaefer develops suspense in *Shane's* plot.

2. Discuss how Samuel builds suspense in the story of David and Goliath (1 Samuel 18).

3. Compare the way suspense is created in *Shane* and in *The Call of the Wild*.

Look Ahead for Friday

- Turn in a final copy of essay or take it as a test
- Optional objective test

Lesson 1

Suspense: "The Tell-Tale Heart"

Daily Assignment

- Warm-up: Did you like *Shane*? Why or why not?
- Students will complete Concept Builder 29-A.
- Prayer journal: Students are encouraged to write in their prayer journal every day.
- Students need to review their material for the next assignment
- Students should systematically review their vocabulary words daily.

CONCEPT
BUILDER
29-A

Predicting or Foreshadowing

Most authors are quite intentional about the way they structure their literary piece. A clever reader, however, will discern the outcome/resolution long before the literary piece ends. Find as many hints as possible in *Shane* (if possible before you finish reading it) and offer an informed prediction.

Shane Arrives

Foreshadowing Incident 1

A stranger named Shane drifts into an isolated western valley. It soon becomes apparent that he is a former gunslinger, and he finds himself drawn into a conflict between the humble farmer Joe Starrett and powerful cattle baron Rufus Ryker, who wants to force Starrett and every other homesteader in the valley off the land.

Foreshadowing Incident 2

As tensions mount between the factions, Ryker hires Jack Wilson, a hired gun.

Foreshadowing Incident 3

After Wilson kills another homesteader who had stood up to him, Joe Starrett decides to take it upon himself to go kill Wilson and Ryker and save the town; however, he is stopped by Shane, who insists on going himself.

Shane Rides into the Sunset

Lesson 2

Sample Essay: Suspense

Daily Assignment

- Warm-up: Did Shane do the right thing (supporting the family with violence)?
- Students will complete Concept Builder 29-B.
- Prayer journal.
- Students should outline all assigned essays for the week.

CONCEPT
BUILDER
29-B

Foils

Foils are used by an author to develop his main character, in this case, Shane. Discuss how the author uses foils to develop Shane.

Foil	Joe	Marian	Joey	Ryker
How the author develops Shane	Joe invites Shane to a cause. He is a moral, stubborn farmer who needs help. This brings out the best in Shane.	Marian shows the soft side of Shane, but, at the same time, she allows the author to show how strong Shane is in the face of temptation.	Joey shows the gentle, patient side of Shane.	Ryker reminds the reader that Shane is a skilled killer and will not be provoked too far.

Lesson 3

Grammar Review: Problems in Style

Daily Assignment

- Warm-up: Did you like the ending? If not, write a more satisfying ending. If you liked the ending, why did you like it?
- Students will complete Concept Builder 29-C.
- Prayer journal.
- Students should write rough drafts of all assigned essays and speech.

CONCEPT
BUILDER
29-C

Generalizations

Slowly, as the story unfolds, the reader makes observations, forms conclusions, and ultimately makes generalizations about Shane. Note some of those here.

Fact/Observation 1	Shane is not afraid to be connected to poor, unimportant people.
Fact/Observation 2	*Shane is not too busy, not too important, to spend time with Joey.*
Fact/Observation 3	*Shane could take advantage of the farmer's wife, but he chose not to do so.*
Fact/Observation 4	*Although he is reluctant to do so, Shane will not allow the hired hand to kill anyone else.*

Generalization: Shane is a very brave man, a fair man, and a just man.

Lesson 4

Student Essay

Daily Assignment

- Warm-up: What Hollywood actor would you like to see as Shane? Why?
- Students will complete Concept Builder 29-D.
- Prayer journal.
- Review the assigned text. Keep vocabulary cards.
- This is the day that students should write, and then rewrite, the final drafts of their assigned essay.

CONCEPT
BUILDER
29-D

Theme

The theme is the central purpose of a literary piece. It is the central idea that an author wants to share with a reader. The author mostly uses the plot and characters to advance a theme.

The author develops several plots, but, notably, is the plot of "redemption." Shane is literally healed and redeemed by helping a family overcome adversity. How does the author develop this theme?

Plot Details	Character Details
A conflict — farmers vs. the ranchers — exists before the story begins.	*Shane is a man struggling with his violent past.*
Shane is obviously shy and quiet. He seems to be hiding something.	*He is hiding his past. The reader does not know, never knows, much about that past. That adds to the suspense.*
Shane has an awkward relationship with Marian.	*The reader cannot tell if Shane loves her or not; but that is irrelevant. Shane acted in an entirely respectful way.*
The ranchers are openly antagonistic to the farmers.	*Shane tries to ignore this problem. He does not want to get involved. He knows that his presence could escalate the whole affair.*
One of the farmers is killed.	*Now Shane has no choice but to intervene.*
Shane will have to fight the ranchers himself or Joe will.	*Shane fights and wins.*

Theme - Redemption

Chapter 29 Test Answer

OBJECTIVE TEST (50 POINTS)

A   Shane is (A) a former gunfighter (B) captain in the army (C) an army scout (D) farmer.

B   Shane avoids (A) all physical labor (B) all physical confrontations (C) cattle drives (D) opportunities to marry.

C   Marian is married to (A) Shane (B) Bob (C) Joe (D) David.

B   Marian loves both Shane and Joe but chooses to (A) leave both (B) stay with Joe (C) leave with Shane (D) stay but asks both to leave.

D   At the end of the novel, the boy realizes (A) that Shane is a coward (B) that his mom is a coward (C) that his dad is deaf (D) that his dad is braver than Shane in many ways.

Chapter 29 Essay Answer

ESSAY (50 POINTS)

If your parents will allow you to do so, watch the 1953 movie *Shane*, starring Alan Ladd, and in a one-page essay compare the way the director of the movie develops suspense with the way Schaefer develops suspense. Does the movie closely follow the book?

Summary: The movie does follow the book fairly closely and suspense mounts in a similar fashion.

Character: Internal Conflict — *Shane*
(Jack Warner Schaefer)

Chapter 30

First Thoughts

Shane is full of characters who change. Most of them change because of internal conflict.

Chapter Learning Objectives

In chapter 30 we will examine the way Jack Schaefer uses internal conflict to change characters in *Shane*.

As a result of this chapter study you will be able to . . .

1. Discuss how several characters in the novel *Shane* change because of internal conflict.
2. Discuss the internal conflict that Moses must have felt when he returned to Egypt.
3. Compare the way Bob changes in *Shane* and the way Huw changes in *How Green Was My Valley.*

Look Ahead for Friday

- Turn in a final copy of essay or take it as a test

Lesson 1

Literary Analysis: Internal Conflict in a Character

Daily Assignment

- Warm-up: Is Shane too good to be true? Does he seem like a real person? Why or why not?
- Students will complete Concept Builder 30-A.
- Prayer journal: Students are encouraged to write in their prayer journal every day.
- Students need to review their material for the next assignment
- Students should systematically review their vocabulary words daily.

CONCEPT
BUILDER
30-A

Moral Dilemma

Shane has a moral dilemma, yet it is not unlike many dilemmas we face. Solve the following dilemma.

Joe is a 14-year-old boy who wanted to go to camp very much. His father promised Joe he could go if he saved up the money for it himself. So Joe worked hard at his paper route and saved up the 40 dollars it cost to go to camp, and a little more besides. But just before camp was going to start, his father changed his mind. There was a family emergency and Joe's father asked Joe to give him the money he had saved from the paper route.

ANSWER: Answers will vary.

Lesson 2

Biblical Example of Internal Conflict

Daily Assignment

- Warm-up: Tell the *Shane* story from the perspective of the ranchers.

- Students will complete Concept Builder 30-B.

- Prayer journal.

- Students should outline all assigned essays for the week.

CONCEPT BUILDER 30-B

Moral Dilemma

Your 15-year-old pet, a black lab, is still healthy but struggling. He requires a costly operation to survive. Your family has the money, but they wonder what would be the best solution. Choose one of the solutions below and explain why you chose it.

ANSWER: Answers will vary.

Lesson 3

Grammar Review: Wordy

Daily Assignment

- Warm-up: Compare Shane to a hero you have.
- Students will complete Concept Builder 30-C.
- Prayer journal.
- Students should write rough drafts of all assigned essays and speech.

CONCEPT
BUILDER
30-C

Character Conflicts

Shane struggles through several internal/external struggles. List these below.

Conflict	Internal/External Conflict	Outcome
To stay and help the farmers or not.	Shane will lose his anonymity (internal conflict).	He puts the welfare of the farmer and his family before his own desires.
To give in and be friendly with the farmer's wife or not.	Shane obviously likes the lady, and he is lonely (internal conflict).	Shane again puts the welfare of the farmer and his family before his own desires.
To be close to the boy but not too close; Shane knows he will leave someday.	Shane is lonely and he likes the boy. Shane likes the young man but does not want to get too close. (internal conflict).	The boy is very upset when Shane leaves.
To honor the farmer's courage but to save the farmer's life.	Shane does not want to humiliate the farmer but he wants the farmer to live (external conflict).	He knocks out the farmer so the farmer will not go into town.
To fight the evil ranchers or not.	Shane has no quarrel with the ranchers and tries to ignore them. But he can't. They are threatening innocent people (external conflict).	He fights the ranchers and wins.

Lesson 4

Student Essay: Internal Conflict in *Shane*

Daily Assignment

- Warm-up: Did you guess the ending of *Shane*? Is it predictable? Why or why not?
- Students will complete Concept Builder 30-D.
- Prayer journal.
- Review the assigned text. Keep vocabulary cards.
- This is the day that students should write, and then rewrite, the final drafts of their assigned essay.

CONCEPT BUILDER 30-D

Social Conflict

***Shane* has several central conflicts that propel the plot forward. Complete the following chart.**

Conflict	Participants	Resolution
Farmers versus the ranchers	*The ranchers do not want the farmers to fence the open range. The open range is critical to the ranchers' financial survival.*	*The farmers, this time at least, win.*
Poor, ordinary people versus the privileged, wealthy people.	*The poor farmers are fighting the rich ranchers.*	*The farmers, this time at least, win.*
Shane, the gunfighter, versus ordinary farmers who are not by trade gunmen.	*Joe and his neighbors versus Stryker.*	*Shane more than equals the equation.*
The farmer's wife who urges the strong, righteous Shane to protect her husband.	*Shane, Marian, and Joe*	*Shane knocks out Joe and heads to town.*

Chapter 30 Test Answer

ESSAY (100 POINTS)

Read Matthew 26:31–75 about Peter's betrayal of Jesus. Discuss the internal conflict he must have faced in this darkest hour.

Summary: Answers will vary.

Literary Review: Drama — *A Midsummer Night's Dream* (William Shakespeare)

Chapter 31

First Thoughts

For the remainder of this curriculum, you will be introduced to several other literary genres, and you will be invited to write literary critiques of these works. These genres include: drama, letters, a poem, and a short story.

Our first selection is a play. *A Midsummer Night's Dream* is one of William Shakespeare's most popular and well-written plays. During Shakespeare's time, theater was entertainment (before it was art), much like television functions today. Theater was not merely the pastime of the elite and the educated. It belonged to the people. Shakespeare wrote and performed during the reigns of Queen Elizabeth and King James. The Elizabethan theater highlighted the spoken word. The Elizabethan audience was attentive to the spoken word. They had to be. Theater used few stage properties and almost no scenery. Its outdoor circular theaters surrounded a bare horseshoe-shaped stage. Characters were developed at a fast pace, and what they said indicated who they were. There was neither narrator nor fancy bulletin to help the unwary listener. The audience worked for their treat. Thus, the playwright constantly had to keep his audience interested through the use of bright costumes, numerous action scenes, and frequent scene changes. *A Midsummer Night's Dream* had it all: fairies, creatures, and unicorns. They all invite the reader/viewer to a world of intrigue and entertainment.

Chapter Learning Objectives

In chapter 31 we will analyze an entire literary piece: William Shakespeare's *A Midsummer Night's Dream*.

As a result of this chapter study you will be able to . . .

1. Write a literary analysis of the entire play *A Midsummer Night's Dream*.

2. Analyze what vulgarity is.

3. Discuss the purpose of Puck in this comedy.

Look Ahead for Friday

- Turn in a final copy of essay or take it as a test

- Optional objective test

Lesson 1

Sample Play Review (Not a Full Literary Analysis)

Daily Assignment

- Warm-up: Compare *A Midsummer Night's Dream* to another Shakespeare play you have read or seen.
- Students will complete Concept Builder 31-A.
- Prayer journal: Students are encouraged to write in their prayer journal every day.
- Students need to review their material for the next assignment
- Students should systematically review their vocabulary words daily.

CONCEPT
BUILDER
31-A

Grammar Review: Cogency and Focus

Rewrite the following passages with more cogency and focus.

A. In a morbid condition of the brain, dreams often have a singular actuality, vividness, and extraordinary semblance of reality. At times monstrous images are created, but the setting and the whole picture are so truth-like and filled with details so delicate, so unexpectedly, but so artistically consistent, that the dreamer, were he an artist like Pushkin or Turgenev even, could never have invented them in the waking state. Such sick dreams always remain long in the memory and make a powerful impression on the overwrought and deranged nervous system. (from *Crime and Punishment*)

A. Rewrite:
In the remote parts of the brain, dreams are especially vivid and real. These terrible dreams can be so impressive and awful that they remain forever in the bearer

B. Later on, when he recalled that time and all that happened to him during those days, minute by minute, point by point, he was superstitiously impressed by one circumstance, which, though in itself not very exceptional, always seemed to him afterwards the predestined turning-point of his fate. He could never understand and explain to himself why, when he was tired and worn out, when it would have been more convenient for him to go home by the shortest and most direct way, he had returned by the Hay Market where he had no need to go. It was obviously and quite unnecessarily out of his way, though not much so. It is true that it happened to him dozens of times to return home without noticing what streets he passed through. But why, he was always asking himself, why had such an important, such a decisive and at the same time such an absolutely chance meeting happened in the Hay Market (where he had moreover no reason to go) at the very hour, the very minute of his life when he was just in the very mood and in the very circumstances in which that meeting was able to exert the gravest and most decisive influence on his whole destiny? As though it had been lying in wait for him on purpose! (from *Crime and Punishment*)

B. Rewrite:
He had deja vu of an earlier time when he was at this same place. It was very real to him, and it had a decisive impact on his life.

Lesson 2

Worldview Model

Daily Assignment

- Warm-up: Summarize the plot of *A Midsummer Nights Dream*.

- Students will complete Concept Builder 31-B.

- Prayer journal.

- Students should outline all assigned essays for the week.

CONCEPT
BUILDER
31-B

The Plot

Draw and label the three plots that are occurring in *A Midsummer Night's Dream*.

The play features three interlocking plots, connected by a celebration of the King of Duke Theseus of Athens, and the Amazonian Queen Hippolyta, and set simultaneously in the woodland, and in the realm of Fairyland, under the light of the moon.

Lesson 3

Grammar Review: Exclamation Points

Daily Assignment

- Warm-up: Did you like this play? Why? Why not? Explain.
- Students will complete a daily Concept Builder 31-C.
- Prayer journal.
- Students should write rough drafts of all assigned essays.

CONCEPT BUILDER 31-C

Plot Climax

Draw the climax of *A Midsummer Night's Dream* on this stage.

It would probably be when Oberon releases Titania and orders Puck to remove the ass's head from Bottom. The magical enchantment is removed from Lysander but is allowed to remain on Demetrius, so that he may reciprocate Helena's love.

Lesson 4

Student Essay:
Analysis of *A Midsummer Night's Dream*

Daily Assignment

- Warm-up: Share a dream you had that seemed real until you woke.
- Students will complete Concept Builder 31-D.
- Prayer journal.
- Review the assigned text. Keep vocabulary cards.
- This is the day that students should write, and then rewrite, the final drafts of their assigned essays.

CONCEPT
BUILDER
31-D

Theme Development

The theme of a story is a lesson the author wishes to share with his readers. Complete the following Chart considering a theme centered around love.

A Theme of Love is developed by . . .

Characterization

The characters are colorful, round, and strong. They feel their world deeply. They connect with other characters.

Plot

The fairies make light of love by mistaking the lovers and by applying a love potion to Titania's eyes, forcing her to fall in love with Bottom as an ass. In the forest, both couples are met by problems. Hermia and Lysander are both met by Puck, who provides some comedic relief in the play by confusing the four lovers in the forest. At the end of the play, Hermia and Lysander, happily married, watch the play about the unfortunate lovers Pyramus and Thisbe, and are able to enjoy and laugh about the play, not realizing the similarities between them.

Setting

The mysterious setting — forest at night — adds to the mystery of love.

Chapter 31 Test Answer

OBJECTIVE TEST (50 POINTS)

B   Theseus, Duke of Athens, is preparing for his marriage to (A) Matilda, (B) Hippolyta, (C) Maria, (D) Rosemary, Queen of the Amazons, with a four-day festival of pomp and entertainment.

B   Egeus wishes Hermia to marry Demetrius, who loves (A) Lysander (B) Hermia (C) Puck (D) Demetrius.

C   Egeus asks for (A) Hermia to be forgiven (B) Hermia to be killed (C) the full penalty of law to fall on Hermia if she disobeys her father (D) Hermia to be sent away.

C   Hermia and Lysander plan to (A) commit suicide (B) escape Athens the following night and go to Sparta (C) elope (D) buy a house.

C   The last character the audience sees is (A) Lysander (B) Hermia (C) Puck (D) Demetrius.

Chapter 31 Essay Answer

ESSAY (50 POINTS)

With your parents' permission, attend a live performance of a play, or watch a movie and write a one-page review. In your essay, answer these questions

1. Were the lighting and scenery appropriate?

2. Was the play/movie too long? Too short? Just right?

3. Were the actors and actresses appropriately cast?

4. Did the plot unfold appropriately and in an interesting way?

5. Was there a theme? What was it?

6. Who were the characters? Did they come alive? Were they well developed?

7. Who was the narrator? Was he believable?

8. What was the worldview? Was it ably presented?

9. What was the tone? Was it appropriate for the subject matter?

10. Overall, was it a great play? Why or why not?

Summary: Answers will vary but should include some of the following criteria for judging the value of the play: believable, interesting characters performing actions that have thematic importance in an interesting setting.

Literary Review: Letters — "Letters" (C.S. Lewis)

Chapter 32

First Thoughts

Letter writing is quickly becoming a lost art. With the advent of e-mail and telecommunications, most Americans do not write letters anymore. However, throughout history letter writing has been a powerfully effective way to communicate. For example, Paul's letters to the churches in the New Testament were a powerful and effective means to communicate the gospel.

Chapter Learning Objectives

In chapter 32 we will examine C.S. Lewis's "Letters to Mr. Vanauken."

As a result of this chapter study you will be able to . . .

1. Examine the letters and discuss their style and structure. In other words, how does Lewis persuade his friend to give his life to Christ?

2. Write a letter to a friend or acquaintance who does not know the Lord

3. Discuss the influence of C.S. Lewis on the conversion of Chuck Colson

Look Ahead for Friday

*   Turn in a final copy of essay or take it as a test

Lesson 1

Literary Analysis: Internal Conflict in a Character

Daily Assignment

- Warm-up: Describe a significant religious experience that you have had.
- Students will complete Concept Builder 32-A.
- Prayer journal: Students are encouraged to write in their prayer journal every day.
- Students need to review their material for the next assignment
- Students should systematically review their vocabulary words daily.

CONCEPT
BUILDER
32-A

Active Reading

Read the following personal letter from C.S. Lewis to a friend, and then answer the following questions:

1. Notice the way that Lewis uses rhetorical questions and dialogue. Why?

ANSWER: Isn't the truth this: that it would gratify some of our desires (ones we feel, in fact, pretty seldom) and outrage a good many others? Lewis tries to anticipate doubts and questions.

2. Circle examples of each.

Lesson 2

Biblical Letter

Daily Assignment

- Warm-up: Persuade your parents to let you go to Disneyland.
- Students will complete Concept Builder 32-B.
- Prayer journal.
- Students should outline all assigned essays for the week.

CONCEPT BUILDER 32-B

Writing a Letter

Write an informal letter to an unsaved friend, convincing him to give his life to Christ. Begin with a greeting. Offer some arguments, and evidence to support your arguments. Then, discuss one counter-argument (opposing view) and finish with a Summary and prayer.

ANSWER: Answers will vary.

Lesson 3

Grammar Review: Wordy

Daily Assignment

- Warm-up: Persuade your best friend to eat pizza from the wide (not sharp) end.
- Students will complete Concept Builder 32-C.
- Prayer journal.
- Students should write rough drafts of all assigned essays and speech.

CONCEPT
BUILDER
32-C

Analyze Lewis' Letter

Take excerpts from the text of C.S. Lewis' Letter to complete the boxes below.

Greeting/Introduction

My own position at the threshold of Christianity was exactly the opposite of yours. You wish it were true; I strongly hoped it was not. At least, that was my conscious wish: you may suspect that I had unconscious wishes of quite a different sort and that it was these which finally shoved me in. True: but then I may equally suspect that under your conscious wish that it were true, there lurks a strong unconscious wish that it were not. What this works out to is that all the modern thinking, however useful it may be for explaining the origin of an error which you already know to be an error, is perfectly useless in deciding which of two beliefs is the error and which is the truth.

Argument

For (a.) One never knows all one's wishes, and (b.) In very big questions, such as this, even one's conscious wishes are nearly always engaged on both sides. What I think one can say with certainty is this: the notion that everyone would like Christianity to be true, and that therefore all atheists are brave men who have accepted the defeat of all their deepest desires, is simply impudent nonsense. Do you think people like Stalin, Hitler, Haldane, Stapledon (a corking good writer, by the way) would be pleased on waking up one morning to find that they were not their own masters, that they had a Master and a Judge, that there was nothing even in the deepest recesses of their thoughts about which they could say to Him "Keep out! Private. This is my business?" Do you? Rats! Their first reaction would be (as mine was) rage and terror. And I very much doubt whether even you would find it simply pleasant. Isn't the truth this: that it would gratify some of our desires (ones we feel in fact pretty seldom) and outrage a good many others? So let's wash out all the wish business. It never helped anyone to solve any problem yet. I don't agree with your picture of the history of religion. Christ, Buddha, Mohammed and others elaborating on an original simplicity.

Evidence

I believe Buddhism to be a simplification of Hinduism and Islam to be a simplification of Christianity. Clear, lucid, transparent, simple religion (Tao plus a shadowy, ethical god in the background) is a late development, usually arising among highly educated people in great cities. What you really start with is ritual, myth, and mystery, the death and return of Balder or Osiris, the dances, the initiations, the sacrifices, the divine kings. Over against that are the Philosophers, Aristotle or Confucius, hardly religion at all. The only two systems in which the mysteries and the philosophies come together are Hinduism and Christianity: there you get both the Metaphysics and Cult (continuous with primeval cults). That is why my first step was to be sure that one or the other of these had the answer. For the reality can't be one that appeals either only to savages or only to high brows. Real things aren't like that (e.g. matter is the first most obvious thing you meet milk, chocolates, apples, and also the object of quantum physics). There is no question of just a crowd of disconnected religions. The choice is between (a.) The materialist world picture: which I can't believe. (b.) The real archaic primitive religions; which are not moral enough. (c.) The (claimed) fulfillment of these in Hinduism. (d.) The claimed fulfillment of these in Christianity. But the weakness of Hinduism is that it doesn't really merge the two strands. Unredeemable savage religion goes on in the village; the Hermit philosophizes in the forest: and neither really interfaces with the other. It is only Christianity which compels a high brow like me to partake of a ritual blood feast, and also compels a central African convert to attempt an enlightened code of ethics.

Conclusion

Have you ever tried Chesterton's The Everlasting Man? The best popular apologetic I know. Meanwhile, the attempt to practice Tao is certainly the right line. Have you read the Analects of Confucius? He ends up by saying, "This is the Tao. I do not know if anyone has ever kept it." That's significant: one can really go direct from there to the Epistle of the Romans. I don't know if any of this is the least use. Be sure to write again, or call, if you think I can be of any help.

Prayer

Lesson 4

Student Essay:
Style of Persuasion in C.S. Lewis's "Letters"

Daily Assignment

- Warm-up: Write a letter to someone you love. Tell him/her why.
- Students will complete Concept Builder 32-D.
- Prayer journal.
- Review the assigned text. Keep vocabulary cards.
- This is the day that students should write, and then rewrite, the final drafts of their assigned essay.

CONCEPT
BUILDER
32-D

Background History

First, tell who these people are. Then, look in a reference book and check your answer.

Person in History	Who I think he is . . .	Who he really is. . .
Confucius	*Chinese philosopher*	*A wise religious/philosophical Chinese teacher*
Aristotle	*Greek philosopher*	*An important Greek philosopher who wrote books like* Poetics *and* Rhetoric
Hitler	*Nazi dictator*	*A German dictator who was the head of Germany from 1932–1945*

ESSAY (100 POINTS)

Write a two-page letter to your four-year-old nephew explaining what the Christian life is all about. In your discussion, remember to discuss grace, salvation, righteousness, redemption, sanctification, eternal security (or not), and predestination. Remember your audience, and choose your words and phrases carefully.

Summary: Answers will vary, but language should be simple and appropriate for a four-year-old.

Poetry — "The Midnight Ride of Paul Revere" (Henry Wadsworth Longfellow)

Chapter 33

First Thoughts

During his lifetime, Longfellow was loved and admired both at home and abroad. In 1884, he was honored by the placing of a memorial bust in Poets' Corner of Westminster Abbey in London. He was the first American to be so recognized. Sweetness, gentleness, simplicity, and a romantic vision shaded by melancholy are the characteristic features of Longfellow's poetry. His poetry was not merely good; it was read by almost every literate American. Perhaps no American poet has captured the American heart like Longfellow did.

Chapter Learning Objectives

In chapter 33 we will learn how to write a literary analysis of a poem and will examine Henry David Longfellow's "Midnight Ride of Paul Revere."

As a result of this chapter study you will be able to . . .

1. Write a literary analysis of "The Midnight Ride of Paul Revere."

2. Discuss biblical examples of storytelling.

3. Write a narrative poem about a famous, intriguing, or even difficult event in your family's life, using Longfellow's narrative poem celebrating a famous historical event as an example

Look Ahead for Friday

- Turn in a final copy of essay or take it as a test

Lesson 1

"The Midnight Ride of Paul Revere"

Daily Assignment

- Warm-up: What is your favorite poem? Why?

- Students will complete Concept Builder 33-A.

- Prayer journal: Students are encouraged to write in their prayer journal every day.

- Students need to review their material for the next assignment

- Students should systematically review their vocabulary words daily.

CONCEPT BUILDER 33-A

Writing Poetry

Read the poem and then answer the following questions.

1. What is the central image Simic presents?

ANSWER: A fork

2. What metaphors does he use to compare the fork?

ANSWER: It resembles a bird's foot work around the cannibal's neck.

3. Is this poem humorous? Why?

ANSWER: Yes. His images are foreign to the ordinary fork. They are exaggerations.

4. Create a similar poem entitled: "The Spoon."

ANSWER: Answers will vary.

Lesson 2

Literary Analysis: Poetry

Daily Assignment

- Warm-up: What makes a great poem?
- Students will complete Concept Builder 33-B.
- Prayer journal.
- Students should outline all assigned essays for the week.

CONCEPT
BUILDER
33-B

Writing Poetry

Read the poem and then answer the following questions.

1. Why is the word "Star" on the top?

ANSWER: It is the top of a Christmas tree.

2. Why is huddld misspelled?

ANSWER: So that the poet can keep the shape of the Christmas tree consistent.

3. Using the above poem as a model, write a poem entitled "A Church."

ANSWER: Answers will vary.

Lesson 3

Grammar Review: Review

Daily Assignment

- Warm-up: Imagine you are in your yard. Describe your surroundings.

- Students will complete Concept Builder 33-C.

- Prayer journal.

- Students should write rough drafts of all assigned essays and speech.

> **CONCEPT BUILDER 33-C**

Concrete Poems

Create a concrete poem with one of the following titles: Clouds, Forest, River

ANSWER: Answers will vary.

Lesson 4

The Plot of The Midnight Ride

Daily Assignment

- Warm-up: Describe "loneliness."
- Students will complete Concept Builder 33-D.
- Prayer journal.
- Review the assigned text. Keep vocabulary cards.
- This is the day that students should write, and then rewrite, the final drafts of their assigned essay.

CONCEPT
BUILDER
33-D

Poetry Descriptions

Read the poem and then answer the following questions.

1. What season is Keats describing?

ANSWER: Autumn

2. Draw a picture of this poem.

ANSWER: Answers will vary.

3. Give two examples of effective descriptions in this poem.

ANSWER: SEASON of mists and mellow fruitfulness
    To swell the gourd, and plump the hazel shells

ESSAY (100 POINTS)

Write a one-page analysis of "Holy Sonnet X" by the 17th-century poet John Donne.

Summary: Donne, a country preacher and poet, argues strongly for a Christian view of death. This poem exhibits a theistic worldview. It is an affirmation of faith in the face of imminent death. The author is personifying death. He speaks directly to death. In the final analysis, the life of faith wins out.

Short Story — "The Lady or the Tiger?" (Frank Stockton)

Chapter 34

First Thoughts

The short story is more than a short story; it is a story that makes a succinct point, or promotes a focused point within a 500–15,00 word limitation.

Chapter Learning Objectives

In chapter 34 we will write a literary analysis of the short story "The Lady or the Tiger?" by Frank Stockton.

As a result of this chapter study you will be able to . . .

1. Write a literary analysis of "The Lady or the Tiger?" by Frank Stockton. Discuss the plot, theme, tone, setting, narration, and characters.

2. Explain how "The Lady or the Tiger?" is disturbingly anti-Christian.

3. Analyze the ending of this short story.

Look Ahead for Friday

- Turn in a final copy of essay or take it as a test

Lesson 1

The Lady or the Tiger?

Daily Assignment

- Warm-up: What makes a great short story?
- Students will complete Concept Builder 34-A.
- Prayer journal: Students are encouraged to write in their prayer journal every day.
- Students need to review their material for the next assignment
- Students should systematically review their vocabulary words daily.

CONCEPT
BUILDER
34-A

Conflict and Consequences Equal Suspense

Identify conflicts in "The Lady or the Tiger?" by Frank R. Stockton.

Character	Plot Event	Conflict	Suspense
Protagonist	Meets the young lady, wants to marry the young lady	Internal conflict: *He loves the young lady but has to take a chance that he will get the tiger instead.* External conflict: *The conflict with the king.*	*Will he get the lady or the tiger?*
King (Antagonist)	Meets the young man, offers a challenge to the young man	Internal conflict: *The king does not want to lose his daughter.* External conflict: *He confronts the young man.*	*Will the protagonist get the lady or the tiger?*

Lesson 2

Composition of the Short Story

Daily Assignment

- Warm-up: Will the protagonist get the girl? Or will he be eaten by the tiger? Offer textual evidence to support your conclusion.
- Students will complete Concept Builder 34-B.
- Prayer journal.
- Students should outline all assigned essays for the week.

CONCEPT BUILDER 34-B

Plot Development

Identify the exposition, rising action, climax, denouement, and resolution in "The Lady or the Tiger?"

Exposition	*The three principal characters are introduced.*
Rising Action	*The protagonist (young man) loves the young princess.*
Climax	*The king designs a contest for the young man to see if he really loves his daughter.*
Denouement	*When the daughter signals the right door, the reader feels there is going to be a satisfactory resolution. However, as this short story develops, readers are not so sure.*
Resolution	*The reader must guess about the heart of the daughter: does she really love the young man?*

Lesson 3

Grammar Review: Review

Daily Assignment

- Warm-up: Compare "The Lady or the Tiger?" with another short story you have read.
- Students will complete a daily Concept Builder 34-C.
- Prayer journal.
- Students should write rough drafts of all assigned essays.

CONCEPT
BUILDER
34-C

Plot Development

Identify the plot development in "The Lady or the Tiger?"

Hint 1	*Among the borrowed notions by which his barbarism had become semified was that of the public arena, in which, by exhibitions of manly and beastly valor, the minds of his subjects were refined and cultured.*
Hint 2	*When her lover turned and looked at her, and his eye met hers as she sat there, paler and whiter than any one in the vast ocean of anxious faces about her, he saw, by that power of quick perception which is given to those whose souls are one, that she knew behind which door crouched the tiger, and behind which stood the lady. He had expected her to know it. He understood her nature, and his soul was assured that she would never rest until she had made plain to herself this thing, hidden to all other lookers-on, even to the king. The only hope for the youth in which there was any element of certainty was based upon the success of the princess in discovering this mystery; and the moment he looked upon her, he saw she had succeeded, as in his soul he knew she would succeed.*
Hint 3	*The question of her decision is one not to be lightly considered, and it is not for me to presume to set myself up as the one person able to answer it. And so I leave it with all of you: Which came out of the opened door — the lady, or the tiger?*

Lesson 4

Student Essay:
A Review of "The Lady or the Tiger?"

Daily Assignment

- Warm-up: Why does the father create a contest to test his potential son-in-law?
- Students will complete Concept Builder 34-D.
- Prayer journal.
- Review the assigned text. Keep vocabulary cards.
- This is the day that students should write, and then rewrite, the final drafts of their assigned essays.

CONCEPT BUILDER 34-D

Descriptions

Explain what each word picture means and then draw a physical picture of the word picture.

Word Picture	In Your Own Words	Picture
He was a man of exuberant fancy	*He was a man prone to excesses. When he created an event, it was usually full of surprises and excitement.*	*Answers will vary.*
This semi-barbaric king had a daughter as blooming as his most florid fancies.	*This young woman was beautiful, ruddy in complexion, and outgoing in personality.*	*Answers will vary.*
Among his courtiers was a young man of that fineness of blood and lowness of station common to the conventional heroes of romance who love royal maidens.	*This young man was an ordinary man in most ways.*	*Answers will vary.*

ESSAY (100 POINTS)

Write a two-page short story (500–1,000 word limitation with all the elements of a good short story: setting, plot, theme, characterization).

Summary: Answers will vary.

Weekly Essays/Tests

Chapter 1 Test

TRUE AND FALSE (50 POINTS)

___ In the beginning of the novel, Buck lived in rugged Minnesota.

___ In Alaska, there was a great need for hardy dogs to pull sleds.

___ Manuel sold Buck to be mean to Judge Miller.

___ Buck's initial response to cruelty was surprise.

___ Thornton was the best master, by far, that Buck had.

___ The setting was critical to this book.

___ Buck resisted the call of the wild until his master was killed.

___ Mercedes, the only woman in this book, was a very skilled tomboy who lived off the land.

___ Native Americans killed Thornton.

___ Thornton won $1,000 when Buck pulled a very heavy sled.

Chapter 1 Essay

ESSAY (50 POINTS)

Read the passage from Mary Shelley's *Frankenstein* and discuss in a one-page essay how Shelley uses the setting to make her thematic points. (You can access the story at your favorite digital provider or http://www.online-literature.com/shelley_mary/frankenstein The site is free to access without subscription. http://www.gutenberg.org/ or http://books.google.com/ are other free options; this is often part of a collection or you can access the single work.)

It was on a dreary night of November that I beheld the accomplishment of my toils. With an anxiety that almost amounted to agony, I collected the instruments of life around me that I might infuse a spark of being into the lifeless thing that lay at my feet. It was already one in the morning; the rain pattered dismally against the panes, and my candle was nearly burnt out, when, by the glimmer of the half-extinguished light, I saw the dull yellow eye of the creature open; it breathed hard, and a convulsive motion agitated its limbs.

How can I describe my emotions at this catastrophe, or how delineate the wretch whom with such infinite pains and care I had endeavoured to form? His limbs were in proportion, and I had selected his features as beautiful. Beautiful! Great God! His yellow skin scarcely covered the work of muscles and arteries beneath; his hair was of a lustrous black, and flowing; his teeth of a pearly whiteness; but these luxuriances only formed a more horrid contrast with his watery eyes, that seemed almost of the same colour as the dun-white sockets in which they were set, his shrivelled complexion and straight black lips.

The different accidents of life are not so changeable as the feelings of human nature. I had worked hard for nearly two years, for the sole purpose of infusing life into an inanimate body. For this I had deprived myself of rest and health. I had desired it with an ardour that far exceeded moderation; but now that I had finished, the beauty of the dream vanished, and breathless horror and disgust filled my heart. Unable to endure the aspect of the being I had created, I rushed out of the room and continued a long time traversing my bedchamber, unable to compose my mind to sleep. At length lassitude succeeded to the tumult I had before endured, and I threw myself on the bed in my clothes, endeavouring to seek a few moments of forgetfulness. But it was in vain; I slept, indeed, but I was disturbed by the wildest dreams. I thought I saw Elizabeth, in the bloom of health, walking in the streets of Ingolstadt. Delighted and surprised, I embraced her, but as I imprinted the first kiss on her lips, they became livid with the hue of death; her features appeared to change, and I thought that I held the corpse of my dead mother in my arms; a shroud enveloped her form, and I saw the grave-worms crawling in the folds of the flannel. I started from my sleep with horror; a cold dew covered my forehead, my teeth chattered, and every limb became convulsed; when, by the dim and yellow light of the moon as it forced its way through the window shutters, I beheld the wretch — the miserable monster whom I had created. He held up the curtain of the bed; and his eyes, if eyes they may be called, were fixed on me. His jaws opened, and he muttered some inarticulate sounds, while a grin wrinkled his cheeks. He might have spoken, but I did not hear; one hand was stretched out, seemingly to detain me, but I escaped and rushed downstairs. I took refuge in the courtyard belonging to the house which I inhabited, where I remained during the rest of the night, walking up and down in the greatest agitation, listening attentively, catching and fearing each sound as if it were to announce the approach of the demoniacal corpse to which I had so miserably given life.

Oh! No mortal could support the horror of that countenance. A mummy again endued with animation could not be so hideous as that wretch. I had gazed on him while unfinished; he was ugly then, but when those muscles and joints were rendered capable of motion, it became a thing such as even Dante could not have conceived.

I passed the night wretchedly. Sometimes my pulse beat so quickly and hardly that I felt the palpitation of every artery; at others, I nearly sank to the ground through languor and extreme weakness. Mingled with this horror, I felt the bitterness of disappointment; dreams that had been my food and pleasant rest for so long a space were now become a hell to me; and the change was so rapid, the overthrow so complete!

Morning, dismal and wet, at length dawned and discovered to my sleepless and aching eyes the church of Ingolstadt, its white steeple and clock, which indicated the sixth hour. The porter opened the gates of the court, which had that night been my asylum, and I issued into the streets, pacing them with quick steps, as if I sought to avoid the wretch whom I feared every turning of the street would present to my view. I did not dare return to the apartment which I inhabited, but felt impelled to hurry on, although drenched by the rain which poured from a black and comfortless sky.

Chapter 2 Test

ESSAY (100 POINTS)

Write short essays discussing the worldviews in these contemporary movies.

A. *Pocahontas*

Disney's account of the Jamestown settlement begins with the noble savage Pocahontas observing the rough, war-like English settlers approaching her unspoiled wilderness. The English are led by Governor Ratcliffe, who is looking to strike it rich — no matter what the cost in human lives or in environmental impact. Irreligious John Smith is looking for girls and adventure. Upon landing and setting up camp in Virginia, Smith sets out to look for "savages" and meets Pocahontas. After their initial awkward encounter, they become friends. Their respective communities, on the other hand, prepare for war. John Smith's community sees the Native Americans as savages who in turn see the explorers as arrogant, self-centered brutes. Pocahontas asks advice from her grandmother-tree (i. e., a tree that speaks) and enters into a serious friendship with Smith.

B. *Scooby-Doo*

Fred, Velma, Daphne, Shaggy, and his talking dog, Scooby-Doo, make up a crime-solving group. Despite the fact that they are all winsome people, they are also selfish people. So, as the movie begins, they are disbanded. The group is now reunited on Spooky Island, a macabre amusement park run by Emile and frequented by hedonistic youth on spring break. It appears that while unwary youth arrive lucid, the students leave in something of a zombie state that makes the team believe something is amiss. The team sets out to get to the bottom of the mystery.

Chapter 3 Test

ESSAY (100 POINTS)

In a one- to-two-page essay, discuss your favorite narrative in a short story or book, focusing on how the main character is developed through the narration, and why you believe this makes the character memorable.

ESSAY (100 POINTS)

In a one-page essay, state the theme of the short story "The Diamond Necklace" by the French writer, Guy de Maupassant. (You can access the story at your favorite digital provider or http://www.online-literature.com/maupassant/206/ The site is free to access without subscription. http://www.gutenberg.org/ or http://books.google.com/ are other free options; this is often part of a collection or you can access the single work.)

Chapter 5 Test

MATCHING (50 POINTS)

Match the characters with the role(s) they assume. Some characters will fulfill more than one role. Be prepared to defend your answer.

___ Joseph   A. Protagonist

___ Jacob   B. Antagonist

___ Potiphar's wife   C. Foil

___ Pharaoh

___ The baker

___ Joseph's brothers

Match the following:

___ Judah struggles with his feelings about selling Joseph into captivity.   A. External Conflict

___ Joseph physically struggles with his brothers when they put him into the pit.   B. Internal Conflict

___ Jacob worries about sending Benjamin to Egypt.

___ Jacob announces that his brothers are thieves.

Chapter 5 Essay

ESSAY (50 POINTS)

Write a one-page essay discussing characterization in the short story "Luck of the Roaring Camp," by Bret Harte. (You can access the story at your favorite digital provider or http://www.online-literature.com/bret-harte/1681/. The site is free to access without subscription. http://www.gutenberg.org/ or http://books.google.com/ are other free options; this is often part of a collection or you can access the single work.)

ESSAY (100 POINTS)

Write a one-page essay in which you discuss the plot development of a favorite movie, book, or play. In your answer refer to the rising action, climax, falling action, and resolution.

Chapter 7 Test

MULTIPLE CHOICE (25 POINTS)

____ The author of Tom Sawyer is (A) Bret Harte, (B) Huck Finn, (C) Samuel Clemens, (D) William Faulkner.

____ Tom and Huck go to the graveyard to (A) find Injun Joe (B) rid themselves of warts (C) find a dead cat (D) scare Aunt Polly.

____ Tom got in trouble in school for (A) lying about Becky's torn page (B) cheating on a test (C) talking too much in class (D) pretending he was lost on the Mississippi River.

____ Tom and Huck ultimately returned from Jackson Island because (A) Huck was bitten by a snake (B) Tom was sick (C) they were homesick (D) they were hungry.

____ Injun Joe was to die in the cave because (A) the sheriff caught him (B) he was lost (C) Tom shot him (D) his way out was blocked.

Chapter 7 Essay

ESSAY (75 POINTS)

Write a one-page essay in which you discuss how humor is presented in the short story "The Ransom of Red Chief," by O. Henry. (You can access the story at your favorite digital provider or www.online-literature.com/donne/1041/. The site is free to access without subscription. http://www.gutenberg.org/ or http://books.google.com/ are other free options; this is often part of a collection or you can access the single work.)

Chapter 8 Test

ESSAY (100 POINTS)

In a one-page essay, describe the use of symbolism in the following powerful scene from Victor Hugo's *Les Miserables.* (You can access the story at your favorite digital provider or http://www.online-literature.com/ victor_hugo/les_miserables/. The site is free to access without subscription. http://www.gutenberg.org/ or http:// books.google.com/ are other free options; this is often part of a collection or you can access the single work.)

Jean Valjean, an escaped criminal, has been apprehended for stealing silver from a priest. His captors bring him to the priest. . . .

"Monseigneur, Monseigneur!" she exclaimed, "does your Grace know where the basket of silver is?"

"Yes," replied the Bishop.

"Jesus the Lord be blessed!" she resumed; "I did not know what had become of it."

The Bishop had just picked up the basket in a flower-bed. He presented it to Madame Magloire.

"Here it is."

"Well!" said she. "Nothing in it! And the silver?"

"Ah," returned the Bishop, "so it is the silver which troubles you? I don't know where it is."

"Great, good God! It is stolen! That man who was here last night has stolen it."

In a twinkling, with all the vivacity of an alert old woman, Madame Magloire had rushed to the oratory, entered the alcove, and returned to the Bishop. The Bishop had just bent down, and was sighing as he examined a plant of cochlearia des Guillons, which the basket had broken as it fell across the bed. He rose up at Madame Magloire's cry.

"Monseigneur, the man is gone! The silver has been stolen!"

As she uttered this exclamation, her eyes fell upon a corner of the garden, where traces of the wall having been scaled were visible. The coping of the wall had been torn away.

"Stay! yonder is the way he went. He jumped over into Cochefilet Lane. Ah, the abomination! He has stolen our silver!"

The Bishop remained silent for a moment; then he raised his grave eyes, and said gently to Madame Magloire:

"And, in the first place, was that silver ours?"

Madame Magloire was speechless. Another silence ensued; then the Bishop went on:

"Madame Magloire, I have for a long time detained that silver wrongfully. It belonged to the poor. Who was that man? A poor man, evidently."

"Alas! Jesus!" returned Madame Magloire. "It is not for my sake, nor for Mademoiselle's. It makes no difference to us. But it is for the sake of Monseigneur. What is Monseigneur to eat with now?"

The Bishop gazed at her with an air of amazement.

"Ah, come! Are there no such things as pewter forks and spoons?"

Madame Magloire shrugged her shoulders.

"Pewter has an odor."

"Iron forks and spoons, then."

Madame Magloire made an expressive grimace.

"Iron has a taste."

"Very well," said the Bishop; "wooden ones then."

A few moments later he was breakfasting at the very table at which Jean Valjean had sat on the previous evening. As he ate his breakfast, Monseigneur Welcome remarked gayly to his sister, who said nothing, and to Madame Magloire, who was grumbling under her breath, that one really does not need either fork or spoon, even of wood, in order to dip a bit of bread in a cup of milk.

"A pretty idea, truly," said Madame Magloire to herself, as she went and came, "to take in a man like that! and to lodge him close to one's self! And how fortunate that he did nothing but steal! Ah, mon Dieu! it makes one shudder to think of it!"

As the brother and sister were about to rise from the table, there came a knock at the door.

"Come in," said the Bishop.

The door opened. A singular and violent group made its appearance on the threshold.

Three men were holding a fourth man by the collar. The three men were gendarmes; the other was Jean Valjean.

A brigadier of gendarmes, who seemed to be in command of the group, was standing near the door. He entered and advanced to the Bishop, making a military salute.

"Monseigneur" said he.

At this word, Jean Valjean, who was dejected and seemed overwhelmed, raised his head with an air of stupefaction.

"Monseigneur!" he murmured. "So he is not the cure?"

"Silence!" said the gendarme. "He is Monseigneur the Bishop."

In the meantime, Monseigneur Bienvenu had advanced as quickly as his great age permitted.

"Ah! here you are!" he exclaimed, looking at Jean Valjean. "I am glad to see you. Well, but how is this? I gave you the candlesticks too, which are of silver like the rest, and for which you can certainly get two -hundred francs. Why did you not carry them away with your forks and spoons?"

Jean Valjean opened his eyes wide, and stared at the venerable Bishop with an expression which no human tongue can render any account of.

"Monseigneur," said the brigadier of gendarmes, "so what this man said is true, then? We came across him. He was walking like a man who is running away. We stopped him to look into the matter. He had this silver —"

"And he told you," interposed the Bishop with a smile, "that it had been given to him by a kind old fellow of a priest with whom he had passed the night? I see how the matter stands. And you have brought him back here? It is a mistake."

"In that case," replied the brigadier, "we can let him go?"

"Certainly," replied the Bishop.

The gendarmes released Jean Valjean, who recoiled.

"Is it true that I am to be released?" he said, in an almost inarticulate voice, and as though he were talking in his sleep.

"Yes, thou art released; dost thou not understand?" said one of the gendarmes.

"My friend," resumed the Bishop, "before you go, here are your candlesticks. Take them."

He stepped to the chimney-piece, took the two silver candlesticks, and brought them to Jean Valjean. The two women looked on without uttering a word, without a gesture, without a look which could disconcert the Bishop.

Jean Valjean was trembling in every limb. He took the two candlesticks mechanically, and with a bewildered air.

"Now," said the Bishop, "go in peace. By the way, when you return, my friend, it is not necessary to pass through the garden. You can always enter and depart through the street door. It is never fastened with anything but a latch, either by day or by night."

Then, turning to the gendarmes: "You may retire, gentlemen."

The gendarmes retired.

Jean Valjean was like a man on the point of fainting.

The Bishop drew near to him, and said in a low voice:

"Do not forget, never forget, that you have promised to use this money in becoming an honest man."

Jean Valjean, who had no recollection of ever having promised anything, remained speechless. The Bishop had emphasized the words when he uttered them. He resumed with solemnity:

"Jean Valjean, my brother, you no longer belong to evil, but to good. It is your soul that I buy from you; I withdraw it from black thoughts and the spirit of perdition, and I give it to God."

Chapter 9 Test

ESSAY (100 POINTS)

In a one-page essay, discuss the way the author creates memorable characters in the following passage.

Southern Arkansas was a generous but exhausted land. The house in which I now lived was a natural addition to this magnificent land. Built during the depression years of cheap labor, the House — so named by Helen — reflected my grandparent's unbounded optimism. They had built it with a profitable business and Depression-priced labor. They shamelessly flaunted their prosperity in a culture that was painfully impoverished. No one seemed to mind. The South has always been kind to its elitists. They were a chosen people, or so they claimed with every offering of ebullience. No one questioned their credentials — especially when my grandmother imported bricks from New Orleans streets, painted wicker chairs from replete Havana shops, and crystal chandeliers from abandoned Liverpool mansions. I remember that the bricks surrounding our fireplace evoked a faint smell of horse manure every winter as we enjoyed our winter fires.

The House was a testimony both to my grandmother's generosity and to her eccentricity. Five thousand square feet, six bedrooms and five full baths, and a full basement — the only full basement in my below sea level community — the house appeared in Southern Living in 1931 and 1932. The kitchen was built of cool New Orleans bricks and attached to the house by a closed walkway.

Helen was no Civil Rights activist, nor did she pretend that she had any high moral standards. Helen was no hypocrite. She was a cold realist, and she cared for no one more than herself. She loved us all dearly, but she loved herself more. She knew a propitious place to build a house and was not going to let the absence of money or the pretension of Southern society stop her.

Old man John John Parker at first denied her request. But Helen walked into his business, the Fitzgerald County stock exchange, sat on his lap, kissed him on the mouth (not the cheek!), and asked in her most polished and sophisticated Southern accent, "Please, Mr. John John, will you lend me the money to build my house?" Whether from warm enticement of further benefits or from cold fear that she would do something else to embarrass him, Old Man Parker lent her the money at no interest. The deal was sealed when Helen promised to bake him a Christmas pecan pie for the rest of his life. And she did. Parker ate pecan pie every Christmas until he died. Only once did Helen fail to live up to her bargain — one season the pecan crop was abysmally bad, and she had to substitute Vermont walnuts. Helen did not like to cook — nor did she have to cook. But when she did anything, cooking, building a house, playing hide and seek with her grandchildren, she played and cooked to win.

(James P. Stobaugh)

Chapter 10 Test

MULTIPLE CHOICE (50 POINTS)

___ While at the Admiral Benbow, Billy Bones fears (A) a one-legged man (B) the police (C)a tax-collector (D) pneumonia.

___ The protagonist of this novel is (A) Jim (B) Long John Silver (C) Billy Bones (D) Blackbeard.

___ The black spot means that the bearer (A) has won the lottery (B) has been drafted (C) is marked to die (D) will soon assume is place on board a ship.

___ Israel Hands is killed by (A) Long John (B) Jim (C) Mary Sue (D) Dr. Livesey.

___ At the end, Long John (A) returns to England to stand trial (B) dies (C) marries a young lady (D) deserts.

Chapter 10 Essay

ESSAY (50 POINTS)

In a one-page essay, discuss the way H.G. Wells introduces his protagonist in *The Invisible Man*. (You can access the story at your favorite digital provider or http://www.online-literature.com/wellshg/invisible/. The site is free to access without subscription. http://www.gutenberg.org/ or http://books.google.com/ are other free options; this is often part of a collection or you can access the single work.)

ESSAY (100 POINTS)

In a one-page essay, discuss the way H.G. Wells creates suspense in this chapter of his novel, *War of the Worlds*. (You can access the story at your favorite digital provider or www.online-literature.com/wellshg/warworlds/. The site is free to access without subscription. http://www.gutenberg.org/ or http://books.google.com/ are other free options; this is often part of a collection or you can access the single work.)

An alien space ship has landed in England, and the aliens are now appearing out of their space ship.

When I returned to the common the sun was setting. Scattered groups were hurrying from the direction of Woking, and one or two persons were returning. The crowd about the pit had increased, and stood out black against the lemon yellow of the sky — a couple of hundred people, perhaps. There were raised voices, and some sort of struggle appeared to be going on about the pit. Strange imaginings passed through my mind. As I drew nearer I heard Stent's voice:

"Keep back! Keep back!"

A boy came running towards me.

"It's a movin'," he said to me as he passed; "a-screwin' and a-screwin' out. I don't like it. I'm a-goin' home, I am."

I went on to the crowd. There were really, I should think, two or three hundred people elbowing and jostling one another, the one or two ladies there being by no means the least active.

"He's fallen in the pit!" cried someone.

"Keep back!" said several.

The crowd swayed a little, and I elbowed my way through. Every one seemed greatly excited. I heard a peculiar humming sound from the pit.

"I say!" said Ogilvy; "help keep these idiots back. We don't know what's in the confounded thing, you know!"

I saw a young man, a shop assistant in Woking I believe he was, standing on the cylinder and trying to scramble out of the hole again. The crowd had pushed him in.

The end of the cylinder was being screwed but from within. Nearly two feet of shining screw projected. Somebody blundered against me, and I narrowly missed being pitched onto the top of the screw. I turned, and as I did so the screw must have come out, for the lid of the cylinder fell upon the gravel with a ringing concussion. I stuck my elbow into the person behind me, and turned my head towards the Thing again. For a moment that circular cavity seemed perfectly black. I had the sunset in my eyes.

I think everyone expected to see a man emerge—possibly something a little unlike us terrestrial men, but in all essentials a man. I know I did. But, looking, I presently saw something stirring within the shadow: greyish billowy movements, one above another, and then two luminous disks—like eyes. Then something resembling a little grey snake, about the thickness of a walking stick, coiled up out of the writhing middle, and wriggled in the air towards me—and then another.

A sudden chill came over me. There was a loud shriek from a woman behind. I half turned, keeping my eyes fixed upon the cylinder still, from which other tentacles were now projecting, and began pushing my way back from the edge of the pit. I saw astonishment giving place to horror on the faces of the people about me. I heard inarticulate exclamations on all sides. There was a general movement backwards. I saw the shopman struggling still on the edge of the pit. I found myself alone, and saw the people on the other side of the pit running off, Stent among them. I looked again at the cylinder, and ungovernable terror gripped me. I stood petrified and staring.

A big greyish rounded bulk, the size, perhaps, of a bear, was rising slowly and painfully out of the cylinder. As it bulged up and caught the light, it glistened like wet leather.

Two large dark-coloured eyes were regarding me steadfastly. The mass that framed them, the head of the thing, was rounded, and had, one might say, a face. There was a mouth under the eyes, the lipless brim of which quivered and panted, and dropped saliva. The whole creature heaved and pulsated convulsively. A lank tentacular appendage gripped the edge of the cylinder, another swayed in the air.

Those who have never seen a living Martian can scarcely imagine the strange horror of its appearance. The peculiar V-shaped mouth with its pointed upper lip, the absence of brow ridges, the absence of a chin beneath the wedgelike lower lip, the incessant quivering of this mouth, the Gorgon groups of tentacles, the tumultuous breathing of the lungs in a strange atmosphere, the evident heaviness and painfulness of movement due to the greater gravitational energy of the earth—above all, the extraordinary intensity of the immense eye—were at once vital, intense, inhuman, crippled and monstrous. There was something fungoid in the oily brown skin, something in the clumsy deliberation of the tedious movements unspeakably nasty. Even at this first encounter, this first glimpse, I was overcome with disgust and dread.

Suddenly the monster vanished. It had toppled over the brim of the cylinder and fallen into the pit, with a thud like the fall of a great mass of leather. I heard it give a peculiar thick cry, and forthwith another of these creatures appeared darkly in the deep shadow of the aperture.

I turned and, running madly, made for the first group of trees, perhaps a hundred yards away; but I ran slantingly and stumbling, for I could not avert my face from these things.

There, among some young pine trees and furze bushes, I stopped, panting, and waited further developments. The common round the sand pits was dotted with people, standing like myself in a half-fascinated terror, staring at these creatures, or rather at the heaped gravel at the edge of the pit in which they lay. And then, with a renewed horror, I saw a round, black object bobbing up and down on the edge of the pit. It was the head of the shopman who had fallen in, but showing as a little black object against the hot western sky. Now he got his shoulder and knee up, and again he seemed to slip back until only his head was visible. Suddenly he vanished, and I could have fancied a faint shriek had reached me. I had a momentary impulse to go back and help him that my fears overruled.

Everything was then quite invisible, hidden by the deep pit and the heap of sand that the fall of the cylinder had made. Anyone coming along the road from Choban or Woking would have been amazed at the sight—a dwindling multitude of perhaps a hundred people or more standing in a great irregular circle, in ditches, behind bushes, behind gates and hedges, saying little to one another and that in short, excited shouts, and staring, staring hard at a few heaps of sand.

Chapter 12 Test

ESSAY (100 POINTS)

In a one-page essay, discuss how reliable the narrator is in this passage from Daniel Defoe's _Robinson Crusoe_. Next, rewrite the passage from Friday's perspective. (You can access the story at your favorite digital provider or http://www.online-literature.com/defoe/crusoe/. The site is free to access without subscription. http://www.gutenberg.org/ or http://books.google.com/ are other free options; this is often part of a collection or you can access the single work.)

This passage occurs after Friday had been rescued from cannibals and Robinson Crusoe had begun to "civilize" him.

After I had been two or three days returned to my castle, I thought that, in order to bring Friday off from his horrid way of feeding, and from the relish of a cannibal's stomach, I ought to let him taste other flesh; so I took him out with me one morning to the woods. I went, indeed, intending to kill a kid out of my own flock; and bring it home and dress it; but as I was going I saw a she-goat lying down in the shade, and two young kids sitting by her. I catched hold of Friday. "Hold," said I, "stand still;" and made signs to him not to stir: immediately I presented my piece, shot, and killed one of the kids. The poor creature, who had at a distance, indeed, seen me kill the savage, his enemy, but did not know, nor could imagine how it was done, was sensibly surprised, trembled, and shook, and looked so amazed that I thought he would have sunk down. He did not see the kid I shot at, or perceive I had killed it, but ripped up his waistcoat to feel whether he was not wounded; and, as I found presently, thought I was resolved to kill him: for he came and kneeled down to me, and embracing my knees, said a great many things I did not understand; but I could easily see the meaning was to pray me not to kill him.

I soon found a way to convince him that I would do him no harm; and taking him up by the hand, laughed at him, and pointing to the kid which I had killed, beckoned to him to run and fetch it, which he did: and while he was wondering, and looking to see how the creature was killed, I loaded my gun again. By-and-by I saw a great fowl, like a hawk, sitting upon a tree within shot; so, to let Friday understand a little what I would do, I called him to me again, pointed at the fowl, which was indeed a parrot, though I thought it had been a hawk; I say, pointing to the parrot, and to my gun, and to the ground under the parrot, to let him see I would make it fall, I made him understand that I would shoot and kill that bird; accordingly, I fired, and bade him look, and immediately he saw the parrot fall. He stood like one frightened again, notwithstanding all I had said to him; and I found he was the more amazed, because he did not see me put anything into the gun, but thought that there must be some wonderful fund of death and destruction in that thing, able to kill man, beast, bird, or anything near or far off; and the astonishment this created in him was such as could not wear off for a long time; and I believe, if I would have let him, he would have worshipped me and my gun. As for the gun itself, he would not so much as touch it for several days after; but he would speak to it and talk to it, as if it had answered him, when he was by himself; which, as I afterwards learned of him, was to desire it not to kill him. Well, after his astonishment was a little over at this, I pointed to him to run and fetch the bird I had shot, which he did, but stayed some time; for the parrot, not being quite dead, had fluttered away a good distance from the place where she fell: however, he found her, took her up, and brought her to me; and as I had perceived his ignorance about the gun before, I took this advantage to charge the gun again, and not to let him see me do it, that I might be ready for any other mark that might present; but nothing more offered at that time: so I brought home the kid, and the same evening I took the skin off, and cut it out as well as I could; and having a pot fit for that purpose, I boiled or stewed some of the flesh, and made some very good broth. After I had begun to eat some I gave some to my man, who seemed very glad of it, and liked it very well; but that which was strangest to him was to see me eat salt with it. He made a sign to me that the salt was not good to eat; and putting a little into his own mouth, he seemed to nauseate it, and would spit and sputter at it, washing his mouth with fresh water after it: on the other hand, I took some meat into my mouth without salt, and I pretended to spit and sputter for want of salt, as much as he had done at the salt; but it would not do; he would never care for salt with meat or in his broth; at least, not for a great while, and then but a very little.

Having thus fed him with boiled meat and broth, I was resolved to feast him the next day by roasting a piece of the kid: this I did by hanging it before the fire on a string, as I had seen many people do in England, setting two poles up, one on each side of the fire, and one across the top, and tying the string to the cross stick, letting the meat turn continually. This Friday admired very much; but when he came to taste the flesh, he took so many ways to tell me how well he liked it, that I could not but understand him: and at last he told me, as well as he could, he would never eat man's flesh any more, which I was very glad to hear.

The next day I set him to work beating some corn out, and sifting it in the manner I used to do, as I observed before; and he soon understood how to do it as well as I, especially after he had seen what the meaning of it was, and that it was to make bread of; for after that I let him see me make my bread, and bake it too; and in a little time Friday was able to do all the work for me as well as I could do it myself.

I began now to consider, that having two mouths to feed instead of one, I must provide more ground for my harvest, and plant a larger quantity of corn than I used to do; so I marked out a larger piece of land, and began the fence in the same manner as before, in which Friday worked not only very willingly and very hard, but did it very cheerfully: and I told him what it was for; that it was for corn to make more bread, because he was now with me, and that I might have enough for him and myself too. He appeared very sensible of that part, and let me know that he thought I had much more labour upon me on his account than I had for myself; and that he would work the harder for me if I would tell him what to do.

This was the pleasantest year of all the life I led in this place. Friday began to talk pretty well, and understand the names of almost everything I had occasion to call for, and of every place I had to send him to, and talked a great deal to me; so that, in short, I began now to have some use for my tongue again, which, indeed, I had very little occasion for before. Besides the pleasure of talking to him, I had a singular satisfaction in the fellow himself: his simple, unfeigned honesty appeared to me more and more every day, and I began really to love the creature; and on his side I believe he loved me more than it was possible for him ever to love anything before.

Chapter 13 Test

ESSAY (100 POINTS)

Behind this story about a colorful character, Roshanna, is a powerful theme. In a one-page essay, discuss what that theme is.

Roshanna was never subtle. During morning worship in my inner-city, multi-cultural but mostly white, Pittsburgh church, Roshanna had an uncanny ability to find, sit next to, and irritate the most irascible congregants. My 1985, 75-plus urban congregation had more than its share of acrimonious characters.

This particular morning, Roshanna, an interracial child from the neighborhood, was sitting next to Mrs. Musick — a vintage grouch. With adeptness unparalleled in my neighborhood, Roshanna had marked her victim. Roshanna often timed her sneak attack during the silent prayers of confession, while her victim was most contrite and vulnerable. Before the Assurance of Pardon was pronounced, poor Mrs. Musick was hanged and quartered. At the end of the doxology — in celebration of the midpoint of our service — Roshanna deposited her used Bazooka bubble gum on Mrs. Musick's open red-letter Bible. The awful mess was placed between "He" and "multitudes" in Matthew 5:1. Poor Mrs. Musick's Bible would sport Bazooka bubble gum for generations to come.

There would be no peace this Sunday morning.

Mrs. Musick, who never suffered in silence, accosted me at the back door. "Pastor, you have to do something about Roshanna. What are we going to do with these people?"

While ingesting lunch, I shamelessly transferred my frustration to my harried and volunteer lay Christian education director (and mother of my four children), "Honey, what are we going to do about these people?"

My wife Karen responded with characteristic alacrity: "Jim, these people are the best thing that ever happened to us."

Twelve-year-old Roshanna grew up on the city streets. Her mother was a Caucasian who worked two shifts at a local restaurant during the week and turned tricks at the Horoscope Bar on Friday nights; her father was African-American and absent. Roshanna, if she lived anywhere, mostly lived with what appeared to be a wizened old grand-mother but who, I heard later, was actually younger than I was when I finished divinity school.

Every summer morning Roshanna was given a wrinkled dollar and told to disappear until bedtime. Often she stood forlornly in front of her house, as if she was hoping her grandmother would change her mind. But she never did.

Roshanna never owned a doll. She ever felt the touch of a kind adult. Her world was full of broken, glass-filled alleys and abandoned smoke-scarred brick houses. Her favorite silver slide with a paint-chipped clown on its ladder was once the final resting place of an overdosed addict. Roshanna had found him one morning while wasting time at the park. She was a tough street veteran acutely aware that she belonged to no one and to no place. (James P. Stobaugh)

Chapter 14 Test

ESSAY (100 POINTS)

Write a one-page Summary that is a parody of Tom Sawyer. Present him as a spoiled, selfish boy who is so full of himself that he cannot see the humor of his situation. In other words, you are being asked to write a parody of a parody. This writing technique is in contrast to Twain's Tom Sawyer, who is full of insights into human characters. (You can access the story at your favorite digital provider or http://www.online-literature.com/twain/tomsawyer/. The site is free to access without subscription. http://www.gutenberg.org/ or http://books.google.com/ are other free options; this is often part of a collection or you can access the single work.)

ESSAY (100 POINTS)

In *Little Women*, Louisa May Alcott is a master at describing characters through dialogue. In a one-page essay, using chapter 1, discuss how Alcott uses dialogue to describe characters. (You can access the story at your favorite digital provider or http://www.online-literature.com/alcott/littlewomen/0/. The site is free to access without subscription. http://www.gutenberg.org/ or http://books.google.com/ are other free options; this is often part of a collection or you can access the single work.)

ESSAY (100 POINTS)

In Chapter One of Charles Dickens' A Christmas Carol, the reader is presented a memorable figure, Ebenezer Scrooge. In the first few pages, Scrooge comes alive as Dickens introduces him to the reader in a mock-serious tone. In a one-page essay, discuss how Dickens uses tone to present Ebenezer Scrooge. (You can access the story at your favorite digital provider or http://www.online-literature.com/dickens/christmascarol/. The site is free to access without subscription. http://www.gutenberg.org/ or http://books.google.com/ are other free options; this is often part of a collection or you can access the single work.)

Marley was dead to begin with. There is no doubt whatever about that. The register of his burial was signed by the clergyman, the clerk, the undertaker, and the chief mourner. Scrooge signed it. And Scrooge's name was good upon 'Change, for anything he chose to put his hand to.

Old Marley was as dead as a door-nail.

Mind! I don't mean to say that I know, of my own knowledge, what there is particularly dead about a door-nail. I might have been inclined, myself, to regard a coffin-nail as the deadest piece of ironmongery in the trade. But the wisdom of our ancestors is in the simile; and my unhallowed hands shall not disturb it, or the Country's done for. You will therefore permit me to repeat, emphatically, that Marley was as dead as a door-nail.

Scrooge knew he was dead? Of course he did. How could it be otherwise? Scrooge and he were partners for I don't know how many years. Scrooge was his sole executor, his sole administrator, his sole assign, his sole residuary legatee, his sole friend, and sole mourner. And even Scrooge was not so dreadfully cut up by the sad event, but that he was an excellent man of business on the very day of the funeral, and solemnised it with an undoubted bargain. The mention of Marley's funeral brings me back to the point I started from. There is no doubt that Marley was dead. This must be distinctly understood, or nothing wonderful can come of the story I am going to relate. If we were not perfectly convinced that Hamlet's Father died before the play began, there would be nothing more remarkable in his taking a stroll at night, in an easterly wind, upon his own ramparts, than there would be in any other middle-aged gentleman rashly turning out after dark in a breezy spot — say Saint Paul's Churchyard for instance — literally to astonish his son's weak mind.

Scrooge never painted out Old Marley's name. There it stood, years afterwards, above the warehouse door Scrooge and Marley. The firm was known as Scrooge and Marley. Sometimes people new to the business called Scrooge Scrooge, and sometimes Marley, but he answered to both names. It was all the same to him.

Oh! But he was a tight-fisted hand at the grind-stone, Scrooge! a squeezing, wrenching, grasping, scraping, clutching, covetous, old sinner! Hard and sharp as flint, from which no steel had ever struck out generous fire; secret, and self-contained, and solitary as an oyster. The cold within him froze his old features, nipped his pointed nose, shrivelled his cheek, stiffened his gait; made his eyes red, his thin lips blue; and spoke out shrewdly in his grating voice. A frosty rime was on his head, and on his eyebrows, and his wiry chin. He carried his own low temperature always about with him; he iced his office in the dogdays; and didn't thaw it one degree at Christmas.

External heat and cold had little influence on Scrooge. No warmth could warm, no wintry weather chill him. No wind that blew was bitterer than he, no falling snow was more intent upon its purpose, no pelting rain less open to entreaty. Foul weather didn't know where to have him. The heaviest rain, and snow, and hail, and sleet, could boast of the advantage over him in only one respect. They often "came down" handsomely, and Scrooge never did.

Nobody ever stopped him in the street to say, with gladsome looks, 'My dear Scrooge, how are you? When will you come to see me?' No beggars implored him to bestow a trifle, no children asked him what it was o'clock, no man or woman ever once in all his life inquired the way to such and such a place, of Scrooge. Even the blind men's dogs appeared to know him; and when they saw him coming on, would tug their owners into doorways and up courts; and then would wag their tails as though they said, 'No eye at all is better than an evil eye, dark master!'

But what did Scrooge care! It was the very thing he liked. To edge his way along the crowded paths of life, warning all human sympathy to keep its distance, was what the knowing ones call 'nuts' to Scrooge.

Once upon a time — of all the good days in the year, on Christmas Eve — old Scrooge sat busy in his counting-house. It was cold, bleak, biting weather foggy withal and he could hear the people in the court outside, go wheezing up and down, beating their hands upon their breasts, and stamping their feet upon the pavement stones to warm them. The city clocks had only just gone three, but it was quite dark already—it had not been light all day—and candles were flaring in the windows of the neighbouring offices, like ruddy smears upon the palpable brown air. The fog came pouring in at every chink and keyhole, and was so dense without, that although the court was of the narrowest, the houses opposite were mere phantoms. To see the dingy cloud come drooping down, obscuring everything, one might have thought that Nature lived hard by, and was brewing on a large scale.

The door of Scrooge's counting-house was open that he might keep his eye upon his clerk, who in a dismal little cell beyond, a sort of tank, was copying letters. Scrooge had a very small fire, but the clerk's fire was so very much smaller that it looked like one coal. But he couldn't replenish it, for Scrooge kept the coal-box in his own room; and so surely as the clerk came in with the shovel, the master predicted that it would be necessary for them to part. Wherefore the clerk put on his white comforter, and tried to warm himself at the candle; in which effort, not being a man of a strong imagination, he failed.

"A merry Christmas, uncle! God save you!" cried a cheerful voice. It was the voice of Scrooge's nephew, who came upon him so quickly that this was the first intimation he had of his approach.

"Bah!" said Scrooge, "Humbug!"

He had so heated himself with rapid walking in the fog and frost, this nephew of Scrooge's, that he was all in a glow; his face was ruddy and handsome; his eyes sparkled, and his breath smoked again. "Christmas a humbug, uncle!" said Scrooge's nephew. "You don't mean that, I am sure?"

"I do," said Scrooge. "Merry Christmas! What right have you to be merry? What reason have you to be merry? You're poor enough."

"Come, then," returned the nephew gaily. "What right have you to be dismal? What reason have you to be morose? You're rich enough."

Scrooge having no better answer ready on the spur of the moment, said "Bah!" again; and followed it up with "Humbug."

"Don't be cross, uncle!" said the nephew.

"What else can I be," returned the uncle, "when I live in such a world of fools as this? Merry Christmas! Out upon merry Christmas! What's Christmas time to you but a time for paying bills without money; a time for finding yourself a year older, but not an hour richer; a time for balancing your books and having every item in 'em through a round dozen of months presented dead against you? If I could work my will," said Scrooge indignantly, "every idiot who goes about with "Merry Christmas" on his lips, should be boiled with his own pudding, and buried with a stake of holly through his heart. He should!"

"Uncle!" pleaded the nephew.

"Nephew!" returned the uncle sternly, "keep Christmas in your own way, and let me keep it in mine."

"Keep it!" repeated Scrooge's nephew. "But you don't keep it."

"Let me leave it alone, then," said Scrooge. "Much good may it do you! Much good it has ever done you!"

"There are many things from which I might have derived good, by which I have not profited, I dare say," returned the nephew. "Christmas among the rest. But I am sure I have always thought of Christmas time, when it has come round — apart from the veneration due to its sacred name and origin, if anything belonging to it can be apart from that — as a good time; a kind, forgiving, charitable, pleasant time the only time I know of, in the long calendar of the year, when men and women seem by one consent to open their shut-up hearts freely, and to think of people below them as if they really were fellow-passengers to the grave, and not another race of creatures bound on other journeys. And therefore, uncle, though it has never put a scrap of gold or silver in my pocket, I believe that it has done me good, and will do me good; and I say, God bless it!"

The clerk in the Tank involuntarily applauded. Becoming immediately sensible of the impropriety, he poked the fire, and extinguished the last frail spark for ever.

"Let me hear another sound from you," said Scrooge, "and you'll keep your Christmas by losing your situation! You're quite a powerful speaker, sir," he added, turning to his nephew. "I wonder you don't go into Parliament."

"Don't be angry, uncle. Come! Dine with us tomorrow. . . ."

Chapter 17 Test

OBJECTIVE QUESTIONS (50 POINTS)

___ Arthur Shelby is willing to break up slave families because (A) he is a cruel man (B) he is tired of farming (C) he is heavily in debt (D) he divorces his wife.

___ One of the slaves sold is (A) Harry (B) Mary (C) Eliza (D) Arthur.

___ Eliza flees to freedom by crossing the frozen (A) Ohio River (B) Mississippi River (C) Raritan River (D) Susquehanna River.

___ Tom is sold to a vicious slaveholder named (A) Homer Jones B) Arthur Shelby (C) Robert E. Lee (D) Simon Legree.

___ Tom Loker is a changed man after (A) being freed (B) getting married (C) being healed by Quakers (D) returning to Africa.

Chapter 17 Essay Answer

ESSAY (50 POINTS)

In a one-page essay, discuss why the following passage is propaganda. It was written by Nazi leaders during World War II (Goebbels, Unpublished,1944 www.gutenberg.org).

It will forever be the greatest shame of the 20th century that England and the United States joined with Communism in their hate-filled battle against our venerable Fatherland. They will not gain victory; to the contrary, at most they will ruin the economic foundations of their own nations. Only shame will remain. Perhaps it must be that way to speed along the inner decay of their selfish government system. One can speak here only of perverse political and military cooperation. Despite that, it is an enormous danger for us and for Europe, and we must gather all forces to meet it. There is no point in hoping for the aid of other threatened peoples and states. They indeed see the danger, but no power in the world can make them do anything about it. They resemble the rabbit that looks hypnotized at the snake until it is devoured. We are mostly dependent on ourselves successfully to conduct this battle for our survival and the survival of Europe. And we will do it. The strength of the Reich has grown greatly since the beginning of the war, when we faced a far greater danger, which the enemy knows. Europe is mostly in our hands. The enemy will leave no method untried in the coming year to steal important land from our Fuhrer. If he is to do this, the state of things requires that he take dangerous risks in the West, which until now he has successfully avoided. He tries to replace them by an air attack, which everyone knows is directed more against our war morale than our war potential. I speak of an air attack, which is a very polite and restrained expression for a singularly unsoldierly way of righting that has no historical parallel in its coarseness and brutality. Through the centuries, it will remain the second great shame of the English and the Americans. During the First World War they tried starvation against women and children. Now they are using phosphorus to beat down a fine and moral nation that requires nothing more than a decent and free life.

ESSAY (100 POINTS)

Write a one-page allegory of your Christian life.

ESSAY (100 POINTS)

Write a one-page essay discussing the development of a character in one of your favorite novels. Support your development by using specific references from the novel.

Chapter 20 Test

ESSAY (100 POINTS)

In a one-page essay, discuss the importance of setting to the short story "An Occurrence at Owl Creek Bridge" by Ambrose Bierce. (You can access the story at your favorite digital provider or http://www.online-literature.com/bierce/175/. The site is free to access without subscription. http://www.gutenberg.org/ or http://books.google.com/ are other free options; this is often part of a collection or you can access the single work.)

Chapter 21 Test

OBJECTIVE TEST (50 POINTS)

____ Silas Marner is a (A) preacher (B) weaver (C) miller (D) policeman.

____ He is an outsider, the object of suspicion because (A) of his special skills and the fact that he has come to Raveloe from elsewhere (B) he is learning disabled (C) he is rich (D) he is poor.

____ He is driven from the town because (A) he has terminal cancer (B) someone gave him some money (C) he won the lottery (D) someone falsely accused him of theft and excommunicated him.

____ Eppie's biological father is (A) Dunster (B) Silas (C) Godfrey (D) George.

____ Eppie decides to (A) live with her biological father (B) stay with Silas (C) move to another town (D) to marry David.

Chapter 21 Essay

ESSAY (50 POINTS)

In Book III, chapter 13 of *A Tale of Two Cities,* by Charles Dickens, one of the most famous coincidences in world literature occurs. The protagonist, aristocrat Charles Darnay, is in a French prison waiting to be executed the next day. An acquaintance, who looks a lot like Darnay, enters the prison to visit Darnay.

Determine whether this coincidence is necessary to the plot of this book. Support your argument with instances from the excerpt. (You can access the story at your favorite digital provider or http://www.online-literature.com/dickens/twocities/. The site is free to access without subscription. http://www.gutenberg.org/ or http://books.google.com/ are other free options; this is often part of a collection or you can access the single work.)

Chapter 22 Test

ESSAY (100 POINTS)

Continuing with the story of Charles Darnay and Sydney Carton, in a one-page essay, examine the final chapter of *The Tale of Two Cities* and argue for or against your opinion of whether the ending is sentimental. Support your arguments with references to the text. (You can access the story at your favorite digital provider or http://www. online-literature.com/dickens/twocities/45/. The site is free to access without subscription. http://www.gutenberg. org/ or http://books.google.com/ are other free options; this is often part of a collection or you can access the single work.)

(Another victim is speaking to Sydney Carton)

"But for you, dear stranger, I should not be so composed, for I am naturally a poor little thing, faint of heart; nor should I have been able to raise my thoughts to Him who was put to death, that we might have hope and comfort here today. I think you were sent to me by Heaven."

"Or you to me," says Sydney Carton. "Keep your eyes upon me, dear child, and mind no other object."

"I mind nothing while I hold your hand. I shall mind nothing when I let it go, if they are rapid."

"They will be rapid. Fear not!"

The two stand in the fast-thinning throng of victims, but they speak as if they were alone. Eye to eye, voice to voice, hand to hand, heart to heart, these two children of the Universal Mother, else so wide apart and differing, have come together on the dark highway, to repair home together, and to rest in her bosom.

"Brave and generous friend, will you let me ask you one last question? I am very ignorant, and it troubles me — just a little."

"Tell me what it is."

"I have a cousin, an only relative and an orphan, like myself, whom I love very dearly. She is five years younger than I, and she lives in a farmer's house in the south country. Poverty parted us, and she knows nothing of my fate — for I cannot write — and if I could, how should I tell her! It is better as it is."

"Yes, yes: better as it is."

"What I have been thinking as we came along, and what I am still thinking now, as I look into your kind strong face which gives me so much support, is this: — If the Republic really does good to the poor, and they come to be less hungry, and in all ways to suffer less, she may live a long time: she may even live to be old."

"What then, my gentle sister?"

"Do you think:" the uncomplaining eyes in which there is so much endurance, fill with tears, and the lips part a little more and tremble: "that it will seem long to me, while I wait for her in the better land where I trust both you and I will be mercifully sheltered?"

"It cannot be, my child; there is no Time there, and no trouble there."

"You comfort me so much! I am so ignorant. Am I to kiss you now? Is the moment come?"

"Yes."

She kisses his lips; he kisses hers; they solemnly bless each other. The spare hand does not tremble as he releases it; nothing worse than a sweet, bright constancy is in the patient face. She goes next before him — is gone; the knitting-women count Twenty-Two.

"I am the Resurrection and the Life, saith the Lord: he that believeth in me, though he were dead, yet shall he live: and whosoever liveth and believeth in me shall never die." The murmuring of many voices, the upturning of many faces, the pressing on of many footsteps in the outskirts of the crowd, so that it swells forward in a mass, like one great heave of water, all flashes away. Twenty-Three.

They said of him, about the city that night, that it was the peacefullest man's face ever beheld there. Many added that he looked sublime and prophetic.

One of the most remarkable sufferers by the same axe — a woman had asked at the foot of the same scaffold, not long before, to be allowed to write down the thoughts that were inspiring her. If he had given any utterance to his, and they were prophetic, they would have been these:

"I see Barsad, and Cly, Defarge, The Vengeance, the Juryman, the Judge, long ranks of the new oppressors who have risen on the destruction of the old, perishing by this retributive instrument, before it shall cease out of its present use. I see a beautiful city and a brilliant people rising from this abyss, and, in their struggles to be truly free, in their triumphs and defeats, through long years to come, I see the evil of this time and of the previous time of which this is the natural birth, gradually making expiation for itself and wearing out.

"I see the lives for which I lay down my life, peaceful, useful, prosperous and happy, in that England which I shall see no more. I see Her with a child upon her bosom, who bears my name. I see her father, aged and bent, but otherwise restored, and faithful to all men in his healing office, and at peace. I see the good old man, so long their friend, in ten years' time enriching them with all he has, and passing tranquilly to his reward.

"I see that I hold a sanctuary in their hearts, and in the hearts of their descendants, generations hence. I see her, an old woman, weeping for me on the anniversary of this day. I see her and her husband, their course done, lying side by side in their last earthly bed, and I know that each was not more honoured and held sacred in the other's soul, than I was in the souls of both.

"I see that child who lay upon her bosom and who bore my name, a man winning his way up in that path of life which once was mine. I see him winning it so well, that my name is made illustrious there by the light of his. I see the blots I threw upon it, faded away. I see him, foremost of just judges and honoured men, bringing a boy of my name, with a forehead that I know and golden hair, to this place — then fair to look upon, with not a trace of this day's disfigurement — and I hear him tell the child my story, with a tender and a faltering voice.

"It is a far, far better thing that I do, than I have ever done; it is a far, far better rest that I go to than I have ever known."

ESSAY (100 POINTS)

Write a one-page essay in which you discuss at least two themes in this portion of the short novel *His New Mittens* by Stephen Crane. (You can access the story at your favorite digital provider or http://www.online-literature. com/crane/his-new-mittens/. The site is free to access without subscription. http://www.gutenberg.org/ or http:// books.google.com/ are other free options; this is often part of a collection or you can access the single work.)

Little Horace was walking home from school, brilliantly decorated by a pair of new red mittens. A number of boys were snow-balling gleefully in a field. They hailed him. "Come on, Horace. We're having a battle."

Horace was sad. "No," he said, "I can't. I've got to go home." At noon his mother had admonished him. "Now, Horace, you come straight home as soon as school is out. Do you hear? And don't you get them nice new mittens all wet, either. Do you hear?" Also his aunt had said: "I declare, Emily, it's a shame the way you allow that child to ruin his things." She had meant mittens. To his mother, Horace had dutifully replied: "Yes'm." But he now loitered in the vicinity of the group of uproarious boys, who were yelling like hawks as the white balls flew.

Some of them immediately analyzed this extraordinary hesitancy. "Hah!" they paused to scoff, "afraid of your new mittens, ain't you?" Some smaller boys, who were not yet so wise in discerning motives, applauded this attack with unreasonable vehemence. "A-fray-ed of his mit-tens! A-fray-ed of his mit-tens." They sang these lines to cruel and monotonous music which is as old perhaps as American childhood and which it is the privilege of the emancipated adult to completely forget. "A-fray-ed of his mit-tens!" Horace cast a tortured glance toward his playmates, and then dropped his eyes to the snow at his feet. Presently, he turned to the trunk of one of the great maple trees that lined the curb. He made a pretense of closely examining the rough and virile bark. To his mind, this familiar street of Whilomville seemed to grow dark in the thick shadow of shame. The trees and the houses were now palled in purple.

"A-fray-ed of his mit-tens!" The terrible music had in it a meaning from the moonlit war-drums of chanting cannibals.

At last Horace, with supreme effort, raised his head. "'Tain't them I care about," he said gruffly. "I've got to go home. That's all."

Whereupon each boy held his left forefinger as if it were a pencil and began to sharpen it derisively with his right forefinger. They came closer, and sang like a trained chorus, "A-fray-ed of his mittens!"

When he raised his voice to deny the charge it was simply lost in the screams of the mob. He was alone fronting all the traditions of boyhood held before him by inexorable representatives. To such a low state had he fallen that one lad, a mere baby, outflanked him and then struck him in the cheek with a heavy snow-ball. The act was acclaimed with loud jeers. Horace turned to dart at his assailant, but there was an immediate demonstration on the other flank, and he found himself obliged to keep his face toward the hilarious crew of tormentors. The baby retreated in safety to the rear of the crowd, where he was received with fulsome compliments upon his daring. Horace retreated slowly up the walk. He continually tried to make them heed him, but the only sound was the chant, "A-fray-ed of his mit-tens!" In this desperate withdrawal the beset and haggard boy suffered more than is the common lot of man.

Being a boy himself, he did not understand boys at all. He had of course the dismal conviction that they were going to dog him to his grave. But near the corner of the field they suddenly seemed to forget all about it. Indeed, they possessed only the malevolence of so many flitter-headed sparrows. The interest had swung capriciously to some other matter. In a moment they were off in the field again, carousing amid the snow. Some authoritative boy had probably said,

"Aw, come on."

As the pursuit ceased, Horace ceased his retreat. He spent some time in what was evidently an attempt to adjust his self-respect, and then began to wander furtively down toward the group. He, too, had undergone an important change. Perhaps his sharp agony was only as durable as the malevolence of the others. In this boyish life obedience to some unformulated creed of manners was enforced with capricious, but merciless, rigor. However, they were, after all, his comrades, his friends.

"'Aw, come on.'"

They did not heed his return. They were engaged in an altercation. It had evidently been planned that this battle was between Indians and soldiers. The smaller and weaker boys had been induced to appear as Indians in the initial skirmish, but they were now very sick of it, and were reluctantly, but steadfastly, affirming their desire for a change of caste. The larger boys had all won great distinction, devastating Indians materially, and they wished the war to go on as planned. They explained vociferously that it was proper for the soldiers always to thrash the Indians. The little boys did not pretend to deny the truth of this argument; they confined themselves to the simple statement that, in that case, they wished to be soldiers. Each little boy willingly appealed to the others to remain Indians, but as for himself he reiterated his desire to enlist as a soldier. The larger boys were in despair over this dearth of enthusiasm in the small Indians. They alternately wheedled and bullied, but they could not persuade the little boys, who were really suffering dreadful humiliation rather than submit to another onslaught of soldiers. They were called all the baby names that had the power of stinging deep into their pride, but they remained firm.

Then a formidable lad, a leader of reputation, one who could whip many boys that wore long trousers, suddenly blew out his cheeks and shouted, "Well, all right then. I'll be an Indian myself. Now." The little boys greeted with cheers this addition to their wearied ranks, and seemed then content. But matters were not mended in the least, because all of the personal following of the formidable lad, with the addition of every outsider, spontaneously forsook the flag and declared themselves Indians. There were now no soldiers. The Indians had carried everything unanimously. The formidable lad used his influence, but his influence could not shake the loyalty of his friends, who refused to fight under any colors but his colors.

Plainly there was nothing for it but to coerce the little ones. The formidable lad again became a soldier, and then graciously permitted to join him all the real fighting strength of the crowd, leaving behind a most forlorn band of little Indians. Then the soldiers attacked the Indians, exhorting them to opposition at the same time.

The Indians at first adopted a policy of hurried surrender, but this had no success, as none of the surrenders were accepted. They then turned to flee, bawling out protests. The ferocious soldiers pursued them amid shouts. The battle widened, developing all manner of marvelous detail.

Horace had turned toward home several times, but, as a matter of fact, this scene held him in a spell. It was fascinating beyond anything which the grown man understands. He had always in the back of his head a sense of guilt, even a sense of impending punishment for disobedience, but they could not weigh with the delirium of this snow battle.

Chapter 24 Test

ESSAY (100 POINTS)

Write a précis (75–150 words) of the following essay.

At the beginning of the 21st century there truly is an exciting phenomenon occurring in American society: homeschooling. As sociologist Peter Berger accurately observes, evangelicals (and Christian homeschoolers) generally subscribe to two strongly held propositions: that a return to Christian values is necessary if the moral confusion of our time is to be overcome and that the Enlightenment is to be blamed for much of the confusion of our time.

In fact, I believe that Christian homeschooling, along with other strains of evangelicalism, is one of the most potent anti-Enlightenment movements in world history. I most assuredly did not say "anti-intellectual." Christian homeschoolers argue that the excessives of Enlightenment rationalism have sabotaged the certitude of classicism and Christian theism that so strongly influenced Western culture long before the formidable onslaught of the likes of David Hume.

Additionally, Christian homeschoolers are quickly filling the ranks of Evangelical Christianity. Higher test scores and functional family units are only two reasons that homeschoolers are capturing the elite culture of America.

The *Washington Post* in 1993 coyly observed that evangelicals are "largely poor, uneducated and easy to command." And, among our own, evangelical professor Mark Noll unkindly observed, "The scandal of the evangelical mind is that there is not much of an evangelical mind."[1] Indeed. Not anymore. Today, more than ever, in the garb of Christian homeschooling, Evangelicalism has gained new life.

By sidestepping the Enlightenment, Christian homeschooling has opened up a whole new arena for debate. While conceding that faith is not a makeshift bridge to overcome some Kierkegaardian gap between beliefs and evidence, homeschooling posits that it still is important that we look beyond our experience for reality. Human needs and aspirations are greater than the world can satisfy, so it is reasonable to look elsewhere for that satisfaction. Worth is the highest and best reality (a decidedly anti-Enlightenment notion) and its genesis and maintenance come exclusively from relationship with God. Homeschooling families, with their sacrificial love of one another and their extravagant gift of time to one another, offer a radical path into this new way of looking at reality.

Christian homeschooling, then, reaches far back in time when intellectualism was not separate from religion. It knocks against the claims of the Enlightenment. Homeschooling has brought stability back into the lives of countless millions of Americans when the majority of Americans are living in a context of clashing reactivities where the very ground of meaning, the foundations and structures of thought, language, and social discourse are up for grabs — where the very concepts of personhood, spirituality, truth, integrity, and objectivity are all being demolished, breaking up, giving way.

Homeschooling. Millions strong. This new cultural revolution is inviting Americans back to those traditional truths that have been with us always and to others that need to be rediscovered. Homeschooling has invited Americans to a comfortable marriage of intellectualism and transcendentalism that fares our culture and our nation well in the years ahead. In that sense, then, perhaps homeschooling families are the new patriots, the hope for our weary nation and our dysfunctional culture. We shall see. . . . (James P. Stobaugh)

---

1   Mark Noll, *The Scandal of the Evangelical Mind* (Grand Rapids, MI: Wm. B. Eerdmans Publ. Co., 1995), p. 3.

Chapter 25 Test

OBJECTIVE TEST (50 POINTS)

____ Anne is (A) an orphan girl (B) a wealthy heiress (C) an accomplished circus rider (D) a relative to Matthew.

____ Matthew arrives at the train station to pick up (A) a package (B) a girl (C) a boy (D) a horse.

____ Anne's favorite childhood friend is (A) Marilla (B) Matthew (C) Deanna (D) Diana.

____ Initially, Anne did not like a boy whose name is (A) Gilbert (B) Martin (C) Matthew (D) David.

____ After Matthew dies, Anne decides to stay at Green Gables to help Marilla because (A) Marilla is poor (B) Marilla is going blind (C) Marilla is lonely (D) Anne is homesick.

Chapter 25 Essay

ESSAY (50 POINTS)

In 75–150 words, discuss how the author creates his character in the following essay.

A father smiles when he hears that one son will soon graduate from Harvard Business School; another son is busily pursuing a successful career in education; and a final son will soon enter Princeton Theological Seminary. His life in Christ is growing, but he stills feels empty, so this budding saint prays that God will turn his life around.

Later, we see this same 49-year-old husband/father lying in a modern hospital. For four years, he has fought the inhumane ravages of cancer. As the doctors frantically practice their incantations and magic formulas, this broken, gentle man looks up from among the tubes, bandages, and IV bottles, and whispers, "I am not enjoying this, to be sure."

A chuckle breaks from his lips.

"In fact, this is a horrible way to die. But, you know, in spite of all the pain, I would not change a thing. Oh, I don't want to die. But if I were healed, and it meant that I lost all that I've learned about the Lord, well . . . I'd rather die just the way I am now."

"Everything," he said with quiet power, "everything I've experienced is worth what I've gained in the knowledge and love in Jesus Christ!"

He died two hours later. This unpretentious, unlikely hero was my father, who died one cloudy, miserable Sunday afternoon — on Father's Day 1982. (James P. Stobaugh)

Chapter 26

ESSAY (100 POINTS)

Write a 75–150 word essay discussing the theme in the following essay.

September 11, 1975, was a particularly warm, promising day even in the South where fall sometimes is lost between tepid, late summer afternoons and frosty winter mornings. My heart was beaming, too, for on this day I was to begin a two-day trip to Boston, where within the month I would begin my seminary studies. My trip began on Rt. 1 North, a rather boring road that wound through white, unharvested cotton fields, and one-grocery-store towns. However, I was not bored. I was euphoric! Finally, finally, I was to begin a new chapter of my life that I had anticipated for almost half a decade. I was to begin my formal training to be an ordained minister. As I stopped at MacArthur and bought a moon pie and RC Cola, I could not know that within an hour I was to enter what the English author Joseph Conrad called "the heart of darkness."

Before I finished my moon pie and RC, I fell asleep, and my little red Fiat curved to the right, made a 45-degree turn, and hit a concrete bridge. It was a dull bridge; besides having an occasional thoughtless Dairy Queen cup thrown over its side, this little 14-foot structure, built in 1962, had never known any excitement.

However, I will never forget this bridge, because against its rain-washed side, my poor compact car crumbled like a cheap, flimsy pop can. At the same time, my dreams were similarly shattered as they were thrust against the vicissitudes of life. The joyful lights in my life were going out.

Before that day was to end I was to experience horror as I had never known it. Besides breaking my hand in two places, I had a severed right foot, compound multiple fractures in my right femur, and a painful fracture in my right hip.

For three months I recovered in my windowless hospital room. I encountered an aspect of life that I innocently had never known. My 22 years on this earth and four years of walking with Christ had scarcely prepared me for the valley I entered. The same God who had saved me and called me to the ministry now seemed to be destroying me. Surely I was in darkness in spite of knowing only light for more than five years! Where was the God of my salvation?

I learned a lesson all Christians will learn at one time or another: inevitably, we must be broken. Steve Brown often says it is hard to hug a muddy kid or a sticky kid, but a stiff, rebellious kid is the hardest kid of all to hug. God is in the business of breaking down our pride so that we will really love Him and so that He can really bless us. It is easier to love a limp, broken saint than to struggle with a stiff one.

I once grew an oak tree from an acorn. I lovingly watered and fertilized it, until it was ready to be transplanted in our front yard. Unfortunately, my loving care had scarcely prepared the little oak tree for the violence of rain storms and the back legs of neighborhood dogs. The oak tree did not survive a week. Without brokenness, we are ill-prepared to face the world we see around us. (James P. Stobaugh)

Chapter 27 Test

OBJECTIVE TEST (50 POINTS)

D   Ivanhoe has recently returned from (A) wars in France (B) exploring China (C) conquering Spain (D) participating in the Crusades.

A   He is disguised as (A) a religious pilgrim (B) a black knight (C) an old man (D) as an army captain.

C   King Richard is (A) dead (B) in England (C) in an Austrian prison (D) fighting in Palestine.

B   King John is (A) Richard's father (B) Richard's brother (C) Richard's cousin (D) no relation of Richard's.

C   The black knight is really (A) Ivanhoe (B) King John (C) King Richard (D) Rowena.

Chapter 27 Essay

ESSAY (50 POINTS)

Write a two-page story exhibiting all the elements of a sound plot (rising action, climax, falling action, resolution).

Chapter 28 Test

ESSAY (100 POINTS)

Read the following poem by T.S. Eliot, and in a one-page essay, discuss its worldview.

The Hippopotamus

The broad-backed hippopotamus
Rests on his belly in the mud;
Although he seems so firm to us
He is merely flesh and blood.

Flesh-and-blood is weak and frail,
Susceptible to nervous shock;
While the True Church can never fail
For it is based upon a rock.

The hippo's feeble steps may err
In compassing material ends,
While the True Church need never stir
To gather in its dividends.

The 'potamus can never reach
The mango on the mango-tree;
But fruits of pomegranate and peach
Refresh the Church from over sea.
At mating time the hippo's voice
Betrays inflexions hoarse and odd,
But every week we hear rejoice
The Church, at being one with God.

The hippopotamus's day
Is passed in sleep; at night he hunts;
God works in a mysterious way-
The Church can sleep and feed at once.

I saw the 'potamus take wing
Ascending from the damp savannas,
And quiring angels round him sing
The praise of God, in loud hosannas.

Blood of the Lamb shall wash him clean
And him shall heavenly arms enfold,
Among the saints he shall be seen
Performing on a harp of gold.

He shall be washed as white as snow,
By all the martyr'd virgins kiss,
While the True Church remains below
Wrapt in the old miasmal mist.[1]

---

1   www.poetry-archive.com/e/the_hippopotamus.html

Chapter 29 Test

OBJECTIVE TEST (50 POINTS)

___ Shane is (A) a former gunfighter (B) captain in the army (C) an army scout (D) farmer.

___ Shane avoids (A) all physical labor (B) all physical confrontations (C) cattle drives (D) opportunities to marry.

___ Marian is married to (A) Shane (B) Bob (C) Joe (D) David.

___ Marian loves both Shane and Joe but chooses to (A) leave both (B) stay with Joe (C) leave with Shane (D) stay but asks both to leave.

___ At the end of the novel, the boy realizes (A) that Shane is a coward (B) that his mom is a coward (C) that his dad is deaf (D) that his dad is braver than Shane in many ways.

Chapter 29 Essay

ESSAY (50 POINTS)

If your parents will allow you to do so, watch the 1953 movie *Shane*, starring Alan Ladd, and in a one-page essay compare the way the director of the movie develops suspense with the way Schaefer develops suspense. Does the movie closely follow the book?

Chapter 30 Test

ESSAY (100 POINTS)

Read Matthew 26:31–75 about Peter's betrayal of Jesus. Discuss the internal conflict he must have faced in this darkest hour.

Chapter 31 Test

OBJECTIVE TEST (50 POINTS)

____ Theseus, Duke of Athens, is preparing for his marriage to (A) Matilda, (B) Hippolyta, (C) Maria, (D) Rosemary, Queen of the Amazons, with a four-day festival of pomp and entertainment.

____ Egeus wishes Hermia to marry Demetrius, who loves (A) Lysander (B) Hermia (C) Puck (D) Demetrius.

____ Egeus asks for (A) Hermia to be forgiven (B) Hermia to be killed (C) the full penalty of law to fall on Hermia if she disobeys her father (D) Hermia to be sent away.

____ Hermia and Lysander plan to (A) commit suicide (B) escape Athens the following night and go to Sparta (C) elope (D) buy a house.

____ The last character the audience sees is (A) Lysander (B) Hermia (C) Puck (D) Demetrius.

Chapter 31 Essay

ESSAY (50 POINTS)

With your parents' permission, attend a live performance of a play, or watch a movie and write a one-page review. In your essay, answer these questions:

1. Were the lighting and scenery appropriate?

2. Was the play/movie too long? Too short? Just right?

3. Were the actors and actresses appropriately cast?

4. Did the plot unfold appropriately and in an interesting way?

5. Was there a theme? What was it?

6. Who were the characters? Did they come alive? Were they well developed?

7. Who was the narrator? Was he believable?

8. What was the worldview? Was it ably presented?

9. What was the tone? Was it appropriate for the subject matter?

10. Overall, was it a great play? Why or why not?

ESSAY (100 POINTS)

Write a two-page letter to your four-year-old nephew explaining what the Christian life is all about. In your discussion, remember to discuss grace, salvation, righteousness, redemption, sanctification, eternal security (or not), and predestination. Remember your audience, and choose your words and phrases carefully.

Chapter 33 Test

ESSAY (100 POINTS)

Write a one-page analysis of "Holy Sonnet X" by the 17th-century poet John Donne.

Death, be not proud, though some have called thee Mighty and dreadful,

for thou art not so;

For those whom thou think'st thou dost overthrow,

Die not, poor Death, nor yet canst thou kill me.

From rest and sleep, which but thy pictures be,

Much pleasure; then from thee much more must flow,

And soonest our best men with thee do go,

Rest of their bones, and soul's delivery.

Thou art slave to fate, chance, kings, and desperate men,

And dost with poison, war, and sickness dwell;

And poppy or charms can make us sleep as well

And better than thy stroke; why swell'st thou then?

One short sleep past, we wake eternally,

And death shall be no more; Death, thou shalt die.[1]

---

1   http://www.poets.org/viewmedia.php/prmMID/15836

ESSAY (100 POINTS)

Write a two-page short story (500–1,000 word limitation) with all the elements of a good short story: setting, plot, theme, characterization.

Optional Written Assignments

CHAPTER 1

Literary Analysis

Write a one-page literary analysis essay describing how important the setting is to Jack London's novel *The Call of the Wild*.

As previously stated, a literary analysis paper is a paper that takes apart a literary work and then makes judgment calls about how well the literary piece is written.

Biblical Application

Jack London believed that man evolved from apes. What does the Bible have to say about this? What is the danger of this worldview? How would London's worldview influence his opinion about such moral/ethical issues as abortion and euthanasia?

CHAPTER 2

Literary Analysis Question

Write a worldview for yourself. Use the following questions to guide you.

What is the priority of the spiritual world?

Authority: Is the Bible important to you? Do you obey God and other authority — your parents — even when it is uncomfortable to do so?

Pleasure: What do you really enjoy doing? Does it please God?

What is the essential uniqueness of man?

Fate: What/who really determines your life? Chance? Circumstances? God?

What is the objective character of truth and goodness?

Justice: What are the consequences of your actions? Is there some sort of judgment? Do bad people suffer? Why do good people suffer?

(Carl F. Henry, *Toward a Recovery of Christian Belief: The Rutherford Lectures* (Wheaton, IL: Crossway Books, 1990), p. 20–21.)

Challenge

In a two-page essay, compare the worldviews of each of the following passages.

So God created man in His own image, in the image of God.

Gatsby believed . . . tomorrow we will run faster, stretch out our arms farther. . . .

And one fine morning — So we beat on, boats against the current, borne back ceaselessly into the past (F. Scott Fitzgerald, *The Great Gatsby* (New York: Charles Scribner's Sons, 1925), p. 182.)

For mere improvement is not redemption . . . God became man to turn creatures into sons: not simply to produce better men of the old kind but to produce a new kind of man (C.S. Lewis, *Mere Christianity* (Newe York: Touchstone Books, 1980), p. 183).

If it feels good, do it! — The world is totally insane, out of control, stupid!

All my friends do it, so it must be ok.

CHAPTER 3

Biblical Application

Naturalism was a literary movement that had become very popular by 1900. Define this movement and discuss why it is not biblical.

Challenge

The Call of the Wild only has one female in the whole novel. Who is she and how does she set women's liberation back about 150 years?

CHAPTER 4

Literary Analysis

Write a literary analysis essay describing the theme in Jack London's novel *The Call of the Wild*. If you need help writing an essay, you can follow the guide provided in the appendix of this book. Also, remember to check other grammar texts.

Biblical Application

Read chapter 6, "The Love of Man," and discuss what biblical themes Buck exemplifies.

Challenge

The Call of the Wild is clearly not a Christian theistic book. Yet, millions of Christian believers read it. Should they fill their minds with alternative, even hostile, worldviews? What criteria, if any, should Christians employ to guide their reading choices?

CHAPTER 5

Literary Analysis

Write a literary analysis essay describing characterization in the Joseph narrative. In your paper, identify the protagonist, antagonist(s), internal conflict, and external conflict. How did Moses develop these characters? Use evidence from the text. If you need help writing an essay, you can follow the guide provided in the appendix of this book. Also, remember to check any good grammar text.

Biblical Application

Write a list of all the wonderful characteristics that Joseph manifests (e.g., steadfastness, forgiveness, etc.) and make a similar list of the characteristics that God manifests in the same story (e.g., mercy toward Joseph in prison).

Challenge

Write a portion of the story of Joseph from the perspective of an Egyptian historian under the employment of pharaoh.

Next, write a portion of the story from the perspective of Joseph's half-brother Judah.

CHAPTER 6

Literary Analysis

Write a literary analysis essay describing plot development in the Joseph narrative. In your paper, identify the rising action, crisis or climax, falling action, and resolution. If you need help writing an essay you can follow the guide provided in the appendix of this book.

Biblical Application

Rewrite portions of the Joseph story with the following changes: Joseph is angry at his brothers and kills them, Joseph lies to get out of prison, and Joseph gives up his faith to serve the Egyptian gods.

CHAPTER 7

Literary Analysis

Write a literary analysis essay describing the way Mark Twain develops humor in this novel. Find at least one example of satire. If students need help writing an essay, they can follow the guide provided in the appendix of their book. The following is a discussion of tone in C.S. Lewis's *The Screwtape Letters*.

Biblical Application

All jokes aside, Tom Sawyer plays fast and loose with the truth. In fact, he even lies at times. When, if ever, is a lie acceptable?

Challenge

Chapter 8 in *Tom Sawyer* is a parody of a romantic novel. Explain.

CHAPTER 8

Literary Analysis

Write a literary analysis essay describing the way Tennyson uses symbolism in the final passage, "The Passing of Arthur," in *Idylls of the King*.

Biblical Application

Was Alfred, Lord Tennyson a Christian? What do his writings tell you? Consider the way he describes heaven in the last section in his poem.

CHAPTER 9

Literary Analysis

Analyze several characters in *Idylls*. Is King Arthur a realistic hero for this epic poem? Compare and contrast Guinevere and Elaine. And, finally, discuss the wonderful foil Lancelot. If you need help writing an essay, you can follow the guide provided in the appendix of this book. As a result of this lesson, you should understand how an author develops characters in his writing, and you should be able to compare and contrast two or more. The following is a characterization paper.

Biblical Application

Compare and contrast King Arthur with King David. Consider their strengths and weaknesses and kinds of leadership.

Challenge

Idylls of the King is based roughly on the Arthurian legend. Describe the historical King Arthur and how his story evolved over time. You will need to do a bit of research to trace the development of the Arthurian legend.

CHAPTER 10

Literary Analysis

Analyze the plot of *Treasure Island*. If you need help writing an essay, follow the guide provided in the appendix of your book. Identify the *Exposition, Rising Action, Crisis* or *Climax, Falling Action* or *denouement*, and *Resolution*.

Biblical Application

Long John Silver is an enigmatic figure. In the beginning of the novel, he is a rather malevolent character; however, by the end of the novel, he shows signs of being a decent person. Should Long John be released at the end of the novel? Is he innocent? Should he be turned over to the police?

Challenge

The plot of *Treasure Island* has been criticized for its inordinate amount of coincidence. What do you think? How does coincidence harm/not harm the novel?

CHAPTER 11

Biblical Application

Based on your knowledge of *Treasure Island*, is Stevenson a *theist* or a *Christian theist*? What is the difference?

Challenge

Compare and contrast the way suspense is created in *Treasure Island* with the way suspense is created in *Kidnapped*.

CHAPTER 12

Literary Analysis

Analyze the narration of *How Green Was My Valley*. How reliable are Huw's remembrances?

Biblical Application

Closely examine Huw's family and discuss how the family members exhibit Judeo-Christian characteristics toward one another.

Challenge

Every character has a purpose in a plot. Huw is of course the main character or protagonist. All the other characters function as foils — characters who develop the protagonist. How does the pastor function? Is he really necessary?

CHAPTER 13

Literary Analysis

Analyze the theme(s) of *Alice in Wonderland*. (Hint: Alice's challenges in many ways represent the problems of maturation.)

Biblical Application

Some define maturity as learning to delay gratification. Using this definition, find biblical characters who were mature and immature.

Challenge

Find examples of puns and other word plays in *Alice in Wonderland* and explain why Carroll uses them in his book.

CHAPTER 14

Literary Analysis

Analyze the use of parody in *Alice in Wonderland*.

Biblical Application

Lewis Carroll is poking fun at the stuffy morality of Victorian England. However, in light of the moral shortcomings of many contemporary Americans, a little Victorian morality couldn't hurt! Explore what the Bible has to say about morality.

Challenge

Parody is a fairly popular theme in 20th-century literature. Notably, George Orwell wrote *Animal Farm* (1946) as a parody of what was then the communist Soviet Union. Read this short book and compare it with *Alice in Wonderland*.

CHAPTER 15

Literary Analysis

How does Chesterton use dialogue to advance his plot and to develop his characters?

Biblical Application

Everyone agrees that Christians should share their faith with unbelievers. The question is how far can Christians go to be "accepted" before they compromise their witness? How does a Christian be "in" the world but not "of" the world?

Challenge

Find examples of coincidence in "Oracle of the Dog." Is coincidence used with good effect? Why or why not?

CHAPTER 16

Literary Analysis

What is the difference between satire and humor? In this essay, explain how Lewis makes his parlous subject Gilbertian (i.e., the type of humor a reader would find in a Gilbert and Sullivan opera — understated humor). *The Screwtape Letters* is a humorous work on a saturnine (i.e., serious) subject, but it is not satiric.

Biblical Application

Compare this passage from *The Voyage of the Dawn Treader* (*Chronicles of Narnia* by C. S. Lewis) to John 14:1–7:

> "You are too old, children," said Aslan very gently, "and you must begin to come close to your own world now."

> "It isn't Narnia, you know," sobbed Lucy. "It's you. We shan't meet you there. And how can we live, never meeting you?"

> "But you shall meet me, dear one," said Aslan.

> "Are — are you there too, Sir?" said Edmund.

> "I am," said Aslan. "But there I have another name. You must learn to know me by that name. This is the very reason why you were brought to Narnia, that by knowing me here for a little, you may know me better there."

Challenge

The Screwtape Letters was written during World War II when England and most of the civilized world was involved in a life and death struggle with evil. The struggle for a young man's soul becomes the way Lewis deals with evil on a more personal level.

Based on *The Screwtape Letters*, and to a greater degree based on the Bible, how does a Christian believer overcome and resist evil temptations?

CHAPTER 17

Literary Analysis

Using the text as evidence, show how Uncle Tom's Cabin is propaganda. End your essay with a paragraph discussing whether Stowe's propaganda is "good" or "bad" propaganda.

Challenge

While Stowe was clearly in favor of emancipating the slaves, she, like most Americans, was ambivalent about what should happen to them after emancipation. Should they be assimilated into white America? Sent back to Africa? Harriet Beecher Stowe was unsure. Look at her story of George Harris (chapter XLIII), concluding remarks (XLV), and other passages, and then summarize her argument. Why do you agree or disagree with her conclusions?

CHAPTER 18

Literary Analysis

Discuss the use of allegory in *Uncle Tom's Cabin*. Discuss how Stowe symbolizes the Christian motifs of journey, entrance into the promised land, sin, and others.

Challenge

Compare and contrast this novel with John Bunyan's *Pilgrim's Progress*.

CHAPTER 19

Literary Analysis

Anne Frank is both the narrator and the main character in her non-fiction book. She is a dynamic character (a character who changes) verses a static character (a character who does not change). She also is a teenager who is experiencing typical adolescent insecurities. For instance, Anne first is infatuated with Peter. As the story progresses, though, her interest in Peter decreases. Next, as most teenagers, Anne feels that her parents — particularly her father — do not understand her. As her story unfolds, however, it is clear that Anne is maturing into a normal, well-adjusted young lady.

Using the perspective that Anne is a maturing young lady, discuss her views on boys, fate, loneliness, war, and parents. Show how she matures as a character.

Biblical Application

Toward the end of her captivity, Anne Frank is reflecting on how difficult it has been to be in hiding for so many months. ". . . would it not be better if we had not gone into hiding," she says. "Then it would all be over and we would all be dead." Using the Bible as a reference, what would you say to Anne?

Challenge

Pretend that Anne Frank did not die; pretend that she survived. In a 4 to 5 page essay describe her life from the end of World War II until the present. Write your essay as if Anne were continuing to keep a diary.

CHAPTER 20

Biblical Application

The biblical Book of Esther is another story of a Jewish Holocaust. The authorship of Esther is unknown. It must have been written after the death of Ahasuerus (King Xerxes of the Persians), which took place B.C. 465. The writer was a contemporary with Mordecai and Esther and intimate with both. Hence we may conclude that the book was written approximately B.C. 444–434, and that the author was one of the Jews of the Babylonian captivity. This book is more purely historical than any other book of Scripture, and it is remarkable that the name of God does not occur in it. Nonetheless, it is an incredibly powerful testimony to God's faithfulness. Concentrating on chapters 4 and 5, discuss how Esther saved the Jewish nation from a terrible holocaust.

Challenge

Compare and contrast ways the setting of *Call of the Wild* by Jack London develops Buck, and the way Anne Frank's setting affects her. Why is the setting critical to both books?

CHAPTER 21

Literary Analysis

Coincidence plays a large part in the plot. In fact, the plot would not progress at all without coincidence. Silas coincidentally is out of his cottage when Dunstan passes the cottage. Eppie coincidentally sees the light in the cottage. Molly coincidentally dies before Godfrey is exposed. Does the story lose all credibility? Are the coincidences necessary and appropriate to the plot's development?

Biblical Application

Mary Ann Evans (i.e., George Eliot) turned her back on the Lord and rejected her faith. Rejecting Christianity was a daring thing for any person to do in 19th-century England. Nonetheless, she replaced her faith with good works and a Judeo-Christian ethical code, exhibiting a natural way that many romantics reacted to their world.

How does Eliot present organized religion in *Silas Marner*?

According to Eliot, what is the main metaphysical force in this world?

Challenge

Research Eliot's (Evan's) life. Compare and contrast her own childhood to Eppie's childhood. If you are unfamiliar with writing comparison and contrast papers, consult a good composition handbook.

CHAPTER 22

Literary Analysis

Did Eliot use too much sentimentality?

Biblical Application

Compare a biblical figure to Godfrey Cass. Then, discuss Godfrey's weaknesses.

Challenge

Eliot was particularly belligerent toward the Lantern-Yard Christian group, which appears to be a fundamentalist group — perhaps the Plymouth Brethren. The very name suggests that its faith casts only a dim light (a lantern) of knowledge in a closed-in space (a yard). This metaphor is ironic. She says that the group gives its members a sense of security, but she describes their unhappy beliefs with heavy irony.

Discuss why this passage about groups in chapter 1 is so ironic.

Why is it ironic that Silas finds his pocketknife where the bag of money should have been? Describe at least one other instance of irony in *Silas Marner*.

Finally, compare irony in this novel to *Pride and Prejudice*, by Jane Austin. One example of irony in this book is when Mr. Bennet thinks about the money his brother-in-law has spent to bring about this marriage of his daughter to one of the least admirable young men in England — a great irony. At the same time, he worries about how he can ever repay Edward Gardiner. Expecting always to have a son who would inherit his estate and keep it in the family, he has never saved any part of his income. This is only one instance. Find others and compare them to instances of irony in *Silas Marner*.

CHAPTER 23

Literary Analysis

Discuss several themes in *Silas Marner* and show how George Eliot (i.e., Evans) uses plot, setting, and characterization to develop them.

Biblical Application

One important theme in *Silas Marner* is redemption. Using copious textual examples, discuss the biblical understanding of redemption.

Challenge

Compare a character in *Silas Marner* to a biblical character.

CHAPTER 24

Biblical Application

What Christian values did Washington advance in this essay even though he was not overtly writing a Christian essay?

Challenge

Several African American leaders criticized Washington for being too passive in the face of blatant racism. They would have preferred Washington take a more critical and aggressive stand against racism. Why do agree or disagree with their criticism?

CHAPTER 25

Literary Analysis

Using copious references from the text, discuss the way Maude Montgomery develops her protagonist Anne Shirley.

Biblical Application

Discuss how the author of the Book of Job creates his main character (i.e., Job).

Challenge

Anne of Green Gables is replete with rich characters. Discuss how Montgomery uses at least three characters (or foils) to develop Anne.

CHAPTER 26

Literary Analysis

Discuss several themes in *Anne of Green Gables* and show how Maude Montgomery uses the plot, setting, and characterization to develop them.

Biblical Application

One important theme in *Anne of Green Gables* is adoption. Using a number of textual examples, discuss the biblical understanding of adoption.

CHALLENGE

As *Anne of Green Gables* unfolds, the characters change in significant and permanent ways. Discuss these changes in the following characters: Anne, Marilla, Matthew, Gilbert, and Rachel.

CHAPTER 27

Literary Analysis

Discuss the plot of *Ivanhoe*. In your discussion, reference the structure of the plot: rising action, climax, falling action.

Biblical Application

Ivanhoe and other literary figures (e.g., Beowulf) exhibit Christ-like tendencies. On the other hand, they are war-like. Discuss the ways that Ivanhoe is Christ-like and the ways that he is not.

Challenge

Write a 3,000-word adventure story.

CHAPTER 28

Literary Analysis

Discuss how Scott uses the plot and characters to communicate his worldview in *Ivanhoe*.

Biblical Application

In *Ivanhoe*, women are one-dimensional and somewhat shallow. Compare the way Scott presents women with the way the virtuous woman is presented in Proverbs 31.

Challenge

Should Christians read literature that does not have a Christian theistic worldview? Why or why not?

CHAPTER 29

Literary Analysis

Discuss how Schaefer develops suspense in *Shane*'s plot.

Biblical Application

Discuss how Samuel builds suspense in the story of David and Goliath (1 Samuel 18).

Challenge

Compare the way suspense is created in *Shane* and in *Call of the Wild*. Which author is more effective? Why?

CHAPTER 30

Literary Analysis

Discuss how several characters in the novel *Shane* change because of internal conflict.

Biblical Application

Discuss the internal conflict that Moses must have felt when he returned to Egypt.

Challenge

Compare the way Bob changes in *Shane* and the way Huw changes in *How Green Was My Valley*.

CHAPTER 31

Literary Analysis

Write a literary analysis of the entire play *A Midsummer Night's Dream*. Remember to discuss the theme, plot, characters, setting, and tone. (If you need help. check the details of writing in a substantial writing handbook). If possible, compare this play to another play that you may have seen.

Challenge

Discuss the purpose of Puck in this comedy.

CHAPTER 32

Literary Analysis

Examine the letters and discuss their style and structure. In other words, how does Lewis persuade his friend to give his life to Christ?

Biblical Application

Write a letter to a friend or acquaintance who does not know the Lord. Try to persuade him to commit his life to Christ. What form and style will you employ?

CHALLENGE

Chuck Colson in *Born Again* describes how the Holy Spirit used C.S. Lewis's *Mere Christianity* to lead him to Christ. What was it that Lewis said that drew Colson to the Lord?

CHAPTER 33

Literary Analysis

Write a literary analysis of "The Midnight Ride of Paul Revere," using guidelines 1–7 above.

Biblical Application

Storytelling is a favorite form of teaching in the Old and New Testaments. But did these stories really happen? Did Jesus really walk on water? How do we know? Obviously I believe the stories really happened. What do you think? Why is this question so important?

Challenge

Longfellow's poem is a narrative poem celebrating a famous historical event. Write a narrative poem about a famous, intriguing, or even difficult event in your family's life.

CHAPTER 34

Literary Analysis

Write a literary analysis of "The Lady or the Tiger" by Frank Stockton. Discuss the plot, theme, tone, setting, narration, and characters.

Biblical Application

"The Lady or the Tiger" is disturbingly anti-Christian. Explain.

Challenge

Some critics think "The Lady or the Tiger" is a "cheap shot." They argue that Stockton is dishonest in his presentation. In other words, readers are expecting a conclusion that they don't get, and therefore they become frustrated. Agree or disagree.

Optional Written Assignment Answers

Chapter 1

Literary Analysis

ANSWER: The cold, harsh Yukon was one of the few places in rapidly developing America where Jack London could still use the literary style of naturalism. Naturalism is an extreme form of realism in which the author tries to show the relationship of man to his environment. Often the author finds it necessary to show the base or ugly side of that relationship. This place of ice and snow was the perfect setting for his book *The Call of the Wild*.

Buck is an aloof friend of Judge Miller, the guardian of the judge's children, and the king of a ranch in the Santa Clara Valley of California. He is ruthlessly yanked from this easy life of a "sated aristocrat" and flung into the Yukon as a sled dog during the Klondike gold rush. The rest of the book is about Buck's life. He watches owners come and go while the call of the wild, the call of his ancestors, the call of things primordial grows within him. Eventually, Buck is ruled by a master whom he truly loves. Then the man is killed. Now with nothing to hold him to civilization, he answers this call and joins a wolf pack.

The fierceness of the Alaskan territory fits the book, for where else are there dogs, men, ice, and snow? Where else are there woods, mountains, wolves, and rabbits, bears and moose, all ruled by the law of club and fang; the law that weeds out the weak, old, and sick? Jack London chose one of the few settings where this could be done and then masterfully tied it all together to make the book *The Call of the Wild*. (Nick)

London's settings mostly occur in the inhospitable far north. However, wherever the story occurs, London emphasizes the ubiquitous presence of nature. Also, London is an agnostic, and he uses nature to emphasize the impersonal nature of God in the lives of his characters. London's naturalistic tendencies are revealed when he presents Buck in the same light as any human being. For instance, London first presents Buck as a domesticated "pet." Once Buck's environment changes, Buck very quickly reverts back, in London's viewpoint, into a savage creature. The difference between Buck and his human masters is incidental. The setting creates Darwinist monsters of both! Ironically, Buck is more compassionate and human than humans! Of course, compassion would be considered a weakness.

Biblical Application

ANSWER: The Bible is clear that there is a chasm between man and animals that cannot be breached. Mankind is created in the image of God. Animals are not. What is the danger of this worldview? If we believe that man is no more than an animal, we may dispose of mankind as if he was an animal. Thus, this view will lead us to accept the abomination that abortion is. Several philosophers brought much confusion into this fray. Notably, these men were Charles Darwin, Arthur Schopenhauer, Frederick Nietzsche, and others. Arthur Schopenhauer (1788–1860) was a true pessimist. He believed pain and suffering are unavoidable. Only the will, he argued, would overcome the unavoidable tragedy that life ultimately became. Friedrich Nietzsche (1844–1900) boldly announced that God is dead. He believed creative humans can use their own strength and intelligence to give life meaning. He further argued that only the strong survive and only by the strength of will. Nietzsche believed that "supermen" would ultimately dominate the race and would lead mankind from the darkness and confusion of religion and Western culture into ultimate triumph. In *Principles of Psychology* (1855) Herbert Spencer, a British philosopher, took Darwin's theory into the social realm. He influenced a generation of sociologists. He wrote that all organic matter originates in a unified state and that individual characteristics gradually develop through evolution. The evolutionary progression from simple to more complex and diverse states was an important theme in most of Spencer's later works. In summary, Spencer argued that the strongest individuals and social systems survive.

Chapter 2

Literary Analysis Question

ANSWER: Answers will vary.

Challenge

ANSWER:

Of course this biblical passage is a Christian theistic statement.

The author F. Scott Fitzgerald had strong romantic and naturalist tendencies that are reflected in this passage. "So we beat on, boats against the current, bore ceaselessly into the past." The implication is that people are captured in a beautiful, perhaps altruistic, but ubiquitous nature. However, this nature is in total control, and it sometimes bores "people ceaselessly into the past" when they might not want to go there. By the way, if you think romantic naturalist is an oxymoron, you are correct. One of the ironies of all worldviews, except Christian theism, is the fact that they readily exist together in the same artistic piece with other worldviews, even opposing worldviews. Christian theism, on the other hand, cannot coexist with any other worldview. It ipso facto claims superiority over all other worldviews. The God of theism will not share His rule with any other worldview.

This Christian theistic worldview shows something that makes it remarkably unique and appealing: it offers redemption for those who adhere to this worldview. No other worldview makes that claim. Romanticism argues for a "heightened consciousness," but it does not offer salvation like Christian theism does.

This absurdist worldview, popular among many contemporary artists, invites the participant to embrace a mindless nihilism that releases participants from all responsibilities for their actions. This is typical evidence for absurdism (and existentialism).

This subjective worldview has elements of romanticism — subjective decisions are appropriate — but in the final analysis is more an existentialist worldview that promises the participants that it is okay to do what feels good, particularly if it is universally embraced.

Chapter 3

Biblical Application

ANSWER: The notion that nature is somehow a transcendent deity is ridiculous. If one accepts the naturalistic worldview, then one is forced to see God as an ineffectual, impersonal power. The Christian knows that God is clearly connected to His people and very much in control of circumstances and events. At the same time, the romantic and the naturalist cannot have it both ways: one cannot be moral in all places and in all circumstances without a Christian theist conversion (i.e., salvation). Being "good" in the face of so much evil requires more than sincerity and good intentions — it requires the supernatural intervention of God (in Jesus Christ). While the Christian theist will concede that perfection is not a reality this side of heaven, redemption is. The believing, converted Christian theist is redeemed — or in right relationship with God — even if he has not yet attained perfection. It is a free gift by virtue of a sacrifice by God — He sent His only begotten Son to die for human sins. Christian theism makes the bold claim that it deals with human sin, yet at the same time, it invites human beings to unimaginative human pleasure — the pleasure of walking and talking with God Himself, the pleasure of being a whole, loved man. No other worldview can make that claim. No other worldview can claim a deity, without sin, who sent his only begotten son, also without sin, to die for sinful man. The problem with human beings, the Christian theist claims, is not that man does not know how to love. It is the haunting fear that man is not loved at all. That makes the truth of John 3:16 particularly satisfying.

Challenge

ANSWER: Naturalist writers do not know what to do with women. Should women be presented as helpless, docile creatures? Should they be presented as liberated, self-sufficient, sexless creatures? The former causes the naturalist writer to flirt with a form of theism that honors women in a subservient role. The latter implies that the weaker sex is equal to animalistic male. To a naturalist, it seems that in every species the male dominates the female. So what does London do? He creates Mercedes. Mercedes is hardly a woman to inspire readers. She is certainly no Emma (Jane Austen) or even a Lucy (*A Tale of Two Cities*, Charles Dickens). London has no time for women, and if Mercedes is an indication of his views, he thinks women are weak and amoral. Mercedes is hardly developed at all.

Chapter 4

Literary Analysis

ANSWER: Actually, O. Henry is stating a moral: the notion that one "gets when one gives" or "it is better to give than to receive." Of course, there are themes of generosity and unselfishness that are implied.

Biblical Application

ANSWER: Buck exemplifies loyalty, courage, and self-sacrifice. How ironical but characteristically naturalistic it is that an animal exemplifies more Judeo-Christian characteristics than many people! Buck unselfishly loves a man who on the surface only uses Buck to advance his purposes (i.e., pull a dog sled). Later, Thornton loves Buck the way Buck loves him. Buck, then, is the Jesus Christ figure who unselfishly is willing to give his life for someone else.

Challenge

ANSWER: R.C. Sproul, C.S. Lewis, G.K. Chesterton, and other Christian apologists argue that Christians should read classical literature. Many people do not find the written or spoken Word to be relevant anymore. Teaching the classics invites participants to accept the notion that there is an authority higher than personal desires. In that sense alone, teaching the Classics is vitally important to the future of Western civilization. At the same time, Christians should show some discretion. They must also be able to discern the worldviews of the author. Christians may elect to read something of enduring artistic value even if the worldview, and perhaps even some of the language, is objectionable.

Chapter 5

Literary Analysis

ANSWER: Answers will vary.

Biblical Application

ANSWER: God is eternally hopeful, eternally patient. He provides direction and protection for Joseph, but He provides scant hope. Joseph has to be hopeful through his own faith. Joseph has to draw from what the theologian Walter Brueggemann calls "hope in history." What that means is that through pain and suffering Joseph learns that God is always there, always faithful, always the Deliverer. His response to those around him — especially his brothers — evidence how profoundly God had changed this spoiled little boy into a mighty man of God.

Challenge

ANSWER: Joseph's brothers would want to point out Joseph's boasting and self-centeredness. The Egyptians would be interested in the providential emphasis of Moses' (the author of Genesis) narrative, but they would give credit to their own polytheistic panoply.

Chapter 6

Literary Analysis

ANSWER:

Rising Action: the introduction of Joseph's family

    Joseph is sold to Midianite slavers who take him to Egypt

    Potiphar throws Joseph in prison

    Joseph is released and tells Pharaoh what his dreams mean

    Joseph rises to leadership in Egypt

    Joseph's family returns

Crisis or Climax: Joseph identifies himself to his family

Falling Action: Joseph's family returns to get their father

Resolution: Joseph's family joins him in Egypt

Biblical Application

ANSWER: Answers will vary.

Chapter 7

Literary Analysis

ANSWER: See the examples. Answers will vary.

Biblical Application

ANSWER: This is a knotty question. Frivolous lying, as Tom Sawyer so gratuitously practiced, seems to be unacceptable. However, the lies told by Corrie Ten Boom to save Jewish guests hiding in her home, seem more acceptable.

Challenge

ANSWER: Tom Sawyer, the protagonist, is the quintessential Romantic. He is constantly "pretending" to be something he is not. This is even more pronounced in Twain's later work, *The Adventures of Huckleberry Finn*.

Chapter 8

Literary Analysis

ANSWER: In the last battle near Lyonnesse, a thick fog covers all the combatants. The fog represents the confusion and tentativeness that have entered Arthur's injured heart. Next, at the end of the battle, Arthur wins, but he stands among hundreds of corpses. Victory that leads to the death of loved ones and friends is no victory at all. Finally, after Arthur dies, the beautiful sword is retained as a memorial to King Arthur.

Biblical Application

ANSWER: Tennyson was certainly moralistic; certainly he embraced Judeo-Christian morality, but he did not necessarily embrace Jesus Christ as Lord. At least I cannot find any evidence in his personal life or writings that Tennyson was a born-again Christian. As one critic explains, Tennyson believed that "both men and their societies must be founded on faith — or, more accurately, on many faiths, on faith between ruler and ruled, man and woman, worshipper and God; and that such faith, however essential, is necessarily a tenuous, subjective, nonrational matter."

George P. Landow, "Closing the Frame: Having Faith and Keeping Faith in Tennyson's 'The Passing of Arthur.'" (1974), 423–42.

Chapter 9

Literary Analysis

ANSWER: Without question, Arthur is the greatest and most heroic figure in this story and in English mythology (surpassing Sir Gawain and Beowulf). He is also the spiritual leader of his nation (see his speech in "The Holy Grail"). He is larger than life. He is a very realistic character for Tennyson's epic poem — if "Idylls" is read as an epic quest. To Tennyson's credit, Guinevere is portrayed as a selfish and cruel woman, contrasting with contemporary versions of Camelot that portray Guinevere as a victim. Lancelot is an enigma. He is an honorable man who behaves honorably around Arthur. However, when he is with Guinevere, his character weakens.

Biblical Application

ANSWER: Both were strong but had noticeable weaknesses. (Students could elaborate on both the strengths and weaknesses of these two leaders.) Both were also the spiritual leaders of their nations. They were not merely military leaders — they invested a great deal of their lives in building a strong moralistic society around them.

Challenge

ANSWER: Arthur was a king of the Celtic Britons who resisted the Anglo-Saxon invaders. After a valiant struggle, Arthur was ultimately defeated. Early Roman histories mention Arthur. Later, in the Middle Ages, songs and legends arose. The most well-known of the Arthurian prose accounts is Mallory's *Morte d'Arthur*. Students can add many more details as they research and become more familiar with the Arthurian legend.

Chapter 10

Literary Analysis

ANSWER: The plot of *Treasure Island* is essentially a treasure hunt during the story of a young man who comes of age. The climax is reached when the pirates are defeated, which occurs toward the end of the book.

Biblical Application

ANSWER: Answers will vary but should consider the definition of justice. What mitigating/moral circumstances, if any, justify disobeying the law? Certainly this is a question Martin Luther King Jr. had to ask in the 1960s; it is a question early Christians also had to ask; and I wonder if Christians in the future will not also have to ask this question.

Challenge Question

ANSWER: To a certain degree, coincidence is inevitable. The action will never advance without it. Besides, this is more of a juvenile adventure story than a literary masterpiece.

Chapter 11

Biblical Application

ANSWER: All the characters are subject to a higher power of good, very similar to the Golden Rule. The moral characters prosper; the immoral decline. Some characters change. For example, Long John Silver changes into a fairly moral person. The reader suspects, even from his first entrance onto the stage, that Long John is not totally bad. On the other hand, there is no hint of "Christian" theism. This is not to denigrate Stevenson's own faith. It is merely to say that this novel is not overtly Christian in its tone or theme.

Challenge

ANSWER: The novel *Kidnapped* is set in the Lowlands and the Highlands of Scotland. David Balfour, a young man much like the protagonist in *Treasure Island*, is the protagonist in *Kidnapped*. David is, of course, kidnapped, but he is kidnapped by the spiteful Mr. Ebenezer Balfour, a relative who wants David's estate. Both protagonists, then, are young ship hands held against their will on renegade ships. David spends a number of days on the high seas on the *Covenant*, where he meets Alan Breck Stewart, who is a Long John Silver type. When he is thrown overboard during a dangerous crossing, David escapes and eventually returns home. The novel, therefore, ends where it begins, in the Lowlands.

Chapter 12

Literary Analysis

ANSWER: Huw is the perfect narrator. A reliable narrator, like a reliable speaker in any setting, is presumably someone who is objective and mature. Huw seems to fit the requirements. Innocent, but precocious enough to know his subject matter, Huw guides the reader through a highly emotional plot. The reader is grateful to have such a narrator.

Biblical Application

ANSWER: To exhibit Judeo-Christian characteristics would be to exhibit the fruit of the Spirit (Gals. 5). Huw's family was not perfect. For one thing, his dad could be stubborn. Nonetheless, the family tried to live moral, godly lives in very difficult times. Huw's mom and dad were wonderful people; the family worked together; they were patient, kind, and long-suffering; they went to church together. They were faithful to one another and to God. They were truly a godly family that exhibited Judeo-Christian characteristics. Contrast this family with some of the families seen on television today.

Challenge Question

ANSWER: Throughout the novel, the community sustains and supports all its members. However, in the pastor's life the reader observes how the community can injure its most faithful members. The community tolerated or participated in vicious, untrue gossip that ended the pastor's ministry. The author uses this incident to show how a seemingly perfect community can have faults. It also shows how Huw's family, especially his sister, acted appropriately.

Chapter 13

Literary Analysis

ANSWER: Evidence for this theme includes her confusion and forgetfulness, her change in size, her struggle with self-control, her struggle to mature.

Biblical Application

ANSWER: Joseph showed great restraint all his life as he stood firm in the face of adversity and struggle. There are other examples: Moses, David, and Peter among others.

Challenge Question

ANSWER: In Chapters 8–10, Alice is encouraged by the Cheshire cat. Unlike other characters, he does not act in an absurd manner. The duchess speaks in a sinister way. She speaks in Victorian clichés. One of them, "Take care of the sense and the sound will take care of themselves" (a twist on the old English proverb, "Take care of the pence and the pounds will take care of themselves") warns Alice of consequences that can occur for thoughtless acts. There are other examples.

Chapter 14

Literary Analysis

ANSWER: The characters are caricatures of real public officials (e.g., the King and Queen of Hearts are King Albert and Queen Victoria). The whole book itself is a parody of a futile Victorian quest toward perfection. Parodies, of course, are very subjective — other Victorian scholars could have and did disagree with Carroll's vision.

Biblical Application

ANSWER: Carroll is poking fun at Victorian society in an appropriate way; however, today, with so many public officials behaving in such immoral ways, many people would welcome more "stuffy" morality. The Bible is clear that there is a moral standard (i.e., the Ten Commandments) that absolutely must be obeyed.

Challenge

ANSWER: George Orwell uses animals to represent the dysfunctional Soviet Communist system in post-World War II Russia. The pigs, for instance, represent one particularly virulent Communist sect. The story begins by having the animals, led by the pigs, take over the farm. By the end of the book, however, the pigs ironically look unnervingly like the men whom they originally replaced. Carroll's *Alice in Wonderland* also uses animals to create a parody of Victorian England. The books are very similar in tone, although the journey motif does not occur in Orwell's *Animal Farm*.

Chapter 15

Literary Analysis

ANSWER: The story is basically a dialogue between Father Brown and Fiennes. A common strategy in this genre, a brilliant detective discusses a case with a trusted, if somewhat dense partner. Several examples include (1) the discussion about the dog — it has significant ramifications for the case but is nowhere indicated in the text, and (2) Feinnes' responses to Father Brown's questions — his excitement is an indication that the case is close to being solved.

Biblical Application

ANSWER: Christians should go to the world and share their faith; however, that does not mean they have to be "in" the world. If Christians are obeying Scripture and living godly lives, their witness will only be enhanced if they go to the Greek and "become a Greek."

Challenge

ANSWER: One coincidence is that the dog happened to be on the walk (with good effect!). Coincidence in this short story makes the ultimate outcome possible. Therefore, coincidence is appropriate to this plot resolution. Only when coincidence is superfluous in order to tease or to provoke is it inappropriate. An example of superfluous coincidence is in O. Henry's short stories (e.g., "Gift of the Magi"), where the literary value is diminished by coincidence. One more example of unnecessary coincidence: Charles Dickens' plots are full of unnecessary coincidence (e.g., *A Tale of Two Cities*).

Chapter 16

Literary Analysis:

ANSWER: Lewis has a fun-loving uncle, writing to a dutiful nephew. This format, the narrative technique of the author, adds credibility to what is being said: the reader will believe a man writing to his nephew — he must have the nephew's best interest in mind. Also, in light of what is being written, it allows C.S. Lewis to employ situational irony in wholesale fashion. For instance, the notion that Christians are their worst enemies — an argument advanced by the devil — is full of raucous humor and irony. In sincere earnestness, the devil speaks to his nephew. The reader of course realizes that this sincerity is meant in a satiric, albeit mildly satiric, tone. Satire often is used in sincere earnestness as the devil speaks to his nephew. Often, satire is used to belittle. C.S. Lewis is not trying to belittle or to make light of this situation or of Satan. He is merely trying to make a serious point by using humor — perhaps one of the most effective ways to communicate serious matters. It certainly works for C.S. Lewis.

Biblical Application

ANSWER: In John 14, the disciples want to know more about where, why, and when Jesus is leaving them. They are seeking knowledge, whereas Jesus is asking them to base their hope on faith. The disciples appear disoriented. They want assurance that they cannot have yet. To Edmund and to Lucy, to the Disciples, and to the reader, the only real assurance we have of eternal life comes by faith in God and His words of promise, not some wishful dream. Finally, faith demands obedience. No obedience means there is no faith. This message appears in both these passages.

Challenge Question

ANSWER: C.S. Lewis deals with evil in a mature and orthodox, Church of England, way. Evil is very real to Lewis. He understands that we will be overcomers by the blood of the Lamb, by the word of our testimony, and by our willingness to give up our lives if necessary for the truth (Rev. 12). Lewis does not wish to privatize life — especially in light of the horrible war being waged around him, but he understands fully the importance of a personal relationship with Christ. That is the beginning point — as he makes clear here and in his later book *Mere Christianity*.

Chapter 17

Literary Analysis

ANSWER: There is no justification for slavery. All modern scholars agree that slavery was a situation that existed during another time and is unacceptable today. Certainly Paul, in Philemon, begrudgingly accepts its existence. It is an evil system of control and a regrettable epoch in American history. However, at times Mrs. Stowe exaggerates to make a point (the reader does not think that the godly woman Mrs. Stowe is anything but sincere). In fact, slave family members are not separated from their families with as much frequency as Mrs. Stowe implies. Nonetheless, even one case — and there were many — is onerous. Overall, propaganda is the exaggeration of a truth to make a case. Propaganda, by the way, was considered a good idea until the Nazis so grievously and excessively employed it in World War II.

Challenge

ANSWER: Answers will vary. Not all Americans who were in favor of abolition of slavery were also in favor of equal rights for all races. Intermingling between the white and black races was anathema to most Americans, north and south. While race mixing is acceptable biblically speaking — the Bible nowhere prohibits marriage between whites and blacks; it only prohibits marriage between non-believers — it still was difficult for Mrs. Stowe, and all Americans, to accept. Race mixing remains the single most controversial aspect of racial discussions. George, in chapter XLIII, wants to return to Liberia, Africa, a course chosen by many African-Americans. Even though he was a mixed-race man, he embraced his African roots. In chapter XLV, Stowe calls the nation to repentance for the wrongs it has committed. She also calls them to prayer — clearly, to Stowe prayer was one key to overcoming these injustices.

Chapter 18

Literary Analysis

ANSWER: The protagonist and her family are escaping to the promised land where they will be free. There is a sense of journey as they do so. Like the Children of Israel, they may be journeying, but they are not lost. They are pilgrims. There is sin in *Uncle Tom's Cabin*. On one hand, the slave hunters are individually sinful. At the same time, they represent a system full of sin — slavery itself is a mark against the whole nation.

Challenge

ANSWER: There are many similarities. Christian, the protagonist in *Pilgrim's Progress*, is journeying to the Celestial City. The journey motif and episodic plot are similar to both. Both books are Christian allegories, more or less, although *Pilgrim's Progress* is much stronger in this direction than *Uncle Tom's Cabin*. On one level, *Uncle Tom's Cabin* is historical fiction. *Pilgrim's Progress* is not historical at all.

Chapter 19

Literary Analysis

ANSWER: At first, the adventure of hiding was interesting. However, Anne writes that she is growing more bored in the annex and tires of listening to the same stories over and over again. The adults constantly repeat the stories they have heard from Mr. Kleiman, Jan, and Miep, which are mainly stories about other Jews who are in hiding. Now, though, she grows closer to God. For the first time, she finds solace in her faith. Anne also looks back over her time in the annex and distinguishes different periods in her growing maturity. Both in her faith journey and in her maturation in general, Anne finds life accelerating in ways that are unnatural and uncomfortable. By early 1944, Anne is reflecting on her faith, her relationship with young men, and even on her death.

Biblical Application

ANSWER: The Bible is clear that all life, even difficult life, is a precious gift from God and not ours to end (Deut. 30:19). Human life is sacred because God made people in His own image (Gen. 1:26, 28). God even proclaimed life precious before people are born (Ps. 139:13–16; Job 10:8–13). Therefore, to terminate life in any way — suicide, abortion, euthanasia — is to violate the above-mentioned Scripture. In light of Anne's voracious appetite for life, however, it appears unlikely she ever seriously considered taking her life.

Challenge

ANSWER: Answers will vary.

Chapter 20

Biblical Application

ANSWER: The Jewish nation is facing imminent extinction. They stand at the brink of annihilation, genocide. They are the victims of the vitriolic and uncontrolled hatred of one man, Haman, and the whimsical irresponsibility of the foolish king, Ahasuerus. Esther's cousin Mordecai comes to warn Esther than she must give up her anonymity and take a stand, or they will all perish. All Esther wants to do is slip back into the safety of her role. Who can blame her? However, for the sake of the nation, Esther will risk everything to do what is necessary. Though her knees must be shaking, she determines to stare death in the face and stand up for her people — which is what she does. Unless summoned by her husband, Esther faces certain death by approaching him, for one never approaches an Oriental monarch unsummoned — especially if one is a lowly woman — even a beautiful wife. Why should she help her relatives and countrymen? What had they done for her lately? No doubt they had scorned her for her fraternization with the enemy. Esther could have known much condemnation and rejection. Why should she put herself and her children in jeopardy for people who may have rejected and derided her? The Scripture does not give great insight into her motivation. For fear of God, for love of her family, perhaps both, she put herself in harm's way as she responded in "such a time as this."

Challenge

ANSWER: Both books have themes that are directly tied to their settings. In *Call of the Wild,* the setting moves from the hospitable California environs to the inhospitable north. The inhospitable north is critical to London's naturalistic novel. As the novel moves geographically, the naturalistic themes emerge (i.e., survival of the fittest). The setting, then, makes the evolution (no pun intended) of this Darwinist theme possible. Likewise, World War II sets the scene for *Anne Frank*. Although *Anne Frank* is not a fictional novel, there nonetheless are thematic components. Namely, the theme of urgent mutability is made possible by the fact that Anne and her friends and family are always in danger from the hostile German army. In that sense, without a doubt, the setting — the World War II occupation of the Netherlands by the German army — is crucial to this book.

Chapter 21

Literary Analysis

ANSWER: Indeed, there is a great deal of coincidence. However, it does not harm the plot, for how else can the plot progress in an economical way? The powerful writing of Eliot causes the reader to forget this element. Besides, in the literary period in which Eliot wrote (i.e., romanticism), coincidence was standard fare and only enhanced the value of the literary piece. The incident where Eppie coincidentally sees the light in the cottage has artistic significance, too. It is more than a coincidence. As Christians see the light and commit their lives to Christ, Eppie finds her "salvation" in a friendly, lonely man's life. So a coincidence also supports a thematic emphasis of this novel.

Biblical Application

ANSWER: At times, Eliot implies that religion is no better than superstition. At other times, she sympathetically describes how church rituals comfort the faithful. Religion binds a community like Raveloe together — even Silas feels lost when he breaks with his sect, yet he seems stronger for having lost his faith. Silas never really regains a belief in God, even after he joins the church in Raveloe. His "redemption" is a product of human, rather than heavenly, love. Eliot is a theist, but she rejects all organized religion.

Challenge

ANSWER: Evans felt orphaned and unloved as a youth. She was reared in a Christian home, apparently, but felt that her religion was too harsh. Like other women (e.g., Mary Shelley) she was deeply impacted by the social situation in England, which to her and to others appeared unjust toward women. Her frustration both with her faith and with her society is manifested in this heartwarming story. Like Billy Budd in Melville's *Billy Budd*, the characters obtain salvation in efficacious relationships rather than in relationship with Christ. This is a romantic vision of life, a modern vision of life that supposes one can be saved by "subjective" feelings. In that sense, *Silas Marner*, and especially *Middlemarch*, both by Eliot, presage the modern novel.

Chapter 22

Literary Analysis

ANSWER: The tone is about what a reader would expect in this era before ascorbic realism emerges in the late 19th century. Especially for this time, Eliot's tone, which does at times appear sentimental, is appropriate. As long as the tone does not take away from the plot, it is appropriate. The reader should ask himself: "Does the tone detract from, add to, or appropriately fit the action of the artistic work?"

Biblical Application

ANSWER: Godfrey was a self-centered, indolent aristocrat, who nonetheless showed some backbone at the end of the novel. Samson, for one, comes to mind. Another biblical parallel might be Ahab.

Challenge

ANSWER: In a serious but mocking tone, Eliot condemns the religious fanatics (in her estimation) who condemn Marner. Notice how long and roundabout her sentences get, mocking the brethren's interpretation of Silas's fits. She also shows how they persuaded Silas to give up his herbal studies, which he enjoyed. Her description of Dane's views is sarcastic, while she pities Silas for his sincerity.

Chapter 23

Literary Analysis

ANSWER: The following are major themes of *Silas Marner*:

1. Fate: Are some people simply more blessed than others? Why *do* bad things happen to good people? Is there an overall justice ruling life? Dunstan Cass lives a charmed existence, or so it seems, while Godfrey nervously waits for the next bad thing to happen to him. Likewise, Silas seems to be cursed — until Eppie enters his life.

2. Faith: Eliot attacks organized religion, both the joyless (in her opinion) fundamentalist church and the hypocritical high church. Silas's "redemption" is a product of human, rather than heavenly, effort (a modern theme).

3. Mutability: In Eliot's view, all change is the product of a multitude of disconnected factors. No one is in control. To examine this theory, Eliot chose for her main setting a community with ingrained old beliefs, a place where change comes slowly. She shows how gradually the collective "mind" of village opinion shifts until it accepts Silas.

4. The disappearance of the small town: Eliot in *Silas Marner*, as Hardy in *The Mayor of Casterbridge*, examined the class system of England in microcosm and the effect the industrial revolution was having on it.

Biblical Application

ANSWER: The New Testament concept of redemption is central to the gospel message. Redemption means a releasing effected by payment of ransom; deliverance, liberation procured by the payment of a ransom. References include Luke 1:68, 2:38, 21:28; Romans 3:24, 8:23; 1 Corinthians 1:30; Ephesians 1:7, 1:14, 4:30; Colossians 1:14; Hebrews 9:12. In *Silas Marner*, Silas is "redeemed" by Eppie, which is not a biblical redemption. In the Bible, redemption concerns a supernatural intervention by God in the life of man. Without God's intervention, no relationship with a person, no matter how efficacious, can bring redemption.

Challenge

ANSWER: Silas in some ways is like Job. He suffered long and was finally blessed. However, the blessing came through totally different channels.

Chapter 24

Biblical Application

ANSWER: Washington advances the notion of honest labor and truth telling. He urges his community to be quick to forgive.

Challenge

ANSWER: In light of all the racism in this country, some may understand Washington's critics' hesitation to embrace Washington's gradualism. However, Washington's position is a strong Christian witness and was radical during his age. Remember: he was writing at the end of the 19th century, not in the middle of the 20th century.

Chapter 25

Literary Analysis

ANSWER: One example of characterization is found in the way Montgomery introduces Anne. Neither the reader nor other characters know Anne is even coming. Along with her new parents, the reader thinks she will be a boy! Then, through extended dialogues and reactions to this dialogue, Anne is slowly revealed. Montgomery develops Anne by taking the reader through one delightful experiential story after another. In this way, Montgomery reveals Anne to the reader, rather than analyzing her. At the same time, the reader grows quite fond of this precocious young lady and Montgomery's intent is established.

Biblical Application

ANSWER: Through a series of adverse situations, the author of Job reveals who this extraordinary man is. The author uses Job's family members and close friends to address probable causes of Job's misfortune to him. Ultimately, the reader finds himself speculating. This is masterful writing.

Challenge

ANSWER: Montgomery uses a panoply of well-developed characters to develop Anne. Matthew Cuthbert, painfully shy and a little eccentric, is the balm of Gilead to Anne. He lives with his unmarried sister on his family's farm in Avonlea. Although Matthew is terrified of females, he instantly likes Anne — "an interesting little thing" — whom he pressures Marilla to adopt. Anne calls him a "kindred spirit" and always turns to him when she wants a sympathetic ear (or to manipulate Marilla). Marilla Cuthbert is Anne's adoptive, spinster mother. Marilla's appearance reveals her personality — all angles and straight lines, with a severe face and tightly knotted hair. Diana Barry is a full-figured, attractive girl who is Anne's age and lives next door. She develops Anne's mischievous side. Montgomery uses Anne's classroom competition and neighboring sidekick, Gilbert, to further her characterization.

Chapter 26

Literary Analysis

ANSWER: One theme is "growing up." All the plot incidences and characters conspire to help Anne grow up. Also, the theme of "unconditional love" is strong. We can see that characteristic in Anne's parents, as well as in other characters (e.g., Diana).

Biblical Application

ANSWER: One important theme in *Anne of Green Gables* is adoption. Using a number of textual examples, discuss the biblical understanding of adoption.

Challenge

ANSWER: As *Anne of Green Gables* unfolds, the characters change in significant and permanent ways. Discuss these changes in the following characters: Anne, Marilla, Matthew, Gilbert, and Rachel.

Chapter 27

Literary Analysis

ANSWER: *Ivanhoe* is set in England in the last years of the 12th century. The plot is the story of a knight returning from the Crusades, the long wars during which the forces of Christian Europe sought to conquer the Holy Land of Jerusalem from its Muslim occupants, to find that his King Richard is not on the throne of England after all. Richard has been supplanted by evil Prince John. Richard has returned to England, but no one knows it (rising action). Ivanhoe disguises himself as a poor knight and fights in a great tournament. Here, with the help of a mysterious Black Knight, he vanquishes his great enemy, the Templar Brian de Bois-Guilbert, and wins the tournament. He names Rowena the Queen of Love and Beauty and reveals his identity to the crowd. However, he is badly wounded and collapses on the field. At the last moment, Ivanhoe appears to defend Rebecca, but he is so weak that the evil de Bois-Guilbert unseats him in the first pass. Nevertheless, Ivanhoe ultimately wins when de Bois-Guilbert falls dead from his horse. In the meantime, the mysterious Black Knight has defeated an ambush carried out by Waldemar Fitzurse and announced himself as King Richard, returned to England at last — the climax of the novel. All other action is falling action.

Biblical Application

ANSWER: Ivanhoe is loyal and faithful to a monarch who is not present and may even be dead. He is chivalrous and kind. On the other hand, he is a vicious warrior. The juxtaposition of these two characteristics creates the tension that drives this novel. This tension is the very essence of the chivalric code and makes Ivanhoe a quintessential medieval hero. Thus, like Beowulf in Anglo-Saxon legend, like Roland in French legend, Ivanhoe is the Christian warrior.

Challenge

ANSWER: Students should be certain to include all the elements of a good story: rising action, climax, falling action, and conclusion.

Chapter 28

Literary Analysis

ANSWER: All the characters in this novel are theists. Although Scott employs an early romantic style of writing (i.e., choosing the spectacular in which to conceptualize life), his characters all exhibit Judeo-Christian morality based on a corpus of absolute truth that is determined by an inspired written resource (viz., the Bible). This morality is at the heart of chivalry and medieval culture of which Ivanhoe was a part.

Biblical Application

ANSWER: Scott's characters have virtually no personality. They are archetypes of Scott's own view of women. The woman in Proverbs 31 is a central part of a home and is vitally important to her husband and children. Their connection to Scott's vision is only circumstance. The reader should not confuse voluntary submission (Prov. 31) with monolithic passivity (Scott) — one-dimensional characters whose primary role is to flatter male protagonists (Scott).

Challenge

ANSWER: Answers will vary. Students should consider such issues as whether or not the literary piece has vulgarity or other objectionable material, and the artistic value of the literary piece.

Chapter 29

Literary Analysis

ANSWER: Shane, who has taken a job at this farm because he wished to escape his dangerous gunfighting life, now finds himself tempted to employ old patterns of behavior again. A local rancher wishes to remove or destroy his employer and his farming family. Shane unsuccessfully avoids trouble, and the book is about how that trouble unfolds. Suspense is generated in each character in the small novel. In their essay, students should cite examples of suspense from some of the characters.

Biblical Application

ANSWER: A most unlikely deliverer of Israel, young David arrives in camp as the nation is arrayed in battle against the Philistines. The Philistines challenge the Israelites to have a contest between their greatest champions. Of course, this challenge builds suspense. Then the plot grows more suspenseful when no one comes forth to answer Philistine Goliath's challenge. Finally, the little shepherd boy stands up to the challenge. From earlier descriptions, the reader is well aware of Goliath's ferocity.

Challenge Question

ANSWER: Suspense in *Shane* is based essentially on one incident and arises out of moral indignation. *Call of the Wild*, on the other hand, is a much longer novel than *Shane*, and suspense grows out of several episodes that arise in the novel. One example would be when Buck saves Thornton from drowning. Another would be when Buck pulls the heavy sled and helps Thornton win a bet. Normally, the suspense grows out of a person or creature pitting himself against outside, often-hostile forces. Typically, the nature of the suspense concerns man versus nature and results from naturalistic patterns.

Chapter 30

Literary Analysis

ANSWER: Shane does not wish to fight again but chooses to do so. Marian loves two men but eventually stays with her husband. Joe is struggling to measure up to his friend Shane. Bob loves his dad but recognizes that Shane is special.

Biblical Application

ANSWER: Having left everything he knew, everyone he loved, Moses must have felt profound ambivalence about going home. True, he wanted to serve God, but he loved the pharaoh and his family — his adopted family. No doubt, too, he worried about his own punishment for the murder of an Egyptian. On the other hand, he knew about and would re-establish relationship with his biological family. All these feelings and concerns conspire to make Moses' internal conflict acute.

Challenge Question

ANSWER: Both boys love their dads, but recognize their shortcomings. Eventually, both mature to adulthood in the respective novels.

Chapter 31

Literary Analysis

ANSWER: Look at the play review of *A Midsummer Night's Dream* in the text.

Challenge

ANSWER: Puck is the interpreter who also offers comic relief as the play advances. Puck is also a perfect foil: he develops all the characters. His primary purpose, however, is to offer comic relief to the audience. He is the interpreter to the Elizabethan audience.

Chapter 32

Literary Analysis

ANSWER: Like any effective apologist, Lewis speaks in ordinary language, using ordinary metaphors. He avoids "God talk" and complicated theological terms. He draws from his experience and tries to connect it with his friend; then Lewis unequivocally states the Word of God. Finally, Lewis's abiding care for his friend is evident throughout the letters. His letters are personal and persuasive.

Biblical Application

ANSWER: Presumably, the student will use the personal form of letter writing and will use Lewis's techniques of connection through experience, of use of God's word without "formal God talk and clichés," and with loving care.

Challenge Question

ANSWER: Lewis's brilliance coupled with his humility was a tool that the Holy Spirit used to draw Colson to the Lord. *Mere Christianity*, in particular, deeply affected Colson.

Chapter 33

Literary Analysis

ANSWER: Students should answer all the questions to the best of their ability. Most critics conclude that this is an inferior poem for the very reason many enjoy it — its meter and rhythm, which are pronounced and consistent.

Biblical Application

ANSWER: The Bible is the inspired and inerrant Word of God. It is without equal. There is no other written authority that matches it. Therefore, to question the historical efficacy of an event is to undermine the authority of the Bible itself. For example, creation either did or did not happen the way the Bible says. If we suggest that it did not, then we are denying the inspiration and the inerrancy of the Word of God. If we are not created in the image of God, then there is an implication that Jesus did not really die for our sins.

Challenge

ANSWER: Answers will vary.

Chapter 34

Literary Analysis

ANSWER:

I. PROTAGONIST — Youth

ANTAGONIST — the King

II. SETTING — a kingdom long ago

III. POINT OF VIEW — third person omniscient

IV. BRIEF SUMMARY OF THE PLOT — a young man must choose between life and death, between a woman and a tiger, and he has no control over the outcome of this decision

V. CLIMAX OF THE SHORT STORY — when the door is opened

VI. THEME (THE QUINTESSENTIAL MEANING/ PURPOSE OF THE BOOK IN ONE OR TWO SENTENCES) — this suspense story examines the effect of fate on human future

VII. AUTHOR'S WORLDVIEW — naturalism — fate controls the future

Biblical Application

ANSWER: The notion that someone would so flippantly take chances with a life is unacceptable to the Christian. Likewise, the notion of "fate" and "chance" determining the future is anti-biblical. Of course, Stockton never intended this short story to be anything but entertainment.

Challenge

ANSWER: Answers will vary.

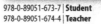
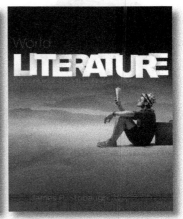